Optimize
Public Law

D0414792

OPTIMIZE LAW REVISION

Titles in the series:
Contract Law
The English Legal System
Equity and Trusts
EU Law
Land Law
Public Law

Forthcoming:
Criminal Law
Tort Law

The Optimize series' academic advisors are:

— Michael Bromby, Higher Education Academy Discipline Lead for Law 2011–2013, Reader in Law, GCU.

'The use of visualisation in Optimize will help students to focus on the key issues when revising.'

— Emily Allbon, Law Librarian and creator of Lawbore, City University.

'Partnering well-explained, comprehensive content with visual tools like maps and flowcharts is what makes the Optimize series so unique. These books help students take their learning up a notch; offering support in grappling with the subject, as well as insight into what will help make their work stand out.'

— Sanmeet Kaur Dua, Lecturer in Law, co-creator of Lawbore, City University.

'This series sets out the essential concepts and principles that students need to grasp in a logical way by combining memorable visual diagrams and text. Students will find that they will not easily forget what they read in this series as the unique aim higher and interaction points will leave a blueprint in their minds.'

— Zoe Swan, Senior Lecturer in Law, University of Brighton.

'The wide range of visual material includes diagrams, charts, tables and maps enable students to check their knowledge and understanding on each topic area, every step of the way... When combined with carefully explained legal principles and solid, understandable examples, students will find this series provides them with a win-win solution to the study of law and developing revision techniques.'

Optimize
Public Law

Ursula Smartt

Routledge
Taylor & Francis Group

LONDON AND NEW YORK

First published 2014
by Routledge
2 Park Square, Milton Park, Abingdon, Oxon OX14 4RN

and by Routledge
711 Third Avenue, New York, NY 10017

Routledge is an imprint of the Taylor & Francis Group, an informa business
© 2014 Ursula Smartt

British Library Cataloguing in Publication Data
A catalogue record for this book is available from the British Library

Library of Congress Cataloging in Publication Data
A catalog record for this book has been requested.

ISBN: 978-0-415-84492-5 (pbk)
ISBN: 978-1-315-84903-4 (ebk)

Typeset in TheSans
by RefineCatch Limited, Bungay, Suffolk

Printed and bound by CPI Group (UK) Ltd, Croydon, CR0 4YY

Contents

Optimize – Your Blueprint for Exam Success

Why Optimize?

In developing the *Optimize* format, Routledge have spent a lot of time talking to law students, lecturers and examiners about assessment, about teaching and learning, and about exam preparation. The aim of our series is to help you make the most of your knowledge to gain good marks – to optimize your revision.

Students

Students told us that there was a huge amount to learn, and that visual features such as diagrams, tables and flowcharts made the law easier to follow. Learning and remembering cases was an area of difficulty, as was applying these in problem questions. Revision guides could make this easier by presenting the law succinctly, showing concepts in a visual format and highlighting how important cases can be applied in assessment.

Lecturers

Lecturers agreed that visual features were effective to aid learning, but were concerned that students learned by rote when using revision guides. To succeed in assessment, they wanted to encourage them to get their teeth into arguments, to support their answers with authority, and show they had truly understood the principles underlying their questions. In short, they wanted them to show they understood how they were assessed on the law, rather than repeating the basic principles.

Assessment criteria

If you want to do well in exams, it's important to understand how you will be assessed. In order to get the best out of your exam or essay question, your first port of call should be to make yourself familiar with the marking criteria available from your law school; this will help you to identify and recognise the skills and knowledge you will need to succeed. Like course outlines, assessment criteria can differ from school to school and so if you can get hold of a copy of your own criteria, this will be invaluable. To give you a clear idea of what these criteria look like, we've collated the most common terms from 64 marking schemes for core curriculum courses in the UK.

reading research Understanding Evidence Structure Engagement Critical Argument Analysis Organisation Application Use sources Accuracy Originality Knowledge Presentation

Common Assessment Criteria, Routledge Subject Assessment Survey

Optimizing the law

The format of this Optimize Law volume has been developed with these assessment criteria and the learning needs of students firmly in mind.

❖ **Visual format:** Our expert series advisors have brought a wealth of knowledge about visual learning to help us to develop the books' visual format.

❖ **Tailored coverage:** Each book is tailored to the needs of your core curriculum course and presents all commonly taught topics.

❖ **Assessment-led revision:** Our authors are experienced teachers with an interest in how students learn, and they have structured each chapter around revision objectives that relate to the criteria you will be assessed on.

❖ **Assessment-led pedagogy:** The Aim Higher, Common Pitfalls, Up for Debate and Case precedent features used in these books are closely linked to common assessment criteria – showing you how to gain the best marks, avoid the worst, apply the law and think critically about it.

❖ **Putting it into practice:** Each chapter presents example essay or problem questions and template answers to show you how to apply what you have learned.

Routledge and the Optimize team wish you the very best of luck in your exams and essays!

Preface

Dear Reader,

This book aims to help you with revision and coursework in law and to gain higher marks. The text will enhance your knowledge of public law and increase your understanding and decision-making in some of the difficult areas, such as Separation of Powers, the Rule of Law and Judicial Review. It is important that you understand the meaning and function of public law and the remedies and mechanisms that exist for UK citizens to be able to challenge the fairness and legality of decisions of public bodies, such as local government and Government Departments. The text will explain that there are non-court-based remedies such as complaints procedures via the Ombudsman schemes, but also litigation remedies by way of Judicial Review.

One of the best ways to help yourself understand this area of law is that you demonstrate in your coursework and exams that you have read widely, that is not only your prescribed textbook, but also law reports and public law journals (e.g. *Public Law*). There are some excellent discussion papers on the parliamentary website: www.parliament.uk (e.g. on the Royal Prerogative, Standard Note SN/PC/03861) and legal commentary on leading cases which you can access via either Westlaw or LexisNexis. These references are particularly important in a coursework essay or case study and remember you must always cite your sources clearly in both the bibliography and footnotes (or in-text) of your work.

Now for some practical tips on examination technique:

1. Before you go into the examination room, make a mental note of how long you can spend on each question. If it is a three-hour examination and you have to answer four questions, you have forty-five minutes for each answer, although this will include time for reading the examination paper at the beginning and reading through your answers at the end. Try to ensure that you give equal time to each answer.
2. The reason it is important to do this is that it is easier to attain the first 50% of marks on an answer than the second 50% of marks, and it follows that you do not want to run out of time before you can finish that last answer and gain at least those first 50% of marks for it.

3. It is always a good idea, whether it is a problem question or an essay question, to draft a rough answer plan. This can be difficult to do when everyone around you seems to be busy writing an answer but if you can discipline yourself to do this, you will probably produce a far better paper. By giving some preliminary thought to your answer, you are less likely to leave points out and your answer will undoubtedly have a better structure.

4. If you are answering an essay question, remember to keep that question in mind throughout, tailor your knowledge to that question and refer back to the question/statement where you can. This is because it is a common mistake to regurgitate lecture notes on a topic without reference to the wording or niceties of the question.

5. Finally, it is a good idea to answer your favourite question first because it will inspire you.

Guide to Using the Book and the Companion Website

The Routledge *Optimize* revision series is designed to provide students with a clear overview of the core topics in their course, and to contextualise this overview within a narrative that offers straightforward, practical advice relating to assessment.

Revision objectives

These overviews are a brief introduction of the core themes and issues you will encounter in each chapter.

Chapter Topic Maps

Visually link together all of the key topics in each chapter to tie together understanding of key issues.

Illustrative diagrams

A series of diagrams and tables are used to help facilitate the understanding of concepts and interrelationships within key topics.

Up for Debate

Up for Debate features help you to critique current law and reflect on how and in which direction it may develop in the future.

Case precedent boxes

A variety of landmark cases are highlighted in text boxes for ease of reference. The facts, principle and application for the case are presented to help understand how these courses are used in legal problems.

Aim Higher and Common Pitfalls

These assessment-focused sections show students how to get the best marks, and avoid the most common mistakes.

Table of key cases

Drawing together all of the key cases from each chapter.

Companion Website

www.routledge.com/revision

Visit the Law Revision website to discover a comprehensive range of resources designed to enhance your learning experience.

Resources for Optimize Law revision

❖ Revision tips podcasts
❖ Topic overview podcasts
❖ Subject maps for each topic
❖ Downloadable versions of Chapter Maps and other diagrams
❖ Flashcard Glossary
❖ MCQ questions

Table of Cases and Statutes

■ Cases

■ Statutes and statutory Instruments

■ European and international legislation

1

Introduction to Constitutional Principles

Revision objectives

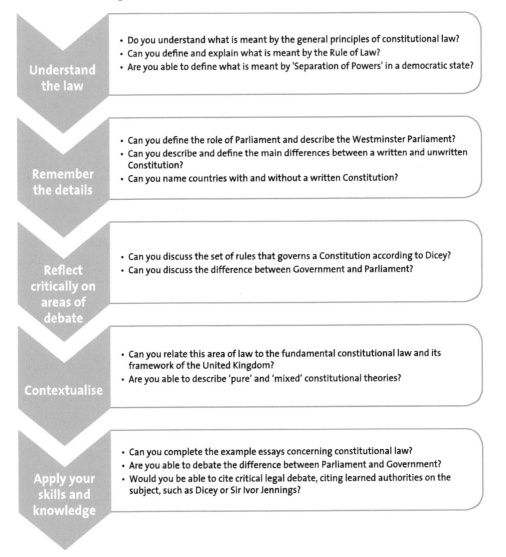

Understand the law
- Do you understand what is meant by the general principles of constitutional law?
- Can you define and explain what is meant by the Rule of Law?
- Are you able to define what is meant by 'Separation of Powers' in a democratic state?

Remember the details
- Can you define the role of Parliament and describe the Westminster Parliament?
- Can you describe and define the main differences between a written and unwritten Constitution?
- Can you name countries with and without a written Constitution?

Reflect critically on areas of debate
- Can you discuss the set of rules that governs a Constitution according to Dicey?
- Can you discuss the difference between Government and Parliament?

Contextualise
- Can you relate this area of law to the fundamental constitutional law and its framework of the United Kingdom?
- Are you able to describe 'pure' and 'mixed' constitutional theories?

Apply your skills and knowledge
- Can you complete the example essays concerning constitutional law?
- Are you able to debate the difference between Parliament and Government?
- Would you be able to cite critical legal debate, citing learned authorities on the subject, such as Dicey or Sir Ivor Jennings?

Chapter Map

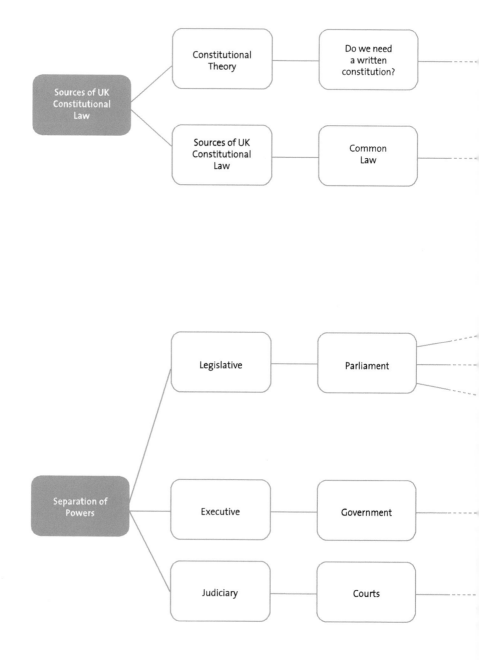

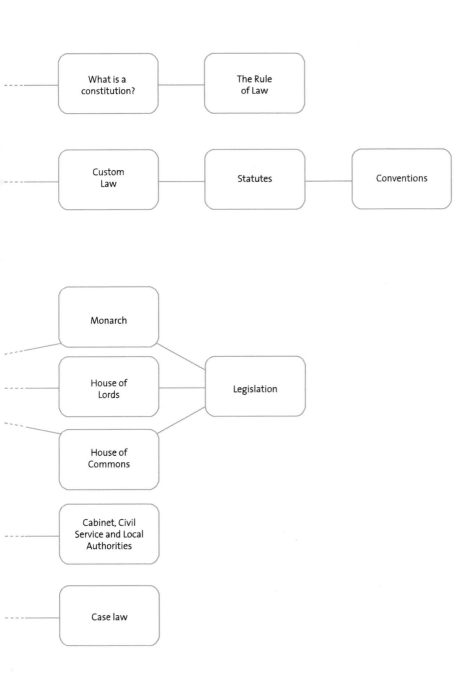

What is a
constitution?

The Rule
of Law

Custom
Law

Statutes

Conventions

Monarch

House of
Lords

Legislation

House of
Commons

Cabinet, Civil
Service and Local
Authorities

Case law

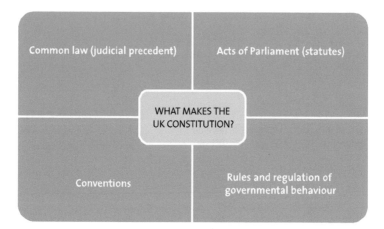

Introduction: general principles

This area of law can be very theoretical and you will generally find essay questions set either as coursework or as part of the Public Law examination. Some institutions will teach this area of law as 'Public Law 1' dealing with **constitutional law**. Part 2 usually deals with **administrative law**, such as Judicial Review, which tends to be more practical in the form of problem questions. Public law also includes criminal law and taxation laws – not covered in this book.

In this chapter, we look at constitutional law, which governs relationships between individuals and the Government, and those relationships between individuals, which are of direct concern to society. It is therefore necessary to look at Government (the Executive – both central and local), which makes decisions about the rights of individuals and on behalf of individuals.

We will look at the Rule of Law doctrine and a number of authorities (in the form of theorists) who have stated that the Executive must act within the law, i.e. that Government must obey the law. For example, a citizen who is unhappy with a decision of an administrative authority (a public body) can ask for the decision to be reviewed by an administrative court (this is called Judicial Review).

Aim Higher

Public law, then, deals with public rights, including welfare benefits, the Health Service, the way prisons and the police are run, how universities should function, and how Government spends money raised through taxes. You need to understand the theoretical basis for this subject in order to debate in class or be able to write a good legal essay on the topic. It is also important that you understand the current politics and political set up of the United Kingdom, so that you have a clear understanding of common law in this area and the difference between public and private law.

What is a Constitution?

Sir Ivor Jennings described a Constitution as a 'document in which are set out the rules governing the composition, powers and methods of operation of the main institutions of Government, and the general principles applicable to their relations to the citizens' (Sir Ivor Jennings, *The British Constitution*, 1967, 5th edn.).

Why do countries need a Constitution?

Why is it important for most democratic states that their Constitution is superior to the ordinary law? **Plato** (348 BC) described constitutionalism in his *The Laws* as follows: 'some body of law should exist on a permanent basis, on a superior plane – neither subject to individual tyranny, nor to a raw majority democracy'. Kenneth Clinton **Wheare**, in his *Modern Constitutions* (1966), investigated the origins of modern Constitutions and found that they were drawn up and adopted because people wished to make a fresh start with a new system of Government. In the case of the United States, because some neighbouring communities wished to unite together under a new Government; or because, as in Austria or Hungary or Czechoslovakia after 1918, communities had been released from an empire as the result of a war and were now free to govern themselves; or because, as in France in 1789 or the USSR in 1917, a revolution had made a break with the past and a new form of Government on new principles was desired; or because, as in Germany after 1918 or in France in 1875 or in 1946, defeat in war had broken the continuity of Government and a fresh start was required after the war.

The American Constitution (1781) is often cited as that which has led many other countries to think it necessary to have a Constitution. The reason why most countries think it necessary to give the Constitution a higher status in law than other rules of law is because they think of it as an instrument by which the Government can be controlled. Wheare believed that Constitutions are able to limit the powers of Government. Most importantly, a Constitution can limit the Executive or subordinate local bodies (i.e. local authorities). At times, it can limit the Legislature, but only so far as the amendment of the Constitution is concerned. In summary, in a truly democratic state, a country's Constitution will be supreme over a Government. Framers of the Constitution will want to ensure that the Constitution is not altered carelessly or at the whim of Government and that the document is not tampered with. There needs to be some special process of constitutional amendment, i.e. that the Legislature can only amend the Constitution by a two-thirds majority or after a General Election.

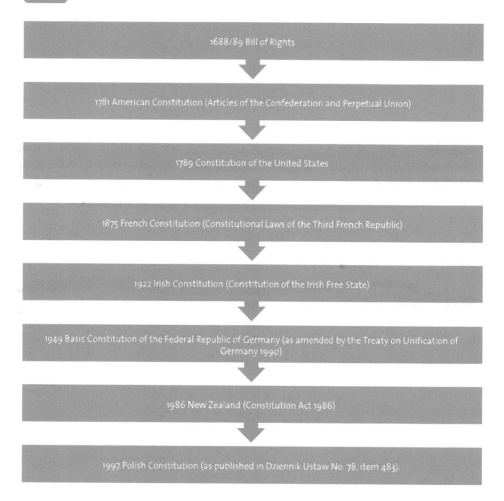

Some constitutions

Is it important to have a written Constitution?

This often forms an essay title and you would do well to read around the topic. It is well known that the United Kingdom does not have a written Constitution. The UK Constitution is a 'whole system of Government ... (with a) ... collection of rules which establish and regulate or govern the Government' (Wheare, K.C., 1966, *Modern Constitutions*). The system is based on a combination of 'Acts of Parliament and judicial decisions ... political practice ... and detailed procedures established by various organs of Government for carrying out their own tasks' (Bradley, A. and Ewing, K., 2011, *Constitutional and Administrative Law*, 15th edn.).

What are the sources of constitutional law in the UK? These include common law, custom law and statutes. Rules and codes of practice are issued by the Prime

Minister to regulate the conduct of ministers (the Ministerial Code). These will be discussed in the following chapters.

The Westminster Parliament has the right to modify the Constitution on the basis of simple majorities in the two Houses of Parliament – the House of Commons and the House of Lords. This means the Constitution has resulted in a very flexible system in which governance depends on political and democratic principles. The UK Constitution is not rigid but flexible, which some regard as its strength but others believe to be a weakness; this has assisted constitutional reform, particularly with regard to the House of Lords and the UK Supreme Court. The Westminster Parliament remains supreme, although some power has been devolved to Northern Ireland, Scotland and Wales.

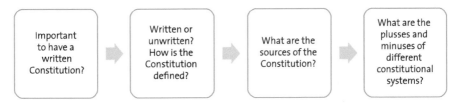

Things to consider

The UK Constitution

The United Kingdom is a constitutional monarchy with a bi-cameral Parliament composed of the House of Commons and the House of Lords. Executive power is vested in the Crown in the person of the Sovereign (the Queen or King), but in reality central Government is carried out in the name of the Crown by Ministers of State. The powers of the Sovereign and the Crown derive either from Acts of Parliament or are prerogative (i.e. recognised in common law). There is no formal separation of the powers of the Legislature and Executive and while legislative authority is vested in the Sovereign in Parliament, ministers responsible for implementing new Acts are also involved in the process of legislation. Since 2009, there is a separate appellate court of final jurisdiction, the UK Supreme Court (UKSC). Until 2009, the House of Lords (or Law Lords) sat as judges in the Appellate Committee of the House of Lords.

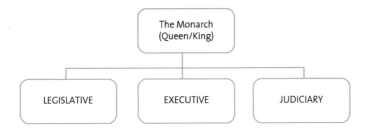

The UK Constitution

Parliament

The origins of Parliament go back to the thirteenth century, and there are many rules and customs that affect how it runs, such as **Standing Orders**. Much of how Parliament conducts its business is not determined by written rules but has become established through continued use over the centuries, known as **Custom and Practice**. One example is of Bills being read three times in both Houses of Parliament. The main work of Parliament is to make laws (also known as the **Legislative**), engage in debate and question Government on how taxes are spent to help run the country. Main issues of debate include health, education, the environment, transport, employment and criminal justice.

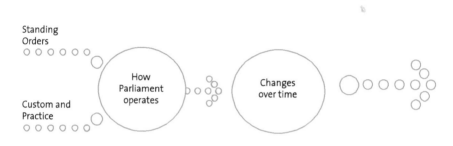

Who works in Parliament?

The UK is a democratic country based on a Constitution. This means Members of Parliament (MPs) are democratically elected by the people. MPs represent the views of the electorate in the **House of Commons**. The House of Commons has the greatest political power. The second part of Parliament is the **House of Lords**, whose **unelected** members complement the work of the House of Commons. The third and final part of Parliament is the **Monarch** (Queen Elizabeth II), who signs the laws that Parliament votes for; this is known as **Royal Assent**. Together with the House of Commons and the House of Lords, **the Crown** is an integral part of the institution of Parliament. The Queen (or King) plays a constitutional role in opening and dissolving Parliament and approving Bills before they become law.

What is the difference between Parliament and Government?

People sometimes confuse Parliament and Government. Both have important powers, but each is responsible for different areas of our democracy. **Government runs/manages the country,** e.g. decides how our taxes are spent. Different Government Departments run different things, e.g. health or transport. Led by the Prime Minister, the UK Government is formed by the political party (or coalition of parties) with the greatest representation in the House of Commons. The Prime Minister selects a team of MPs and members of the House of Lords to help run the country; this is known as the Cabinet (although the Prime Minister does not select every member of the two Houses to join the Government). All the other MPs and members of the House of Lords carry out the work of Parliament. MPs are responsible for keeping an eye on the work of Government (known as 'scrutiny'), e.g. members of both Houses scrutinise Government spending.

What happens in Parliament?

The main work of Parliament is to make laws, debate topical issues and look at how our taxes are spent to help run the country. The issues that are discussed in Parliament affect us all: health, the environment, transport, jobs, schools, crime. For instance, Parliament debated and voted on how long people could be arrested on suspicion of terrorism and held without being charged following the atrocious terrorism attacks in New York on 11 September 2001 (known as '9/11'). In summary, Parliament's main responsibility is law-making (also known as the Legislature). It is responsible for approving and changing the country's laws. Most new laws presented to Parliament are suggested by the Government. To pass a new law, both the House of Commons and the House of Lords must agree.

THE UK PARLIAMENT is made up of:

HOUSE OF COMMONS
- ❖ The House of Commons is made up of 650 MPs. UK citizens vote for MPs and whoever wins represents everyone in their local constituency

HOUSE OF LORDS
- ❖ The House of Lords has over 700 members, who are not elected but selected by the Prime Minister and appointed by the Monarch

THE MONARCH
- ❖ The Queen (or King) opens and closes Parliament each year, asks the winning party in a General Election to form the Government and officially signs all the laws that Parliament votes for (Bills before Parliament). The Monarch grants Royal Assent to a Bill, which then becomes a statute (Act of Parliament)

Aim Higher

For a detailed explanation of how Parliament works, see the interactive website for the UK Parliament at Westminster. You can even follow a Bill passing through Parliament (click on 'Bills before Parliament') and sign up for a Bill by email and follow its passage through both Houses (House of Lords and House of Commons) at: www.parliament.uk

Devolution

Since 1999, some powers of the UK institutions have been devolved to decentralise Government. This means certain legislative and executive powers have been handed over to the three nations, which, together with England, make up the United Kingdom. These devolved national and regional governmental bodies are in Scotland (the Scotland Act 1998), Wales (Government of Wales Act 1998) and Northern Ireland (the Belfast (or Good Friday) Agreement 1998 set out an ambitious institutional template for devolution designed to provide cross-community safeguards through a power-sharing – or 'consociational' – form of Government) (see also Chapter 6).

Scottish Parliament, Edinburgh (Pàrlamaid na h-Alba)	Welsh Assembly, Cardiff (Llywodraeth Cymru)	Northern Ireland Assembly, Stormont Castle, Belfast
❖ Scotland Act 1998 ❖ Makes Scottish law on devolved matters ❖ First Minister of Scotland + 129 Members of the Scottish Parliament (MSPs) and civil servants	❖ Government of Wales Act 1998 and Government of Wales Act 2006 ❖ First Minister of Wales + 60 elected Welsh Assembly Members and civil servants ❖ Welsh law-making powers (e.g. education, health)	❖ Belfast (or Good Friday) Agreement 1998 – Northern Ireland Act 1998 ❖ First Minister for NI + 108 elected NI Assembly Members ❖ Standing Orders

Devolution: Developed government in the UK

The Rule of Law

The Rule of Law, according to Albert Venn **Dicey** (1835–1922) – also referred to as 'the Rule of Law and the Protection of the Individual' – is a fundamental principle of the English Constitution. Dicey's concept of the Rule of Law proposes that Government should be restrained and not have discretionary powers; that there should be legal checks and balances by way of the Judiciary over the Executive (of Government), and no one – including the most senior persons of Government – should be above the law. If these principles are successfully obtained and inherent in a society, this will then result in a true democratic and stable state, resulting in the security of all citizens. Failing to follow the principles of the Rule of Law can result in tyranny. Although the idea of the Rule of Law was not pioneered by Dicey, he is usually credited for popularising it. In his book, *Law of the Constitution* (1885), he defends Britain's **unwritten Constitution**, arguing that this is a positive thing.

Dicey's Rule of Law

Dicey summarised the Rule of Law under three headings:

No punishment without law	❖ No one can be punished or lawfully interfered with by the authorities except for breaches of the law ❖ All Government actions must be authorised by law
No man is above the law	❖ Everyone, regardless of rank, is subject to the ordinary laws of the land
Judicial decisions determine the rights of the private person	❖ The rule of law prevails ❖ There is no need for a Bill of Rights

Formal and substantive conceptions of the Rule of Law

There is a large body of academic literature on the Rule of Law examining the concept from almost every conceivable perspective. The main debate concentrates on the formal and substantive meanings of the Rule of Law. **Formal** conceptions address the manner in which the law was disseminated: Was it by authorised persons? Was it clear and did it set sufficient norms to become a clear guide to regulate individual conduct, so that citizens could plan their lives and live according to 'the law'? Formal conceptions of the Rule of Law are not concerned with content; they merely accept that the Rule of Law has formal attributes. They deal with substantive rights. Formal concepts are used to distinguish between 'good' and 'bad' laws.

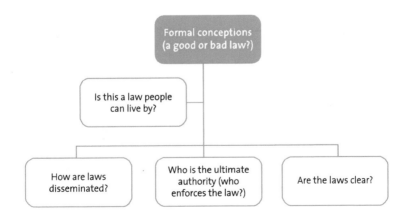

Dicey's conception of the rule of law is essentially **substantive**. Dicey's first limb of the Rule of Law is that no one can be lawfully punished unless he or she has breached the law (no punishment without law). Dicey's second principle concerns equality (everyone is equal before the law) and his third limb of the Rule of Law concerns the concept of substantive and formal right: fundamental human rights must be protected by law (see Dicey, A.V., 1959, *The Law of the Constitution*, 10th edn.).

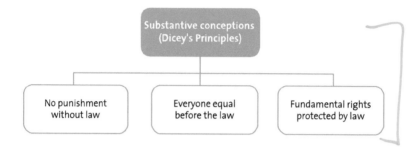

Aim Higher

You might wish to look at Professor Raz's theory of the Rule of Law. Raz articulates the formal conception of the Rule of Law most clearly and explicitly. He argues that a country's regime and laws might be morally objectionable, but they still might have provisions that comply with the formal precepts comprising the Rule of Law. He also cites a democratic regime which may not always necessarily have laws which do measure up to the Rule of Law. This means that the formal concept of the Rule of Law is essentially of negative value, given that the law can empower the state to do all manner of things; the Rule of Law then minimises the danger created by the law itself, as long as the content of the law is open, clear, stable, general and applied by an impartial judiciary (see Raz, J., 'The Rule of Law and its Virtue', 1977 93 LQR 195 at 196).

Professor Trevor Allan adopts an explicitly **substantive** conception of the Rule of Law. Allan firmly believes that the substantive concept is the correct principle in constitutional theory in the context of the British Constitution. He regards formal concepts in relation to the UK Constitution as 'unrealistic' or 'implausible'. This means Allan favours common law as opposed to codified law (such as Continental European law). He firmly believes that common law entails all the substantive principles of the Rule of Law, required by the courts to consider adjunctions of justice and fairness (see Allan, T.R.S., 1993, *Law, Liberty and Justice: The Legal Foundations of British Constitutionalism*).

Aim Higher

It is important that you realise that the Rule of Law is generally regarded as a central principle of constitutional governance and looks at the protection of an individual's fundamental rights. Therefore, it is all the more important that you should be clear about its meaning before tackling an essay on the topic. This is a complex and theoretical concept. By reading around the subject, you may gain greater clarity in this respect, though you will soon realise that public lawyers often contradict each other on this issue of legal theoretical debate. Ultimately, the debate is divided into the **'formal'** and **'substantive'** conceptions of the Rule of Law and the way in which the legal theorists identify legal norms. Their fundamental disagreement concerns the very nature of law and the role of the courts in their adjudication. When discussing or commenting on A.V. Dicey's Rule of Law, it is really important that you establish a sound understanding of the concept of the Rule of Law.

Case precedent – *Entick v Carrington* [1765] 19 State Tr 1029

Facts: On 11 November 1762, the King's Chief Messenger Nathan Carrington, and three other messengers, entered into the home of writer John Entick 'with force and arms' and seized Entick's private papers. Entick was arrested. The messengers said that they were acting on the orders of Lord Halifax 'to make strict and diligent search for . . . the author, or one concerned in the writing of several weekly very seditious papers'. Judge Camden held that Halifax had no right under statute; therefore Carrington was liable for trespass. The immediate and most notable consequences of the decision were that the Executive branch of Government and their agents were limited in what they could do. The court affirmed that a warrant issued by a Home Secretary for entry into private property and seizure of allegedly seditious material was against the law and amounted to trespass:

'*By the law of England, every invasion of private property, be it ever so minute, is a trespass. No man can set foot upon my property without my licence, but he is liable to an action though the damage be nothing*' (Lord Camden said in *Entick v Carrington*).

Principle: Citizens are free to do anything that is not specifically **prohibited** under law and Government agents (executive authorities) are prohibited from doing anything that is not specifically **allowed** by common law or statute.

Application: Use this case when you want to illustrate Dicey's Rule of Law. The case confirms the three branches of Dicey's theory and is still one of the leading civil liberties and human rights cases in English law. The case demonstrates how the courts can limit the scope of Executive power.

Separation of Powers

Separation of Powers is a theory that distinguishes three sorts of powers: **Legislative, Executive** and **Judicial**. These powers are usually exercised by Parliament, Government and judges, respectively. Under this theory, the sign of a 'good' democratic Constitution is one where the persons exercising these powers are separate with as little overlap in functions as possible.

Legislative
(Legislature)
❖ Makes laws
❖ Acts of Parliament or statutes

Executive
❖ Deals with matters of civil and public law
❖ Makes war or peace
❖ Sends or receives embassies
❖ Establishes public security
❖ Provides against invasion of a country

Judiciary
(Judicature)
❖ Punishes criminals (criminal law)
❖ Determines disputes between individuals (civil law)

Aim Higher

If you were required to write a discursive theoretical essay on the Separation of Powers, you might wish to read and cite Walter Bagehot (1826–1877), who wrote *The English Constitution* in 1867. He contrasted the UK Constitution and that of the United States of America. The book focuses in particular on the functioning of the UK Parliament and the British Monarchy, written at the time of the Reform Act 1867. Bagehot states that the British Constitution may be described as 'the close union, the nearly complete **fusion**, of the **executive** and **legislative** powers ... The connecting link is the cabinet.' It is worth noting that Bagehot does not mention the **judicial** power. The book is a classic text and if you enjoy historical legal research, this is the text for you. However, there is plenty of academic discussion on the topic in the form of legal journal articles. Have a look at Westlaw or LexisNexis or the *Public Law* journal.

Separation of Powers and the UK Parliament

So, how can liberty be preserved through the Separation of Powers? By dividing state powers into three separate bodies; each body exercises one power – the Legislative (Parliament), the Executive (Government) and the Judiciary. And why should these be separated? There is the notion of liberty in a democracy, otherwise the Executive can make laws at random which then might lead to a tyrannical state.

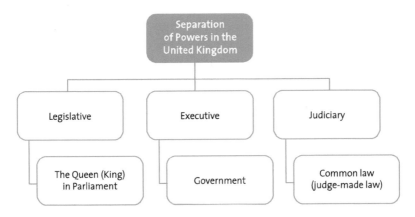

Separation of Powers in the United Kingdom: the UK Parliament

What is meant by the pure theory of the Separation of Powers?

The name most associated with the doctrine of the Separation of Powers is that of Charles Louis de Secondat, Baron de **Montesquieu** ('Montesquieu', 1689–1755). His thoughts on the development of institutions and the Constitution of a democratic state, based on the 'pure' Separation of Powers, have influenced many writers and parliamentarians. Montesquieu did not invent the doctrine of the Separation of Powers; in fact, he based his theory on that of the English philosopher, John Locke (1632–1704) (see Montesquieu's Book XI, Chapter 6 of the *De l'Esprit des Loix* – 'The Spirit of Laws', 1748). In particular, Montesquieu's ideas contributed to the Separation of Powers in relation to the Judiciary, and spheres of governmental activity, especially that of the Executive.

What is meant by the partial theory of the Separation of Powers?

In the partial theory, certain powers within a state are 'fused'. The UK system is a fused system. Historically, the Westminster Parliament was once the High Court of Parliament, but this changed with time when the power of the House of Lords as the highest domestic court of appeal and the power of the Law Lords (who also sat as law-makers in Parliament) was questioned. The Lord Chancellor at the time exercised all three powers: he was a member of Government (Executive), he was also the Speaker of the House of Lords (Legislative) and he also sat as a judge (Judicial) as the Head of Judiciary in England and Wales. The Constitutional Reform Act 2005 changed this. It established the new **UK Supreme Court** (UKSC) as the highest appellate body, and removed the **Justices of the Supreme Court** (still called 'Law Lords') from the Legislature (s. 24 of the 2005 Act). The powers of the Lord Chancellor were removed, i.e. he is no longer the Lord Speaker (s. 18), and he is no longer the Head of Judiciary (role now taken by the Lord Chief Justice) (s. 7).

Case precedent – *Liversidge v Anderson* [1942] AC 206

Facts: The claimant sought damages for false imprisonment. The Secretary of State – Home Secretary Sir John Anderson – had refused to disclose certain documents. The question was as to the need for the defendant to justify the use of his powers by disclosing the documents. Sir John Anderson had used his emergency powers bestowed on him via Regulation 18B of the **Defence (General) Regulations 1939**, which permitted the Home Secretary to intern people if he had 'reasonable cause' to believe that they had 'hostile associations'. The House of Lords had to decide whether the court could investigate the objective basis for the 'reasonable cause'; in other words, could they evaluate the Home Secretary's actions on an objective standard (the reasonable man test)? Or were they to measure them against the personal standard of the Secretary of State?

The House of Lords held that legislation must be interpreted to give effect to Parliament's intention, even if that meant adding to the words to give that effect. Although Parliament had made the power subject to a reasonable belief, they accepted the Home Secretary's statement that he held such a belief; or otherwise, that he believed he had reasonable cause. This was a matter of national security. It was therefore not appropriate for a court to deal with matters of national security, especially as they were not privy to classified information that only the Executive had. Lord Atkin (dissenting) asked whether the defendant should or should not be obliged to give further and better particulars of a paragraph in his pleaded defence asserting that he had reasonable cause to believe that the claimant was a person of hostile associations. Lord Atkin's view was that the phrase 'reasonable cause' in the statute at hand indicated that the actions of the Secretary were meant to be evaluated by an objective standard. As a result, it would be within the court's purview to determine the reasonableness of the Secretary's actions.

Principle: One of the pillars of liberty in English law is the principle that every imprisonment is prima facie unlawful and that it is for a person directing imprisonment to justify his act.

Application: This landmark case is of great public importance and should be discussed in relation to the Separation of Powers. The case concerned the relationship between the courts and the state, and in particular the assistance that the Judiciary should give to the Executive in times of national emergency. The case can also be used when discussing human rights issues such as civil liberties. The reason why the dissenting judgment of Lord Atkin is cited is because it became persuasive precedent not only in the UK but also in various other Commonwealth countries. The potential power of this dissenting judgment was clearly recognised even before it was published. However, in 1977, in the deportation case of *R v Secretary of State ex parte Hosenball* [1977], Lord Denning MR in the Court of Appeal supported judicial non-interference with ministerial discretion in matters of national security. *Ex parte Hosenball* concerned the conflict between a state's national security on the one hand and the freedom of the individual on the other. The Court of Appeal held that such a decision was not for a court of law, but for the Home Secretary to decide. He was entrusted by Parliament with the task. He was answerable to Parliament as to the way he handled the deportation of the young American journalist. Mr Hosenball wrote an article for *Time Out* magazine on 21 May 1976 about 'The Eavesdroppers', concerned with spying, touching on matters of national security (see also *R v Secretary of State for the Home Department, Ex parte Cheblak* [1991] 2 All ER 319).

Putting it into practice

Essay questions are likely to relate to one of the following:

❖ The meaning of constitutional law
❖ What a political Constitution is
❖ The difference between countries' written and unwritten Constitutions
❖ The advantages and disadvantages of a written Constitution
❖ The meaning and application of the Rule of Law
❖ Definitions of the Constitution by legal writers of authority
❖ The Separation of Powers

Essay 1

The UK Constitution is said to be in flux – it is constantly evolving. Is it not about time that the Constitution be codified and written down in a single document, as is already the case in many democratic countries? Discuss.

Feedback on putting it into practice

a) This question requires you to tackle the age-old question, 'Does the United Kingdom have a Constitution' and, if so, what are its characteristics?
b) You should refer to the fact that Constitutions are generally founded to represent a political watershed, following a war or a revolution, and written Constitutions are usually a clear break with the past (e.g. France, Poland, the United States).
c) Cite the following examples and pick your own (written) Constitution as a practical example in your essay, based on, for example:

❖ a political upheaval
❖ an invasion
❖ a revolution.

tate that the UK has not experienced such political upheaval or revolutionary events, has never been invaded or colonised. As a consequence, the citizens have probably not felt it necessary to create a new codified Constitution to mark a watershed. The UK's Constitution has developed incrementally.

e) To gain a high mark you should introduce and discuss the legal debate (journal articles and textbooks) with reference to the fact that the UK has no written Constitution, i.e. there is no one legal written-down document, but that

f) there are special legal rules and sources of law which – in total – make up the UK Constitution. Indicate that the system of Government and state institutions in the UK have not been specifically created by a single authoritative constitutional document or code; instead, they have developed and evolved over the years.

g) Define the key institutions of the state and describe the composition and powers of these institutions; how these institutions interrelate and check and balance one another; how these institutions relate to the individual.

h) How is the Rule of Law safeguarded? For example, discuss the rights and freedoms enjoyed by the individual.

i) Summarise that the UK lacks a formal codified document called the 'British Constitution' but that there is a collection of rules which govern the governing institutions, as it clearly has rules and practices which govern the state (you will need to read the following chapters of this text to write about and discuss the various sources of law of the UK Constitution).

j) Refer to the fact that there has not been a public referendum on a Constitution (or Bill of Rights) in the UK, i.e. UK citizens have never formally ratified any Constitution.

Aim Higher

Additional credit will usually be given for the fact that the UK has:

- ❖ a flexible Constitution;
- ❖ a unitary Constitution;
- ❖ a limited Monarchy;
- ❖ no strict Separation of Powers.

Essay 2

(a) Explain the three limbs of Dicey's theory of the Rule of Law.
(b) Describe an academic (*not* a judicial) criticism of Dicey's theory.
(c) Analyse whether Dicey's theory is still accurate.

Feedback on putting it into practice

a)   Note that the question is divided into three parts. To obtain high marks, you must answer all three parts of the question. If you answer only one part of the question, you will be marked down.

b)   The first part (the headline and part a) is purely descriptive, so it is possible for you to pick up marks by describing and defining what is meant by the Rule of Law (Dicey, etc.) without having to engage in critical legal analysis at this point.

c)   The core of the Rule of Law is an autonomous legal order; i.e. under the Rule of Law, the authority of law does not depend so much on the law's instrumental capabilities, but on its degree of autonomy, that is, the degree to which law is distinct and separate from other normative structures such as politics and religion.

d)   The Rule of Law is a regulator of Government power (the Executive) and grants citizens fundamental rights such as equality before the law (cite the three principles of Dicey's Rule of Law here).

e)   The Rule of Law in the UK means procedural and formal justice.

f)   The opposite of Rule of Law is rule by a person (or few persons); cite some examples of tyranny, dictatorship or oligarchy. Provide examples of states where this is the case (e.g. China, Russia, Singapore). Under the 'Rule of Person', there is no limit to what the rulers (the Government) can do and how they do things.

g)   Summary and conclusion: summarise the main aspects of the Rule of Law. Finish by stating how Government arbitrariness can be constrained.

h)   For a truly democratic state to function, there needs to be a limit to Government impulse or the making of arbitrary laws.

Chapter summary

❖   Public law deals with public rights.

❖   A Constitution is a document with a set of rules governing the composition, powers and methods of operation of the main institutions of Government.

❖   The general principles of a Constitution are applicable in the state's relationship with its citizens.

❖   The UK lacks a formal written (codified) document called the 'British Constitution', although there is a collection of rules that govern the governing institutions, i.e. clear rules and practices that govern the state.

❖   The Rule of Law is a regulator of Government power (the Executive) and grants citizens fundamental rights such as equality before the law.

❖   The Rule of Law requires the supremacy of law as opposed to the supremacy of the Government or any political party.

❖   Separation of power means: the Legislative (or Legislature) makes laws, the Executive makes decisions (such as go to war) and the Judiciary applies the law (i.e. punishes criminals or determines disputes in civil law between individuals).

❖   The UK Parliament (the Palace of Westminster) comprises the House of Commons, the House of Lords and the Queen (or King) in Parliament.

Table of key cases referred to in this chapter

Case name	Area of law	Principle
Entick v Carrington [1765]	Rule of Law	Citizens are free to do anything that is not specifically **prohibited** under law
Liversidge v Anderson [1942]	Separation of Powers	There is a general principle that every imprisonment is prima facie unlawful and that it is for a person directing imprisonment to justify his act
R v Secretary of State ex parte Hosenball [1977]	Separation of Powers; Rule of Law	Where national security is involved, the ordinary principles of natural justice can be modified by the Executive to allow for protection of the realm
R v Secretary of State for the Home Department, ex parte Cheblak [1991]	Separation of Powers; Rule of Law	Matters of national security are exclusively matters for the Government (Executive). In the absence of evidence by the Home Secretary, the courts will accept that the Home Secretary has good reason to make a deportation order on national security grounds without requiring him to produce evidence to substantiate those grounds

---

@ Visit the book's companion website to test your knowledge

❖ Resources include a subject map, revision tip podcasts, downloadable diagrams, MCQ quizzes for each chapter, and a flashcard glossary

❖ www.routledge.com/cw/optimizelawrevision

2

Sources of the UK Constitution

Revision objectives

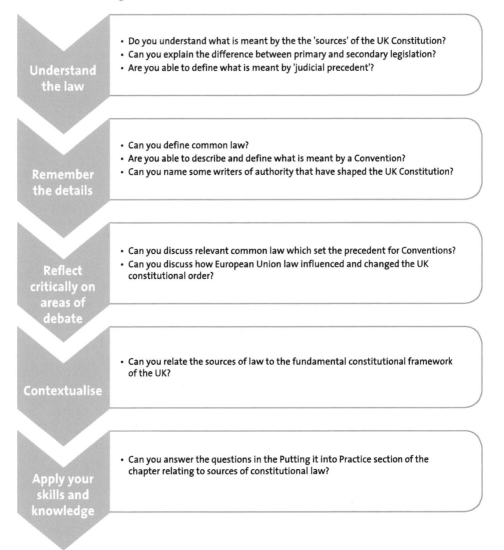

Understand the law
- Do you understand what is meant by the the 'sources' of the UK Constitution?
- Can you explain the difference between primary and secondary legislation?
- Are you able to define what is meant by 'judicial precedent'?

Remember the details
- Can you define common law?
- Are you able to describe and define what is meant by a Convention?
- Can you name some writers of authority that have shaped the UK Constitution?

Reflect critically on areas of debate
- Can you discuss relevant common law which set the precedent for Conventions?
- Can you discuss how European Union law influenced and changed the UK constitutional order?

Contextualise
- Can you relate the sources of law to the fundamental constitutional framework of the UK?

Apply your skills and knowledge
- Can you answer the questions in the Putting it into Practice section of the chapter relating to sources of constitutional law?

Chapter Map

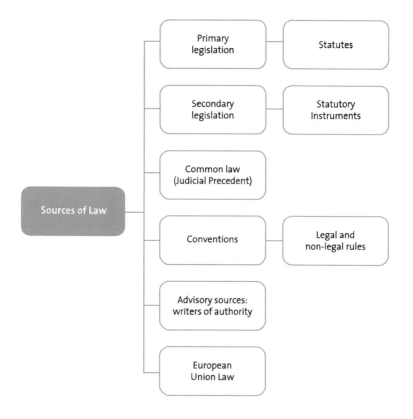

Introduction: what are the sources of law?

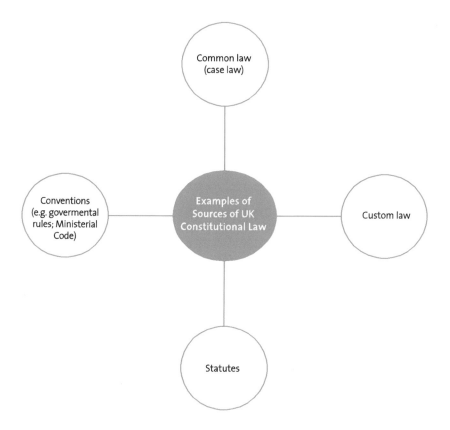

In Chapter 1, you were introduced to the general principles of what makes up a Constitution. You will be aware that these generally form a document that sets out the distribution of powers between, and the principal functions of, a state's organs of Government. Most written Constitutions include a list of the rights which people living in the state enjoy, for example the Constitutions of the United States and France. You will also be aware that the UK Constitution is unwritten or, as European lawyers would call it, 'uncodified'.

In this chapter, we look at UK constitutional law and its sources. It will become clear that the Constitution is not one piece of legislation or charter, but that there are several sources that make up the UK Constitution, dating back to the Bill of Rights 1689. Together with the Act of Settlement 1701, the Bill of Rights is still in effect. It is one of the main constitutional laws governing the succession to the throne of the United Kingdom and a particular part of the realm. The UK Constitution can then be defined as follows: it is more akin to an assemblage of laws, institutions, conventions and customs that compose the general constitutional set-up and system, according to which the British community has agreed to be governed.

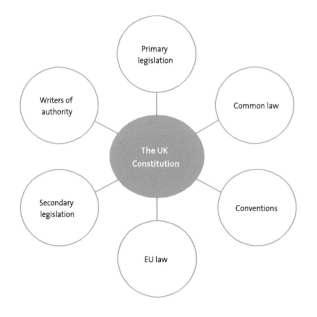

Would you describe the UK Constitution as written or unwritten?

It is often suggested that the UK does not have a written Constitution. This is not strictly true; rather, what it does not have is a **single document** setting out the legal framework and functions of the organs of Government and the rules by which it should operate. Such documents are a declaration of a country's supreme law and have overriding legal force to empower a constitutional court to declare acts of the Legislature illegal if they conflict with the rights embodied in such a formal Constitution. In this, the UK differs from many other countries that have a written Constitution and therefore a Constitutional Court, such as the United States, Ireland, Germany, France, or South Africa.

This means that the UK Constitution is a system of Government with a collection of rules which establish and regulate or govern the Government (see Wheare, K.C., 1966, *Modern Constitutions*). The constitutional system is thus based on a combination of Acts of Parliament and judicial decisions (common law), political practice (Conventions) and detailed procedures established by various organs of Government for carrying out their own tasks. Examples are the law and custom of Parliament and the rules issued by the Prime Minister to regulate the conduct of ministers (Ministerial Code).

Customs and Conventions: the way in which they have shaped the UK Constitution

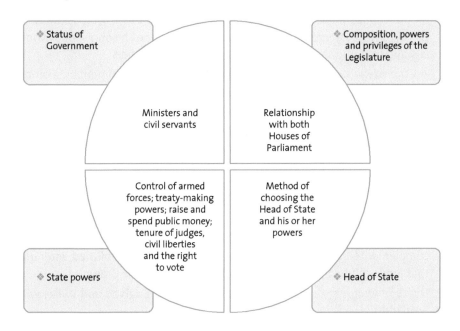

Status of Government

Composition, powers and privileges of the Legislature

Ministers and civil servants

Relationship with both Houses of Parliament

Control of armed forces; treaty-making powers; raise and spend public money; tenure of judges, civil liberties and the right to vote

Method of choosing the Head of State and his or her powers

State powers

Head of State

Primary legislation

The assemblage of laws, institutions and customs in the UK includes numerous items of legislation from medieval to modern times. Major laws in the UK pass through Parliament in the form of Bills. Once Bills have progressed through all of their stages they become Acts of Parliament (a 'statute'). Acts of Parliament often confer powers on ministers to make more detailed orders, rules or regulations by means of Statutory Instruments. Often an Act is only framed generally and rather broadly; Statutory Instruments are then used to provide the necessary detail and 'how to' use and apply the statute. Acts of Parliament can be divided into two types: **public** and **private**. Public Acts are legislation of universal application and change the general law. Private Acts (also known as Local and Personal Acts) affect the powers of individual groups, such as companies or local authorities. Prior to 1798, all Acts, both public and private, were published together, with Private Acts listed as 'local' and Personal Acts considered 'private'. Since 1798, Printed Acts have been divided into two series: 'Public General Acts' and 'Local and Personal Acts'. The following pieces of legislation have significantly shaped the UK Constitution.

↓ Magna Carta 1215. *Magna Carta Libertatum* (the Great Charter of the Liberties of England), granted by King John in 1215. The approved version by the English Parliament was granted by Edward I in 1297. It established certain civil liberties, for example that a person cannot be punished without law and that punishment should only be based on justice.

↓ Petition of Rights 1628. The Act outlawed arbitrary imprisonment or taxation, and the use of martial law in peacetime, except by Acts of Parliament.

↓ Habeas Corpus Act 1679. Habeas corpus is a remedy against unlawful detention. The Act placed stiff penalties on the evasion of the writ by transfer of persons outside the jurisdiction of the English courts.

↓ Bill of Rights 1689. Enacted by the English and Scottish Parliaments in 1689 at the time of the restoration of the monarchy. Laid the foundations for the modern UK Constitution in a series of articles; many of its provisions are still in force.

↓ Act of Settlement 1701. Dealt with succession to the throne and complemented the provisions in the Bill of Rights. It established, *inter alia*, that judges should not hold office at the pleasure of the Crown.

↓ Treaty of Union 1707. Act formalising the union of England and Wales with Scotland.

↓ Parliament Acts 1911 and 1949. Acts including fixing the duration of Parliament, and defining the relations between the House of Lords and House of Commons.

↓ Crown Proceedings Act 1947. The Act established the doctrine of Government according to law. Government Departments and ministers became liable to be sued for wrongful acts and the Sovereign has personal immunity ('Crown immunity').

↓ European Communities Act 1972. Gave effect to the UK's accession to the EEC (European Economic Community). EC law now had direct effect within all Member States. Community law now prevailed over any inconsistent provisions of the national law of Member States, reducing parliamentary sovereignty in the UK. Westminster Parliament now had to legislate according to Community law and the UK courts could not apply any conflicting domestic laws.

↓ Public Order Act 1986. Introduced statutory powers allowing the police to severely limit public processions and assemblies.

↓ Human Rights Act 1998. Came into force in the UK in October 2000. It is composed of a series of sections that have the effect of codifying the protections and articles of the European Convention on Human Rights (ECHR) into UK law. All public bodies (such as courts, police, local governments, hospitals, publicly funded schools) have to comply with Convention rights.

Secondary legislation

Delegated or secondary legislation allows the Government to make changes to the law using powers conferred by an Act of Parliament (or 'statute'). Statutory Instruments form the majority of delegated legislation. Secondary legislation can also be used to amend, update or enforce existing primary legislation.

Statutory Instruments (SI)
- ❖ Form of legislation that allows the provisions of an Act of Parliament to be subsequently brought into force or altered without Parliament having to pass a new Act
- ❖ SIs follow the procedures laid down in the Statutory Instruments Act 1946 (e.g. Orders in Council, regulations, rules and orders)
- ❖ Parliamentary control prescribed in the parent Act (e.g. Prime Minister can alter terms of the Fixed-Term Parliaments Act 2011 by SI, such as polling day)

Church Measures
- ❖ Instrument relating to administration and organisation of the Church of England (Anglican Church)

Special Procedure Orders
- ❖ Delegated legislation applied to parliamentary procedure that gives people or bodies the right to petition (lobby) both Houses of Parliament

Hybrid Instruments
- ❖ SIs that affect some members of a group or individual (Hybrid Bills)

Aim Higher

Make sure you use the correct vocabulary when writing about legislation. Frequently used terms include:

Made – a Statutory Instrument (SI) is 'made' when signed by a minister (or person with authority under the Act); in other words, the instrument is not in draft.

Laid – the procedure that constitutes the laying of a Statutory Instrument is set out in *House of Commons* SO 159. Basically, for a Statutory Instrument to be laid before the House of Commons a copy of the instrument must be 'laid on the table of the House'; this actually means placing a copy of the instrument with the 'Votes and Proceedings' desk in the 'Journal Office'. Most Statutory Instruments are laid in both the House of Commons and House of Lords.

Coming into force – when the provisions in the Statutory Instrument take effect.

Common law and judicial precedent

Prior to the **Norman Conquest of England in 1066**, there was no unitary, national legal system. The English legal system involved a mass of oral customary rules (**Custom**), which varied according to region. Each county had its own local court dispensing its own justice in accordance with local customs. Custom law was enforced in rather arbitrary fashion and local courts dispensed justice such as the tin mining courts of Devon and Cornwall. In 1154, Henry II institutionalised common law by creating a unified court system 'common' to the country through incorporating and elevating local custom to the national level, ending local control, eliminating arbitrary remedies, and reinstating a **jury system** of citizens sworn on oath to investigate criminal accusations and civil claims. Judges of the realm travelled from court to court and began to write down judgments. These became known as 'circuit' judges. The decisions of these 'circuit' courts were recorded and published. The practice developed where past decisions (**precedents**) would be cited in argument before the courts and would be regarded as being of **persuasive authority**. The distinctive feature of common law is that it represents the law of the courts as expressed in **judicial decisions**. The grounds for deciding cases are found in the principles provided by past court decisions, in contrast to a system that is based solely on Acts of Parliament. Originally, supremacy of the law meant that not even the King was above the law; today it means that acts of governmental agencies and ministers can be challenged in the courts. Many examples of judicial decisions have affected the development of the British Constitution, for example the *Case of Proclamations* (1611), where Coke CJ ruled whether the King could create new law without Parliament: 'the King by his proclamation or other ways, cannot change any part of the common law or statute law ...'. Part of the constitutional system – other than judicial precedent – includes trial by jury and the doctrine of the supremacy of Parliament.

Advisory sources: writers of authority

In the absence of a written UK Constitution, the writings of prominent constitutional lawyers have acquired great significance. They include: A.V. Dicey (*The Law of the Constitution*, 1885), Sir William Ivor Jennings (*The Law and the Constitution*, 1933; revised in 1959), Walter Bagehot (*The English Constitution*, 1867) and Stanley Alexander de Smith (*Judicial Review of Administrative Action*, 1959).

One example is Dicey's theory of the Rule of Law. Dicey summarised the **Rule of Law** under three headings: (1) No man can be punished or lawfully interfered with by the authorities except for breaches of law (i.e. Government actions must be authorised by law). (2) No man is above the law and everyone, regardless of rank, is subject to the ordinary laws of the land. (3) Britain does not need a written Constitution or Bill of Rights, because the general principles of the Constitution are the result of judicial decisions determining the rights of private persons (judicial precedent).

Finally, there are so-called legal writers (or in Scotland simply 'Writers') and 'institutional texts' that count as sources of constitutional law. Certain highly respected 'institutional' authors of law texts, written principally in the seventeenth, eighteenth and nineteenth centuries, have such high regard that they have been given a special place in the UK Constitution These books and legal writings are treated by the courts as authoritative statements of the law as it was at the time at which they were written, on the authority of their authors alone. Consequently, they are treated as authoritative statements of the law as it is at the present time, unless it is shown that the law has changed, and may be cited and relied on in court as such. These **books of authority** by legal writers are early **legal authorities** and are treated as such by the courts of England and Wales, and Scotland under common law jurisdiction. Although most of the statements made in these texts are presumed outdated, they can still be cited in some judicial decisions. The primary reason for judges still using some of the writers in their judgments is to demonstrate how the law has changed.

Scots law is a hybrid or mixed legal system, with a mixture of (Roman) civil and common law elements. Together with English law and that of Northern Ireland, it is one of the three legal systems of the United Kingdom. Although it has its own unique sources and institutions, its sources form part of the UK Constitution.

Glanville's Legal Treatise (ca. 1188)

❖ ***Tractatus de legibus et consuetudinibus regni Angliae*** (Treatise on the laws and customs of the Kingdom of England) – the earliest treatise of English common law; Ranulf de Glanfill died 1190

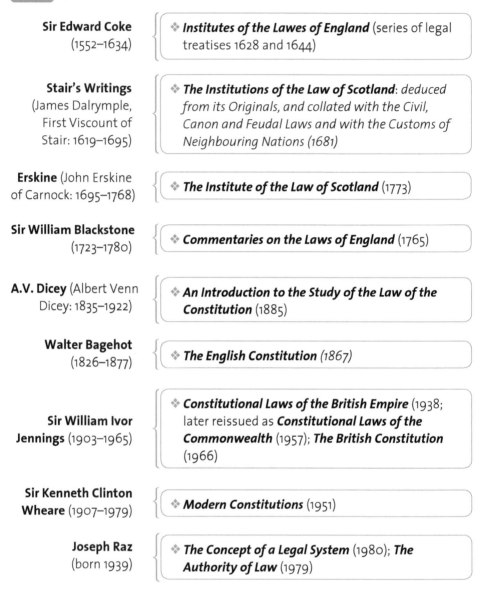

Sir Edward Coke (1552–1634)	❖ *Institutes of the Lawes of England* (series of legal treatises 1628 and 1644)
Stair's Writings (James Dalrymple, First Viscount of Stair: 1619–1695)	❖ *The Institutions of the Law of Scotland: deduced from its Originals, and collated with the Civil, Canon and Feudal Laws and with the Customs of Neighbouring Nations (1681)*
Erskine (John Erskine of Carnock: 1695–1768)	❖ *The Institute of the Law of Scotland* (1773)
Sir William Blackstone (1723–1780)	❖ *Commentaries on the Laws of England* (1765)
A.V. Dicey (Albert Venn Dicey: 1835–1922)	❖ *An Introduction to the Study of the Law of the Constitution* (1885)
Walter Bagehot (1826–1877)	❖ *The English Constitution (1867)*
Sir William Ivor Jennings (1903–1965)	❖ *Constitutional Laws of the British Empire* (1938; later reissued as *Constitutional Laws of the Commonwealth* (1957); *The British Constitution* (1966)
Sir Kenneth Clinton Wheare (1907–1979)	❖ *Modern Constitutions* (1951)
Joseph Raz (born 1939)	❖ *The Concept of a Legal System* (1980); *The Authority of Law* (1979)

Academic writers and advisory sources

Legal writers' authorities can then be used in different ways by parliamentarians, who seek to make a point or discredit others, when they mean that the Executive should not use 'arbitrary' power, i.e. must justify its actions by reference to specific legal rules. Furthermore that all citizens should be treated equally by the courts, and individual rights should be defined by reference to decisions of the courts (legal precedent).

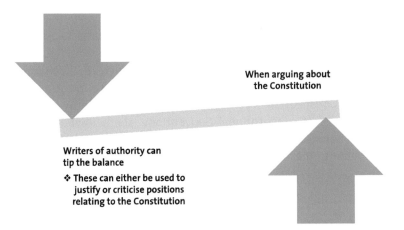

When arguing about the Constitution

Writers of authority can tip the balance

❖ **These can either be used to justify or criticise positions relating to the Constitution**

Conventions

'The flesh which clothes the dry bones of the law; they make the constitution work; they keep it in touch with the growth of ideas.' (Sir Ivor Jennings, 1959)

Conventions can be divided into two categories

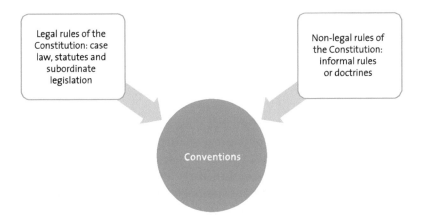

Legal rules of the Constitution: case law, statutes and subordinate legislation

Non-legal rules of the Constitution: informal rules or doctrines

Conventions

How do we know if a Convention exists?

Arguably, there is no clear agreement about what amounts to a constitutional Convention. In order to address an essay question that involves 'Conventions', it is best to look at the definitions of writers of authority, such as Sir Ivor Jennings (*The Law and the Constitution*, 1933), who defined the function or purpose of a Convention within the UK Constitution. You would then need to identify and discuss the different examples of constitutional Conventions (see below) and examine and analyse their characteristics. Only then should you discuss whether Conventions are legally binding rules and how the courts have treated these in common law. Dicey argued that they were not laws at all and would not stand up in courts.

> 'Conventions, understandings, habits or practices which, though they may regulate the conduct of the several members of the sovereign power ... are not really laws at all since they are not enforced by the courts. This portion of constitutional law may, for the sake of distinction, be termed the "conventions of the constitution", or constitutional morality.'   (A.V. Dicey, 1885)

If we accept that Conventions are not strictly 'law', they are nevertheless a characteristic of the UK Constitution and contain some areas that characteristically govern Parliament, the role of the Prime Minister and the Queen or King in Parliament.

> 'Conventions may be roughly defined as non-legal, generally agreed rules about how government should be conducted and, in particular, governing the relations between different organs of government.'
>   (Fenwick, H. and Phillipson, G., 2010, *Public Law and Human Rights*)

Conventions develop over time

The Conventions of the United Kingdom have been adopted by the Constitution over time. They express a desire or rule in order to prevent misconstruction or abuse of powers and extend the ground of public confidence in the Government. Jennings' theory is that a Convention only arises if there is an important 'reason' for its existence, that its provisions have substantial political significance. He argues that Conventions ensure that state institutions run properly. For example, the Convention that the Queen or King will accept the legislation passed by Parliament. This is known as granting **Royal Assent**. Theoretically, the Sovereign could of course refuse to give Royal Assent to a Bill, but this would invariably lead to a constitutional crisis (see also Chapter 6). It is a Convention that a Minister of the Crown should be a

Member of Parliament (and that the Prime Minister is a member of the House of Commons). Some of the best known Conventions include:

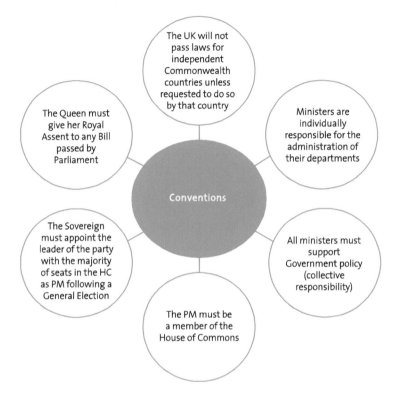

The UK will not pass laws for independent Commonwealth countries unless requested to do so by that country

The Queen must give her Royal Assent to any Bill passed by Parliament

Ministers are individually responsible for the administration of their departments

Conventions

The Sovereign must appoint the leader of the party with the majority of seats in the HC as PM following a General Election

All ministers must support Government policy (collective responsibility)

The PM must be a member of the House of Commons

Sir Ivor Jennings (*The Law and the Constitution*, Ch. III, 1933) devised a simple three-step test, still used today to establish whether a Convention exists:

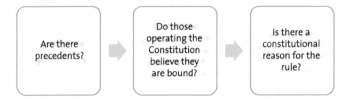

Are there precedents?

Do those operating the Constitution believe they are bound?

Is there a constitutional reason for the rule?

What is the difference between a 'constitutional Convention' and a legal rule?

In summary, the British Constitution consists of legal rules, found in statute, case law (judicial precedent) and subordinate legislation (Statutory Instruments) that generally govern society as a whole. The second category is made up of political and moralistic non-legal rules, also known as constitutional Conventions. Some are accepted as binding within Parliament and society, but they are not enforceable in a court of law. Legal authoritative writers like Jennings and Dicey have argued that Conventions have contributed to the smooth running of Government. Some key

Conventions are frequently asked about in examination or coursework questions. You need to refer to these in order to illustrate a more general point about sources of the Constitution. These are:

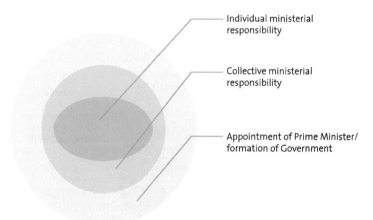

- Individual ministerial responsibility
- Collective ministerial responsibility
- Appointment of Prime Minister/ formation of Government

Collective ministerial responsibility

The Convention (or doctrine) of collective ministerial responsibility obliges all Government Ministers (the Cabinet) to support and defend Government policy. It is expected that ministers 'speak in one voice' and adopt a position of collective responsibility.

'The convention of collective responsibility means that all ministers in the government must accept responsibility for the policies, decisions, and actions of the government, even if they did not personally develop or take them, and even if they personally disagree with them.'
  (Professor Adam Tomkins, 2006, *The Struggle to Delimit Executive Power in Britain*)

Collective ministerial (or Cabinet) responsibility governs the Westminster system, meaning that members of the Cabinet must publicly support all governmental decisions made in Cabinet, even if they do not privately agree with them. This support includes voting for the Government in the Legislature. If, for example, a vote of no confidence were to be passed in Parliament, the Government would be responsible collectively, meaning the entire Government would have to resign, Parliament would be dissolved and a General Election would follow.

The purpose of this Convention is to give an impression of Government unity – moreover, to give the public confidence in governmental policies. Ministers are not expected to be outspokenly critical of Government policy. Those who do are expected to resign from their office. An example of this occurred when Lord Carrington, Foreign Secretary in Mrs Thatcher's first Cabinet, resigned in 1982 over his disagreement with the Falklands War, following the Argentine invasion of the British Falkland Islands.

By Convention, ministers must resign for personal misbehaviour. For example, in 2003 Labour Foreign Secretary Robin Cook resigned over the Iraq War after failing to accept collective ministerial responsibility for the decision to commit Britain to military action and joint invasion of Iraq with the United States, without international agreement or domestic support. Mr Cook publicly criticised the Government's involvement in the Iraq campaign and conventional rules demanded his resignation.

Conservative Cabinet Minister and Foreign Secretary, Cecil Parkinson, was forced to resign in 1983 over his affair with his secretary, Sara Keays, who was expecting his child, despite the personal support of the Prime Minister, Margaret Thatcher.

Case precedent – The Crichel Down Affair of 1954

Facts: It was the big political scandal of 1954 and resulted in the resignation of a Government Minister, Sir Thomas Dugdale, Minister of Agriculture. The case concerned a claim by a landowner of unfair treatment at the hands of the Ministry of Agriculture and the Crown Lands Commissioners. Contrary to wartime promises concerning procedures for resale, the Commissioners held on to 725 acres of his land that had been compulsorily purchased for £12,000 by the Air Ministry in 1937. A public inquiry was set up that was severely critical of official procedures and practices. Sir Thomas – who said he had nothing to do with the original decisions – nevertheless took responsibility and resigned from his office. He told Parliament: 'I, as minister, must accept full responsibility for any mistakes and inefficiency of officials in my department, just as, when my officials bring off any successes on my behalf, I take full credit for them.'

Principle: The resignation of the Government Minister Sir Thomas Dugdale set the precedent for the doctrine of ministerial responsibility.

Application: Today, the 'Crichel Down Rules' still apply and require Government Departments and other statutory bodies to offer back to the former owners, or their successors, any land previously so acquired by, or under the threat of, compulsory purchase (e.g. during World War II). Such an offer is to be at current market value, as assessed by the District Valuation Office. The Rules are non-statutory guidance (Conventions) given to government bodies on the disposal of surplus land.

What happens if a constitutional Convention is breached?

Will a breach of a Convention lead to a breach of law? We established earlier that Conventions are not enshrined in law, that they are merely rules that cannot be enforced in a court of law. Or can they? Dicey wrote that 'conventions are constitutional rules, which are not laws in the strict sense, but which are obeyed because a breach of the rules would ultimately lead to a breach of the law', and that constitutional Conventions 'are designed to control the use of discretionary power by the Crown'.

To summarise, Conventions are unwritten so they are not easy to find or to identify. There is no definitive list of Conventions. Their existence and scope is uncertain. The question before the court in *AG v Jonathan Cape Ltd* (see below) was whether or not the courts would enforce the Convention of cabinet secrecy. Would an injunction be granted to prevent publication of the Crossman Diaries? The court ruled in the negative, reinforcing the view that constitutional Conventions are not enforceable as laws, and thus an injunction to prevent publication was refused.

If the Queen broke a Convention, would she end up in court?

In September 2012, the BBC broke the news that the Queen (Queen Elizabeth II) had lobbied the then Home Secretary over Abu Hamza al Masri. This led to constitutional issues regarding whether the Monarch should become involved in Government policy. It was the Victorian constitutional writer Walter Bagehot who wrote that the Monarch had 'the right to be consulted, the right to encourage and the right to warn'. This Convention suggests that the Monarch has a limited role in Government and that Cabinet Ministers are free to reject his or her advice. In the Abu Hamza case, however, the Queen breached the Convention by encouraging a particular course of action to be taken by the Executive, namely his deportation on allegations of terrorism. Some argued that this action proposed a fundamentally undemocratic alteration to the Constitution since the Queen had not followed the Convention not to interfere in matters of Government. There is nothing objectionable about the Monarch expressing an opinion in private to a friend or even a journalist. But the BBC itself breached the Convention of publishing information that had been divulged in private by the Queen to a journalist, for which the BBC later apologised. However, it does breach a Convention for an unelected Head of State to use his or her position to lobby a Minister of State (like the Home Secretary). Still, Conventions are merely rules of political practice that are regarded as binding, by those to whom they apply, but which are not laws because they are not enforced by the courts and Parliament.

Case precedent – *AG v Jonathan Cape and Others* [1976] 1 QB 752 (The 'Crossman Diaries' case)

Facts: The Attorney-General applied for injunctions restraining the defendant publishers, Jonathan Cape and the Sunday Times, from publishing the contents of the diaries of the late Cabinet Minister, Richard Crossman, which recorded Cabinet discussions and details of advice given by and about civil servants, knowledge which the diarist acquired while a Cabinet Minister. The events described occurred during a period ending some ten years earlier. The Cabinet Secretary had been supplied with a copy of the manuscript prior to publication. The Sunday Times published extracts from the book. The Government via the Attorney-General objected to publication on the grounds that the doctrine of collective ministerial (Cabinet) responsibility would be harmed if discussions held confidentially in Cabinet were disclosed to the public. The courts had to balance the competing interests, namely the public's right to know about Government secrets and indiscretions ('the public interest test') and Cabinet confidentiality. The Court of Appeal refused the applications by the Attorney-General in that the doctrine of collective responsibility could be prejudiced by disclosure of information given in confidence. In this case, the public interest did not require such restraint (injunction of the book) by the court since ten years had elapsed since the events were recorded.

Principle: Expressions of individual opinions by Cabinet Ministers in the course of Cabinet discussion are matters of confidence, the publication of which can be restrained by a court when this is clearly necessary in the public interest. But there must come a time when the confidentiality of the information will lapse, after which the court will not intervene to restrain publication. Disclosure of such events would not tend to damage future operation of collective responsibility or inhibit free discussion in Cabinet.

Application: There is no power in the courts to restrain disclosure of advice given by civil servants or of opinions expressed as to the ability of such civil servants. Collective ministerial responsibility requires a duty of confidence but cannot be restrained from publication indefinitely.

What can be the effect if a constitutional Convention is breached?

A breach of some Conventions will result in conflict with the law and some breaches of the rules will have political consequences. It was established in *Madzimbamuto v Lardner-Burke* [1969] 1 A.C. 645 that UK legislation can overturn a Commonwealth Convention arising out of an international agreement. A Convention can always change or even develop; for example, the Convention that a Member of the House of Lords could not be the Prime Minister developed into one where if one renounced title to the Lords, then the Convention would be satisfied, as with Sir Alec Douglas Home who became Prime Minister.

But the courts have no power to punish a breach of a Convention since they are not 'law'. So, there is no legal mechanism for enforcing a breach of a Convention; for example, if a minister refuses to resign for personal misbehaviour there might be a political crisis, but there is no legislation to avert a political crisis. There are no legal sanctions for breaches of Conventions. Though Dicey would disagree:

> 'Conventions are constitutional rules, which are not laws in the strict sense, but which are obeyed because a breach of the rules would ultimately lead to a breach of the law.   (A.V. Dicey, 1885)

The Convention might cease to exist

A Convention can always change or even develop

A small number of isolated breaches might be treated as exceptions (e.g. Doctrine of Ministerial Responsibility)

The Consequences of Breaching Conventions

May avert political crisis (abandonment of collective responsibility over EC 1975)

May lead to change in law, i.e. be turned into a statute to prevent further breach (e.g. Parliament Act 1911)

If a Convention is breached, then it might cease to be a Convention

Should sources of law and Conventions be codified?

We have established that sources of the UK Constitution can be found in law reports of judicial decisions (common or case law), Acts of Parliament and Conventions. Continental European lawyers would argue, however, that the sheer bulk and complexity of UK law means that it is inaccessible to the ordinary man. They would argue in favour of codification and, of course, a written Constitution (e.g. Spain, France, Germany, Hungary). Since the early 1970s there have been a number of proposals for a codified UK Constitution. They have been produced by individuals and groups holding a wide variety of different political views. The existence of support for codification from such varied standpoints could be interpreted as an argument in favour of such an exercise. Should the law be codified so that it is readily accessible, as in civil law countries such as France or Italy? And if so how? Would such a list ever be definitive? Would codification inhibit flexibility and development? Would such Conventions then be entrenched? Would Conventions form part of a new Bill of Rights? If so, who would decide which of the 'Conventions' discussed above would and could be codified into a Constitution? Who would enforce breaches of the new 'Code' and what would be the penalty for a codified Convention or Constitution? Many countries think it necessary to give the Constitution a higher status in law than other rules of law such as Conventions. In many countries, a Constitution is thought of as an instrument by which Government can be controlled, because they would argue that Constitutions spring from a belief in limited Government (such as Germany or Portugal). The framers of the American Constitution, for example, forbade Congress to pass any ex post facto law, that is, a law made after the occurrence of the action or the situation which it seeks to regulate – a type of law which may render a man guilty of an offence through an action which, when he committed it, was innocent. The framers of the Irish Constitution of 1937 forbade the legislature to pass any law permitting divorce.

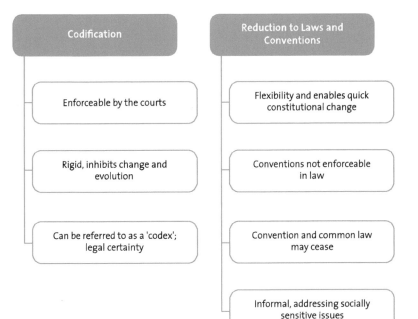

Up for Debate

How significant for the UK is the lack of a codified Constitution? You are discussing the advantages and disadvantages with a fellow student from another country of a codified written Constitution and the UK unwritten Constitution. Discuss the merits of both. Take a look at New Zealand's Constitution or that of Canada and compare it with others which are more codified. What are the advantages and disadvantages for the UK of this informal settlement? What would be the possible impacts of a codification of the UK Constitution, if it were brought about?

European Union law

European Union law (or EU law) became a source of British constitutional law following the enactment by Parliament of the European Communities Act 1972. This Act provides that some European legislation is to be given the same effect as Acts of Parliament passed by the UK Parliament. The EEC (European Economic Community, later renamed the European Community [EC] and again renamed the European Union [EU]) shaped a new legal order in Member States and limited their sovereign rights. EU law now prevails over domestic laws of Member States and has influenced UK laws and its Constitution. Individuals of Member States can rely on EC/EU Treaty Articles in domestic litigation, which is known as the Doctrine of Direct Effect as established in *van Gend & Loos v NV Algemene Transport- en Expeditie Onderneming* (Netherlands Inland Revenue Administration) (1962) Case 26–62.

EU institutions: law-making powers

As from 1 December 2009, the date on which the **Treaty of Lisbon** entered into force, the European Union has legal personality and has acquired the competences previously conferred on the European Community. **Community law** has therefore become **European Union law**. There are three main institutions involved in EU legislation:

* The **Council of the European Union**, which represents the Governments of the individual Member States. The Member States share the Presidency of the Council, on a 6-month rotating basis
* The **European Commission**, which represents the interests of the Union as a whole
* The **European Parliament**, which represents the EU's citizens and is directly elected by them (but has no direct law-making powers)

Together, these three institutions produce through the 'Ordinary Legislative Procedure' the policies and laws that apply throughout the EU. The Commission is the most powerful institution; it proposes new laws. The Council then 'makes' (executes) legislation and the EU Parliament approves (or vetoes) and adopts legislation (in the form of Regulations, Directives or Decisions). The Commission and the Member States then implement them, and the Commission ensures that the laws are properly applied and implemented. The powers and responsibilities of all of these institutions are laid down in the Treaties, which are the foundation of everything the EU does. They also lay down the rules and procedures that the EU institutions must follow. The Treaties are agreed by the Presidents and/or Prime Ministers of all the EU countries, and ratified by their Parliaments.

Policies and legislation set by the **European Council**, which brings together national and EU-level leaders

Directly elected MEPs represent European citizens in the **European Parliament**

The **Commission** is the main legislator and promotes the interests of the EU as a whole. Commissioners are appointed by the Governments of Member States

Governments defend their own country's national interests in the **Council of the European Union**.

The European Union's institutional set-up

Sources of EU Law

There are three sources of European Union law: primary law, secondary law and supplementary law. The main sources of primary law are the Treaties establishing the European Union (see above chart). Secondary sources are legal instruments based on the Treaties and include unilateral secondary law, Conventions and Agreements. Supplementary sources are elements of law not provided for by the Treaties. This category includes European Court of Justice (ECJ) (also known as 'Court of Justice') case law, international law and general principles of law.

Three types of EU Law

Putting it into practice

Essay questions are likely to relate to one of the following:

- ❖ Sources of the UK Constitution
- ❖ The difference between Conventions and laws
- ❖ The importance of constitutional Conventions in the Constitution
- ❖ Breaches of a Convention and how courts have treated such breaches
- ❖ The evolution of the doctrine of ministerial responsibility

Essay 1

Identify at least five examples each of UK primary legislation and case law that have significantly shaped the UK Constitution.

Feedback on putting it into practice

a) Note that the question is divided into two parts. For high marks, you must answer both elements of the question. If you answer only one part of the question, you will be marked down.

b) The British Constitution is founded on statutory and common law rules, made up of Conventions, common law (judicial precedent), legislation (Acts of Parliament) and EU law.

c) The process of Government in the UK is regulated by binding political rules (constitutional Conventions).

d) Discuss the enforceability in law and the distinction between laws and Conventions.

e) Discuss the different viewpoints of legal writers (e.g. Dicey, Jennings, etc.).

f) Conventions are not legally binding and the courts have no jurisdiction to grant a remedy when a Convention is breached (discuss case law here, e.g. 'Crossman Diaries case').

Essay 2

Will a breach of a Convention be a breach of law?

Feedback on putting it into practice

a) Introduce Conventions by citing legal writers' definitions, such as those of Jennings and Dicey.

b) Give reasons why Conventions are obeyed (these are mainly political).

c) Discuss ministerial (Cabinet) responsibility and cite the court's decision in *AG v Jonathan Cape Ltd* (the 'Crossman Diaries case').

d) The question really addresses whether or not courts can enforce Conventions (in the Crossman Diaries case, it concerned the Convention of Cabinet secrecy).

e) Discuss that courts cannot enforce Conventions.

f) Look at the consequences of breaching a Convention and provide examples (e.g. ministers resigning and the role of the Monarch).

g) A blatant breach of a Convention is likely to be criticised by the press and bring the violator into disrepute, as well as tarnish his or her political party's standing in the eyes of the electorate.

h) How are Conventions observed in the UK? Conventions may be observed by force of habit; a desire to conform; a belief that it is right and reasonable; or part of a good structure; fear of political implication, etc. Discuss the political implications.

Chapter summary

❖ Sources of the UK Constitution in the form of common law, legislation and Conventions.
❖ Conventions are a collection of rules that establish and regulate or oversee the Government.
❖ Consequences of breaches of Conventions.
❖ Legal authorities and legal writers' comments on Conventions.
❖ Advantages and disadvantages of codified law.
❖ Are Conventions uncertain and conversely are laws certain?
❖ The (in)flexibility of Conventions and codified law.

Table of key cases referred to in this chapter

Case name	Area of law	Principle
Crichel Down Affair (1954)	Conventions	Doctrine of ministerial responsibility (i.e. the Cabinet must speak with one voice on policy decisions)
AG v Jonathan Cape Ltd [1976] 1 QB 752 ('Crossman Diaries case')	Conventions	Collective ministerial responsibility cannot be enforced by the courts indefinitely
Madzimbamuto v Lardner-Burke [1969] 1 AC	Conventions	Legislation can overturn a (Commonwealth) Convention arising out of an international agreement
Van Gend & Loos v NV Algemene Transport- en Expeditie Onderneming (Netherlands Inland Revenue Administration) (1962)	European Union law	Nationals of a Member State can lay claim to individual rights within and against a Member State (doctrine of direct effect)

@ **Visit the book's companion website to test your knowledge**

❖ Resources include a subject map, revision tip podcasts, downloadable diagrams, MCQ quizzes for each chapter, and a flashcard glossary
❖ www.routledge.com/cw/optimizelawrevision

3

Parliamentary Sovereignty

Revision objectives

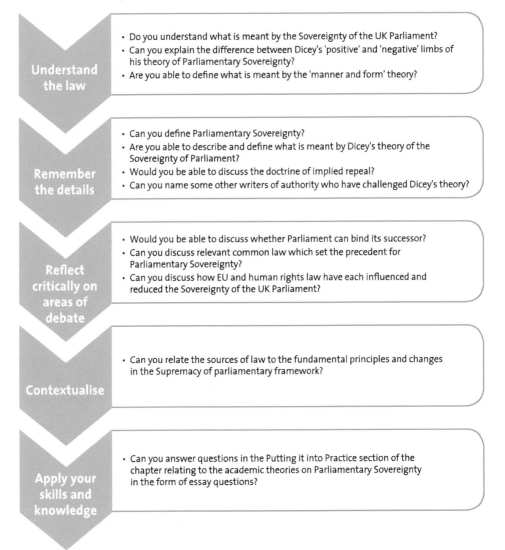

Understand the law
- Do you understand what is meant by the Sovereignty of the UK Parliament?
- Can you explain the difference between Dicey's 'positive' and 'negative' limbs of his theory of Parliamentary Sovereignty?
- Are you able to define what is meant by the 'manner and form' theory?

Remember the details
- Can you define Parliamentary Sovereignty?
- Are you able to describe and define what is meant by Dicey's theory of the Sovereignty of Parliament?
- Would you be able to discuss the doctrine of implied repeal?
- Can you name some other writers of authority who have challenged Dicey's theory?

Reflect critically on areas of debate
- Would you be able to discuss whether Parliament can bind its successor?
- Can you discuss relevant common law which set the precedent for Parliamentary Sovereignty?
- Can you discuss how EU and human rights law have each influenced and reduced the Sovereignty of the UK Parliament?

Contextualise
- Can you relate the sources of law to the fundamental principles and changes in the Supremacy of parliamentary framework?

Apply your skills and knowledge
- Can you answer questions in the Putting it into Practice section of the chapter relating to the academic theories on Parliamentary Sovereignty in the form of essay questions?

Chapter Map

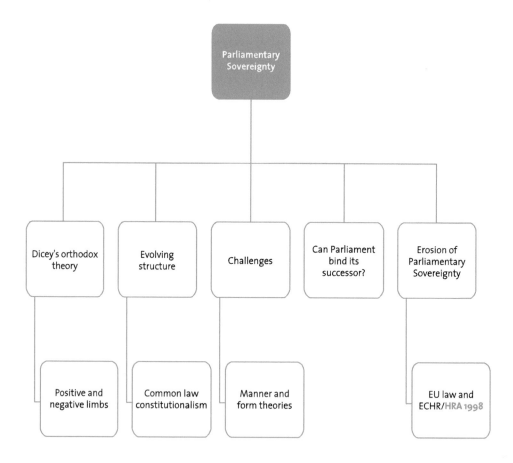

Introduction: the essence of Parliamentary Sovereignty

In the previous two chapters, you were introduced to A.V. Dicey's theories on the general principles of British constitutionalism. In this chapter, we look at the uniqueness of Parliamentary Sovereignty, a fundamental principle of the UK Constitution. In other words, the UK Constitution is dominated by the principle of Parliamentary Sovereignty (also referred to as 'Supremacy'). This doctrine makes Parliament the supreme legal authority in the UK, which can create or end any law. Simply put: Parliament can make and unmake laws as it sees fit. In general, the courts cannot overrule legislation and no Parliament can pass laws that future Parliaments cannot change. Parliamentary Sovereignty is the most important part of the UK Constitution, which we have now established is unwritten (i.e. not wholly codified) but described as 'partly written' founded on a number of sources of law which you read about in Chapter 2. This topic is not easy. It is a discursive one and you need to be absolutely sure about the meaning of Parliamentary Sovereignty before you engage with the topic in a discursive essay. Most importantly, Sovereignty has changed with incoming legislation from EU and human rights law.

> 'The principle of Parliamentary sovereignty means neither more nor less, that this, namely, that Parliament ... has, under the English Constitution, the right to make or unmake any law whatever; and, further, that no person or body is recognised by the law of England as having a right to override or set aside the legislation of Parliament.'
> (A.V. Dicey, 1959, *An Introduction to the Study of the Law of the Constitution*, 10th edn.)

Dicey's 'positive' and 'negative' limbs of Parliamentary Sovereignty

We have already established that Albert Venn Dicey (1835–1922) was one of the greatest writers and academic authorities on the British Constitution. In his major work, *An Introduction to the Study of the Law of the Constitution* (1885), Dicey defines the doctrines of 'Parliamentary Sovereignty' and the 'Rule of Law'. He summarised Supremacy as:

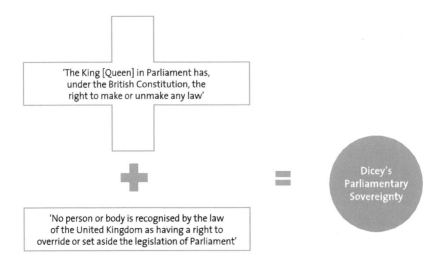

'The King [Queen] in Parliament has, under the British Constitution, the right to make or unmake any law'

'No person or body is recognised by the law of the United Kingdom as having a right to override or set aside the legislation of Parliament'

Dicey's Parliamentary Sovereignty

Dicey's orthodox theory of Parliamentary Sovereignty

Dicey argued that the definition has a positive and a negative dimension (also known as 'positive and negative limb') of Parliamentary Sovereignty. The **positive limb** refers to a power, or set of powers, to bring about valid laws. The **negative limb** refers to an immunity (or set of immunities), against everyone, including the courts, to affect the validity or intended effect of parliamentary laws. This means the UK Parliament enjoys a comprehensive and exclusive immunity of law-making against any other person or body. In any discussion you need to make this point very clearly if you want to argue Dicey's very traditional (orthodox) stance, namely, that laws made by Parliament cannot be changed or unmade except by Parliament. This makes the courts (Judiciary) mere 'interpreters' of legislation (Acts of Parliament). While Dicey did not actually use the terms 'power' and 'immunity', he used the terminology of a 'positive' and 'negative' limb (i.e. aspect) for power and immunity respectively. Dicey's views of Parliamentary Sovereignty are complete and absolute, making Sovereignty a legal fact and a vital part of the UK Constitution.

Positive Limb
* Change and unmake laws
* Law making
* Parliamentary power

Negative Limb
* Courts cannot make laws
* Immunity

Aim Higher

You may wish to undertake additional reading on this topic. Have a look at the scholarly works of Professor Sir William Wade (1918–2004), also known as the 'father' of Public Administrative Law. While Wade was a strong believer in the Dicean theory of Parliamentary Sovereignty, Wade could see that this orthodox concept was moving on. In a well-known and often-cited legal article in *The Cambridge Law Journal* of 1955, Wade pioneered the analysis of a rapidly developing body of common law as well as new parliamentary statutory provisions which regulated the post Second World War Government. Wade's *The Basis of Legal Sovereignty* restated Dicey's 'positive-negative-limb' structure (see above). Wade strongly believed that Parliamentary Sovereignty would bring order into a potentially chaotic post-war world of unregulated ministerial power at the time, also affecting courts, tribunals and inquiries. Professor Wade strongly believed in Dicey's doctrine of Sovereignty (see Wade, *The Basis of Legal Sovereignty* [1955] C.L.J. 177). What is important to note is that Wade strongly argued that the judiciary played a vital role in 'superintending' (keeping in check) the exercise of executive authority (the Executive). For Wade, Parliamentary Sovereignty was the ultimate and unalterable political fact. In later writings, Wade recognised and acknowledged that Britain's accession to the European Economic Community (EEC) in 1972 would bring about change and force a rethink to Dicey's traditional belief in the positive power of Parliamentary Sovereignty (see Wade, H.W.R. and Forsyth, C.F., 2009, *Administrative Law*, 10th edn., first published in 1961).

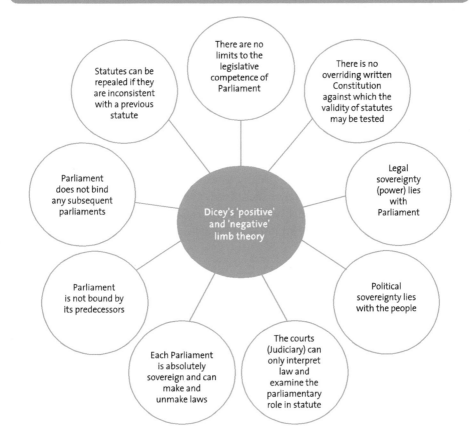

Case precedent – *Liversidge v Anderson* [1942] AC 206 (HL)

Facts: The **Defence (General) Regulations 1939** measure was enacted by Parliament at the start of the Second World War to strengthen the government's powers to protect the country from sabotage, treason and espionage. *Regulation 18B* allowed the Home Secretary to intern (imprison) people if he had 'reasonable cause' to believe that they had 'hostile associations'. The Home Secretary, Sir John Anderson, exercised this power, detaining 1500 people. Robert Liversidge (a Jewish businessman, formerly known as Jacob Perlsweig and a suspected spy) was imprisoned. He sued the Home Secretary for false imprisonment. The question before the court was whether the executive action of Sir John Anderson was 'lawful'? Could the court investigate the objective basis for the reasonable cause, i.e. could they evaluate the Home Secretary's actions on an objective standard (the reasonable man test), or were the courts to measure them against the personal standard of the Home Secretary? By the time the appeal reached the House of Lords, the meaning of Regulation 18B had become uncertain. Four of the five Law Lords accepted the Government's interpretation of the regulation, i.e. the Home Secretary could imprison anyone he thought was 'hostile'. Lord Atkin took a different view (dissented): if Parliament said 'reasonable cause to believe' it must have intended that there was some plausible evidence on which that view was based. He reiterated Dicey's version of the Rule of Law and Parliamentary Sovereignty, and gave Regulation 18B its literal meaning.

Principle: The majority of the House of Lords held that the legislation should be interpreted so as to make effective what Parliament intended, even if that meant adding to or amending the wording of the statute to give that effect. Although Parliament had made the power subject to a 'reasonable belief', they accepted the Home Secretary's statement that he held such a belief; in other words, that Sir John Anderson believed he had reasonable cause to imprison Liversidge. It appears that their Lordships were greatly concerned with the fact that they were dealing with a matter of national security. In their Lordships' view, it was not appropriate for a court to deal with matters of national security, especially as they were not privy to classified information by the Security Services that only the Executive had.

Application: This is a landmark case in constitutional law, concerning the relationship between the courts and the state (the Executive), and in particular the assistance that the judiciary gave to the Executive in times of national emergency (the Second World War). The case concerned civil liberties, the Separation of Powers and the Supremacy of Parliament. The House of Lords judgment in the case became persuasive authority not only in English law but also for a number of Commonwealth nations. It is fair to say that the English courts have gradually retreated from the decision in *Liversidge*. But Lord Atkin's dissenting judgment has since been recognised as a defining statement of the need for courts (the Judiciary) to remain independent of the Executive whatever the prevailing circumstances. In his view, the majority had abdicated their responsibility to investigate and control the Executive. Lord Atkin protested that the courts had given uncontrolled power of imprisonment to the minister.

Challenging Dicey's theory: manner and form theory

According to Dicey's positive limb theory, whatever Parliament wishes, it becomes the law. Dicey's orthodox theory makes Supremacy (or Parliamentary Sovereignty) very simple: by fixing a single source of law (Act of Parliament), the system of Supremacy cannot be challenged by anyone, least of all the courts (Judiciary). This is also known as '**manner and form**' theory. So for Dicey, the Sovereignty of Parliament (and not the Rule of Law) was the dominant characteristic of the British Constitution and its political institutions. This then led Dicey (and to a certain extent Wade) to deny that nothing could change the supreme constitutional traditions of the United Kingdom.

Dicey's Parliamentary Sovereignty and the way statute is enacted has to be in a correct and **appropriate form**. This essentially means that the way Parliament enacts legislation has to be in the **correct manner** that follows the ordinary legislative process, subject to the Parliament Acts 1911 and 1949. For example, how the Queen/King grants Royal Assent to a Bill or how the House of Commons is assembled, has to follow statute in correct manner and form.

In the British constitutional context, this means that the work of the Westminster Parliament depends on the existing rules of public law, developed through the practice of the courts and by previous statutes. According to Dicey, Parliament is a public institution operating under the law, and the same is true of all public institutions and authorities. Further principles and rules in correct manner and form include the rules on Royal succession, the election of Members of the House of Commons and the appointment of Peers in the House of Lords. There are also well-determined principles of procedure how Parliament and its institutions work and decisions are reached, governed by the Parliament Acts 1911 and 1949 (see also Chapter 6). The concept of Parliamentary Sovereignty then holds that the legislative body (the Legislature) may change or repeal any previous legislation, and is therefore not bound by written law or by precedent.

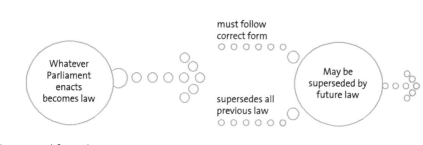

Manner and form theory

Does Dicey's orthodox theory of Parliamentary Sovereignty still apply today?

In 1976, the then Lord Chancellor, Lord Hailsham, described the British system of government as an 'elective dictatorship' in a Richard Dimbleby Lecture at the BBC. What he meant was that the Government, if elected with an absolute majority, is able to behave like a dictator owing to the weakness of Parliament (also known as 'executive dominance'). There is, then, the possibility of political transgressions and the courts can become weak, which means there are not enough checks and balances of the Executive. A Government with an elective majority in the House of Commons can then control Parliament and therefore over-influence legislation. There can be a significant overlap between the Legislature and the Executive that threatens the Separation of Powers.

The reason for executive dominance in most British Governments has been a majority of MPs in the House of Commons, owing to the first-past-the-post electoral system (by convention, ministers sit in one or other House). One example was when (New) Labour came to power in 1997 with a majority, and, despite enormous public opposition, Prime Minister Tony Blair was able to persuade Parliament to support the military invasion of Iraq in 2003. Such majorities, combined with a **whipping system** that disciplines Government backbenchers to support their own side, as well as MPs' loyalty to their own party, means that majority Governments rarely lose. This has changed since the General Election in May 2010 when no absolute majority was achieved, and a coalition Government had to be formed, made up of Conservatives and Liberal Democrats (Prime Minister David Cameron and Deputy Prime Minster Nick Clegg).

The doctrine of implied repeal

Having established that Parliamentary Sovereignty is an absolutely fundamental concept to the understanding of the UK Constitution, we have to accept the doctrine of implied repeal. This is a concept of constitutional theory. If an Act of Parliament conflicts with an earlier one, the later Act takes precedence and the conflicting parts of the earlier Act are repealed (i.e. no longer law).

Which statute takes precedence?

What happens if there has been no express repeal of a statute and the provisions of the (newer) Act of Parliament conflict with the provisions of an earlier one? Which one would take precedence? The Court of Appeal in *Ellen Street v Minister of Health* [1934] 1 KB 590 adopted the **formalist approach** to the doctrine of Parliamentary Sovereignty. The judges (re)stated the formal rule that the courts must unquestioningly obey the most recent Act of Parliament. If that Act appeared inconsistent with previous legislation, the previous Act must give way (lex posterior derogate priori, meaning, a later law overrules an earlier one). A similar approach was taken in *Vauxhall Estates v Liverpool corporation* [1932] 1 KB 133. Both cases focused on the Acquisition of Land (Assessment of Compensation) Act 1919, a slum clearance measure that laid down levels of compensation for property owners whose houses were demolished. The Housing Acts 1925 and 1930 made these provisions less generous in terms of compensation. The landowners then sought to have their compensation levels reassessed on the basis of the 1919 Act. The courts rejected that argument, basing its judgment firmly on the **doctrine of implied repeal**.

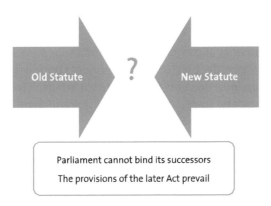

The doctrine of implied appeal

In *Thoburn v Sunderland City Council* [2003] QB 151 (the so-called 'Metric Martyr' cases), Lord Justice Laws ruled that some constitutionally significant statutes held a higher status in UK law and were not subject to the doctrine of implied repeal and would therefore require Parliament to expressly repeal the Act. *Thoburn* dealt with shopkeepers and market traders who found themselves being prosecuted for failure to comply with EC legislation, requiring weights and measures of goods offered for sale to be exclusively in metric scales. The case specifically dealt with s. 2(2) of the European Communities Act 1972, but in his judgment, Laws LJ also named the Parliament Acts 1911 and 1949 and the Human Rights Act 1998 as other 'constitutional statutes' and therefore not subject to the doctrine of implied repeal. Constitutional statutes can still be expressly repealed if Parliament wishes, but unless the words doing so are totally unambiguous, the courts will follow the precedent established in *Thoburn* (see also *Madzimbamuto v Lardner-Burke* [1969] 1 AC 645).

Up for Debate

In January 2011, Conservative MP Bill Cash expressed 'grave concern' in the House of Commons about the extent of judicial involvement in the 'construction and interpretation' of laws applying to the UK, covering areas ranging from the economy to the deportation of suspected terrorists. He argued that Parliamentary Sovereignty was in 'grave danger' due to the large number of laws being made in Europe, which Mr Cash said had turned into a 'tsunami' affecting every aspect of British life. Would you agree? Discuss the erosion of Sovereignty and Mr Cash's allegation that judges are now 'flagrantly disregarding' legislation enacted by the UK Parliament and Britain is on the way to 'judicial supremacy'. He proposed legislation to provide a 'firewall' against further judicial interference.

Developments affecting Parliamentary Sovereignty

Over the years, Parliament has passed laws that limit the application of Parliamentary Sovereignty. These laws reflect political developments both within and outside the UK. These developments do not fundamentally undermine the principle of Parliamentary Sovereignty, since, in theory at least, Parliament could repeal any of the laws implementing these changes.

Up for Debate

An essay question might ask you to debate and examine whether the privileges of Parliament should be codified by an Act of Parliament. You would then argue that such legislation would mean that the Westminster Parliament would give itself more powers. You would further make the point – as a matter of constitutional theory – that the powers of Parliament are unlimited (Dicey). You would argue that, subject to Royal Assent (regarded as a formality), the House of Commons and House of Lords acting together can pass any laws they like. One of the privileges of the Westminster Parliament is freedom of speech in both Houses of Parliament (**Bill of Rights 1689**). Ministers in the House of Commons and Peers in the House of Lords are free to raise any matter in debate without fear of civil or criminal liability. When writing your essay, you need to make a finely balanced argument: On the one hand, parliamentary privileges are unclear and rather limited. On the other hand, it may be easier for Parliament to assert new privileges if things are left as they are.

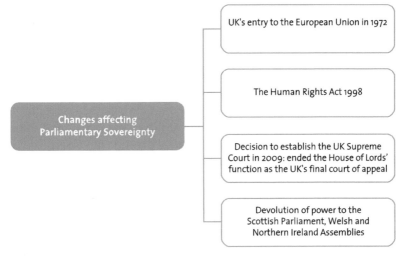

Changes affecting Parliamentary Sovereignty

Parliamentary Sovereignty: EU law and human rights

Certain limitations on Parliamentary Sovereignty have been imposed by **European Union** law since 1972 and the Human Rights Act 1998, as well as by the principles of implied repeal and the rules concerning statutory interpretation (see also Chapter 8). This part of the Constitution defines and limits the powers of Parliament and outlines the way in which Acts of Parliament and the other sources of law are to be understood today. While the orthodox (Dicean) principles of continuously binding precedent are recognised by Parliament, current officeholders also recognise new and ever-evolving principles which have developed in common law, and with the UK's accession to the European Union and the supremacy of EU law. The UK Constitution has thus changed and now specifies the 'disabilities' and liabilities that limit Parliament. Human rights law has shaped the civil liberties and laws as well as the duties of MPs.

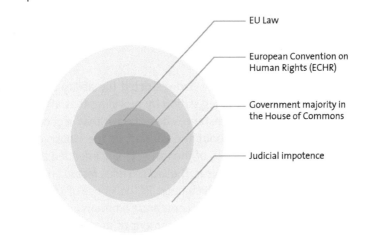

Limitations of Parliamentary Sovereignty

What are the advantages and disadvantages of Parliamentary Sovereignty?

The Constitutional Reform Act 2005 brought about changes to the way the House of Lords was made up (i.e. no more hereditary peers but appointed members such as Baroness Helena Kennedy or Lord Sugar), changes to the office of Lord Chancellor and the creation of the UK Supreme Court, thereby severing the link between the House of Lords/Court of Appeal ('the Law Lords') and Parliament. This increased and strengthened the concept of separation of Powers (the Judiciary from the Legislative) but increasingly brought into question Dicey's doctrine of Parliamentary Sovereignty. This was partly due to the UK's entry into the EEC (i.e. membership of the European Union) and partly brought about by judicial suggestions. The most notable was the Judicial Review case of *R (on the application of Jackson) v Attorney General* [2005] (also known as Jackson), in which a challenge to the validity of the Hunting Act 2004 failed (see below).

Parliamentary Sovereignty (or 'Supremacy') has gradually changed and has arguably been eroded. It is a constitutional concept that requires rethinking, particularly in light of such influences as the Human Rights Act 1998 and EU law. Although there is a range of views about whether it should be abandoned or reformed, undeniably the Sovereignty of Parliament remains a key principle of the UK Constitution.

> ### Case precedent – *R (on the application of Jackson) v Attorney-General* [2005] UKHL 56
>
> **Facts:** The application for Judicial Review was brought by John Jackson, Chairman of the Countryside Alliance, Bicester Hunt member Patrick Martin, and Mair Hughes, the wife of the Master of the Llangeinor Hunt in Mid Glamorgan. Together they challenged the use of the Parliament Acts 1911 and 1949 to enact the Hunting Act 2004 (which banned fox hunting with dogs). The Attorney-General, Lord Goldsmith, insisted that the Hunting Act was lawful and now represented the 'law of the land'.
>
> Section 2(1) of the Parliament Act 1911 had restricted the ability of the House of Lords to prevent the enactment of legislation by providing that after a period of two years had elapsed in the circumstances described in that section, a Bill could become an Act of Parliament without the consent of the House of Lords. The 1949 Act, enacted in reliance on s. 2(1) of the 1911 Act, had amended the 1911 Act by reducing the two-year period to one year. The *Jackson* issue rested on the claim that whereas the two-year delay under which peers in the House of Lords could block but not veto a Bill had been agreed by the Lords and Commons in 1911, the reduction of the delay to one year by the Labour Government of 1949 was not endorsed by Peers. Until the present case, that claim had never been tested in the courts.

Mr Jackson and the other appellants had an interest in fox hunting and challenged the validity of the 2004 Act that banned the hunting of foxes with dogs. Mr Jackson et al. sought declarations that the 1949 Act was not an Act of Parliament and was consequently of no legal effect, and that accordingly the 2004 Act was not an Act of Parliament and was of no legal effect. The appellants claimed that the Parliament Act 1911 could not lawfully be used to pass the Parliament Act 1949, which amended the 1911 Act; the Hunting Act 2004, which was passed only in accordance with the modified as opposed to the original requirements of the Parliament Acts procedure, was therefore invalid. The case reached the House of Lords, which held that it had jurisdiction to examine the validity of the Hunting Act as a question of statutory interpretation: whether the 1911 Act could be used to enact the 1949 Act?

Their Lordships held that there are no limits to the type of legislation that could be passed using the Parliament Acts except for the express limitations contained in the legislation. The Parliament Act 1949 had therefore been validly passed using the 1911 Act and the Hunting Act 2004 was consequently also held to be a valid statute. In *obiter* opinions made in the judgment, Lord Steyn, Lord Hope and Baroness Hale suggested that there might be limits to Parliamentary Sovereignty. But Lord Bingham and Lord Carswell supported the orthodox Dicean view that there are no limits to Parliamentary Sovereignty.

Principle: The House of Lords found that the Parliament Act 1911 did not have any limitations that would prevent it being used to enact the Parliament Act 1949. The 1949 Act had therefore validly amended the requirements for a Bill to use the Parliament Acts procedure and the Hunting Act 2004, which was passed in accordance with these amended requirements, was consequently also held to be valid; the appellants' appeal was dismissed.

Application: The House of Lords in *Jackson* ruled that the Parliament Act 1949 had been validly made under the power contained in the Parliament Act 1911 to enact legislation without the consent of the House of Lords, and therefore the Hunting Act 2004, made pursuant to the 1911 and 1949 Acts, had also been validly made. *Jackson* reaffirmed the doctrine of Parliamentary Sovereignty as a fundamental underpinning of UK democracy. Though Lords Hope and Steyn made the point (*obiter*) that EU law and human rights law had swept aside some of Parliament's supremacy by new protections of civil liberties and human rights, acknowledging that EU law was now supreme over domestic legislation.

Up for Debate

Take a look at the individual opinions of Lord Steyn and Lord Hope in the *Jackson* case (see above). Does either judge accept that Parliament has the ability to make and unmake any laws whatsoever? If not, what reasons do they give for this view?

Putting it into practice

Essay questions are likely to relate to one of the following:

❖ The Dicean (orthodox) theory of the Constitution and Parliamentary Sovereignty
❖ Positive and negative limbs of Dicey's theory
❖ The doctrine of implied repeal
❖ Challenges to Dicey's orthodox theory (Jennings' critique)
❖ Manner and form
❖ Inconsistency with international law (EU and ECHR)

Essay 1

Explain what is meant by the 'positive' and 'negative' limbs of Dicey's theory of Parliamentary Sovereignty. Use examples to illustrate both limbs.

Feedback on putting it into practice

a) Note that the question has three parts. For high marks, you must answer all elements of the question: define A.V. Dicey's positive and negative limbs of Parliamentary Sovereignty and illustrate both limbs by examples using case law.

b) Introduce the essay by defining the nature of the British Constitution (use your notes covered in this text for Chapters 1 and 2).

c) Define legal sovereignty that lies with Parliament, i.e. political sovereignty lies with the people and Parliament ('the Queen or King in Parliament') may make or unmake any law.

d) Parliament may pass any statute making whatever provision it wishes upon any subject matter.

e) The UK (or Westminster) Parliament is 'self-embracing', i.e. it can subsequently bind itself and future parliaments.

f) Common law must give way to statute (self-embracing theory of Parliamentary Sovereignty).

g) Critical constitutional writers such as Professor Ian Loveland have argued that such a theory 'has had no political effect in this country' (Loveland, I., 2012, *Constitutional Law, Administrative Law, and Human Rights*)

h) Discuss Dicey's legal doctrine of Parliamentary Sovereignty, which normatively stipulates that past parliaments cannot bind future ones; that predecessors cannot negotiate on behalf of their successors.

i) Discuss sovereignty is a common law rule which the judiciary (the Judicature) has to obey (i.e. courts interpret and apply laws made by Parliament).

j) The main part of the essay should concentrate on the Dicean theory of the positive and negative branches (or limbs) of Parliamentary Sovereignty.

k) The positive limb asserts that Parliament is capable of making or unmaking any law that it wishes, as no other sovereign body exists to legally prevent it from doing so (implied repeal).

l) The negative limb of Dicey's theory defines the legality of Acts of Parliament, which cannot be challenged in any legal court.

m) You then need to give examples: If a case involves a challenge to the validity of an Act of Parliament, the courts cannot question its validity, let alone judicially review it and declare it void for illegality.

n) Courts may not normally investigate the procedural regularity of a statute beyond confirming that it has been passed according to correct and appropriate parliamentary procedure.

o) Example: at the height of the Troubles in Northern Ireland during the 1970s, the Westminster Parliament introduced compulsory internment of suspected IRA terrorists without trial.

p) Example: the War Damages Act 1965 had retrospective effect and effectively undid the decision in *Burmah Oil Co Ltd v Lord Avocate* (1965), which technically amounted to a breach of the Rule of Law.

Essay 2

Can Parliament bind its successors? Discuss and use examples to illustrate and consider the various theories of Parliamentary Sovereignty.

Feedback on putting it into practice

a) This topic covers implied repeal and the 'manner and form' argument raised ([1931] and [2005]).

b) The question really asks whether Parliamentary Sovereignty is still the 'jewel in the crown' of the UK Constitution?

c) Discuss Dicey's (and Wade's) definition of Parliamentary Sovereignty first (manner and form of laws and the orthodox theory that Parliament can make and unmake laws as it sees fit).

d) You then need to move to the present constitutional doctrine of legal 'dualism', a state of affairs that allows Parliamentary Sovereignty alongside other treaties, such as the European Convention on Human Rights or EU law in the form of the European Communities Act 1972.

e) You may well argue that the Treaty of Rome (*Treaty Establishing the European Economic Community* (TEEC) 1958) and other EU treaties have gradually undermined Parliamentary Sovereignty.

f) Your conclusion should critique Wade's theory that Parliamentary Sovereignty is no longer a regime in which Parliament necessarily binds its successors successfully.

g) The fact that checks and balances by the judiciary are not possible in a majority Government (Wade's worry) is not quite true: there are now checks and balances by way of supreme EU law and the European Court of Justice (see *Costa v ENEL* (1964) ECR 585 (6/64); *R v Secretary of State for Transport exparte Factortame (No 2)* (1991) Case C-213/89 [1991] 1 AC 603).

h) You should make the point that some sovereignty passed from 'Westminster' to 'Brussels' (i.e. to the EU Parliament) but only in those legal areas that are covered by European Community Treaties (i.e. free movement of goods, free movement of workers but not criminal law).

i) For exceptionally high marks you may wish to argue that the UK faces a dilemma if the Scottish people decide to vote for a separate Scottish state in the referendum. Alternatively, whether or not future British courts will be able to find an Act of Parliament that intends to repeal the European Communities Act 1972, therefore the United Kingdom's membership in the European Union (as per the *Treaty of Maastricht 1991*), in order to leave the EU.

Chapter summary

❖ The essence and meaning of Parliamentary Sovereignty.
❖ Dicey's 'positive' and 'negative' limbs of Parliamentary Sovereignty.
❖ Manner and form of statutes that strictly govern Parliament and how laws are made.
❖ Recent challenges to the Dicean theory whether Parliament can bind its successor.
❖ The doctrine of implied repeal.
❖ Developments affecting Parliamentary Sovereignty and limitations of the doctrine by way of EU and human rights law.

Table of key cases referred to in this chapter

Case name	Area of law	Principle
Vauxhall Estates v Liverpool Corporation [1932]	Parliamentary Sovereignty; doctrine of implied repeal	A later Act repeals the earlier statute
Ellen Street Estates v Minister of Health [1934]	Parliamentary Sovereignty; doctrine of implied repeal	A later statute overrules the earlier one
Costa v ENEL (1964)	Supremacy of EU Law	Supremacy of EU law over all Member States of the European Union
Madzimbamuto v Lardner-Buke [1969]	Parliamentary Sovereignty	If Parliament chooses to repeal one Act and replace it with a new Act of Parliament, the courts cannot hold the (new) Act of Parliament invalid
R v Secretary of State for Transport ex parte Factortame (No. 2) (1991)	Supremacy of EU law	The *Factortame* judgment is part of the UK's uncodified body of the Constitution, reinforcing the supremacy of EU law
Thoburn v Sunderland City Council [2003] ('Metric Martyr' cases)	Doctrine of implied repeal; supremacy of EU law	EU law takes precedent over domestic law; UK statutes can still be repealed if Parliament wishes, but unless the words doing so are totally unambiguous, the courts will follow the precedent established in *Thoburn*
R (on the application of Jackson) v Attorney-General [2005]	Parliamentary Supremacy; supremacy of EU law	*Jackson* reaffirmed the doctrine of Parliamentary Sovereignty as a fundamental underpinning of UK democracy. Note the obiter dicta by Lords Hope and Steyn EU and human rights law have swept aside some of the supremacy

@ **Visit the book's companion website to test your knowledge**

❖ Resources include a subject map, revision tip podcasts, downloadable diagrams, MCQ quizzes for each chapter, and a flashcard glossary

❖ www.routledge.com/cw/optimizelawrevision

4

The Royal Prerogative

Revision objectives

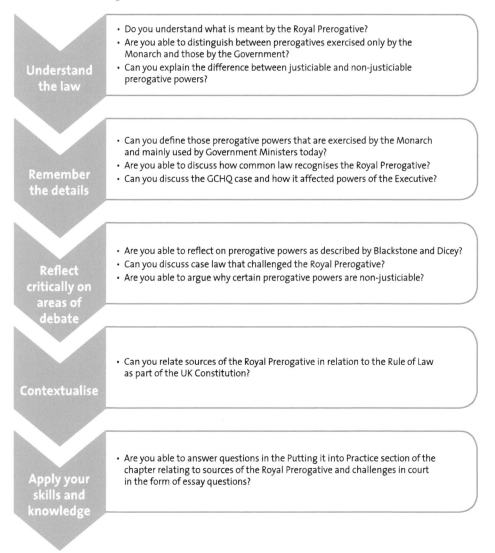

Understand the law
- Do you understand what is meant by the Royal Prerogative?
- Are you able to distinguish between prerogatives exercised only by the Monarch and those by the Government?
- Can you explain the difference between justiciable and non-justiciable prerogative powers?

Remember the details
- Can you define those prerogative powers that are exercised by the Monarch and mainly used by Government Ministers today?
- Are you able to discuss how common law recognises the Royal Prerogative?
- Can you discuss the GCHQ case and how it affected powers of the Executive?

Reflect critically on areas of debate
- Are you able to reflect on prerogative powers as described by Blackstone and Dicey?
- Can you discuss case law that challenged the Royal Prerogative?
- Are you able to argue why certain prerogative powers are non-justiciable?

Contextualise
- Can you relate sources of the Royal Prerogative in relation to the Rule of Law as part of the UK Constitution?

Apply your skills and knowledge
- Are you able to answer questions in the Putting it into Practice section of the chapter relating to sources of the Royal Prerogative and challenges in court in the form of essay questions?

Chapter Map

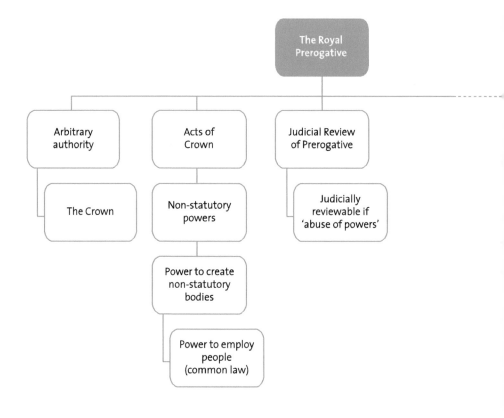

Prerogative by
the Monarch

Prerogative by
Government

Non-justiciable
prerogatives

Summon/dissolve
Parliament

Power to make
war and peace

The appointment
of ministers

Appoint Prime
Minister/Ministers

Power to
enter treaties

The dissolution
of Parliament

Give Royal
Assent to Bills

Power to deploy
armed forces
overseas

The granting
of honours

Right of Royal
Fish, Swans and
Treasure Trove

Power to stop
prosecutions

The prerogative
of mercy

Grant of Mercy
(Royal Pardon)

Defence of the
Realm

The making
of treaties

Introduction: what is the Royal Prerogative?

Historically, the King had special powers to preserve the realm against external forces, amounting to an undefined residue of power that he could use for the public good. This was known as the **Royal Prerogative**, granting the Monarch exclusive powers in respect of his personal decision-making. This meant that certain Royal functions could only be exercised in certain ways. While the King could only exercise questions of the title to land or punish criminals through the common law courts ('the King's courts' or the 'King's Bench'), the Monarch additionally possessed the residual power of administering justice through his Council where the courts of common law were regarded as insufficient. The Bill of Rights 1689 declared illegal certain specific uses and abuses of the Prerogative, followed by the concept of responsible Government and the establishment of a Constitutional Monarchy. Have a look at Dicey's definition of the Royal Prerogative below.

> 'The residue of discretionary or arbitrary authority, which at any time is legally left in the hands of the Crown ... Every act which the executive government can lawfully do without the authority of an Act of Parliament is done in virtue of this prerogative.'
> (A.V. Dicey, 1959, *An Introduction to the Study of the Law of the Constitution*, 10th edn.)

Various electoral reform acts of the nineteenth century established that the bulk of prerogative powers could be exercised only through and on the advice of ministers responsible to Parliament. Although the Monarch retained formal power of appointment and removal of ministers, the development of **collective ministerial responsibility** made it increasingly difficult for the King or Queen to exercise their prerogative freely against the wishes of the Prime Minister and Cabinet.

Definition of the Royal Prerogative

The term is difficult to define. A.V. Dicey defined the Royal Prerogative as 'The residue of discretionary or arbitrary authority, which at any given time is legally left in the hands of the Crown' (see Dicey, A.V., 1959, *Introduction to the Study of the Law of the Constitution*, 10th edn.). The point Dicey was making was the arbitrariness of the Royal Prerogative that is neither in statute nor in common law. William Blackstone described the Royal Prerogative in more detail, as those powers that 'the King enjoys alone, in contradistinction to others, and not to those he enjoys in common with any of his subjects' (see Blackstone, W., 1769, *Commentaries on the Laws of England*). Dicey's definition builds on Blackstone's definition of **Prerogative Powers**, still used by Members of Parliament today.

'... that special pre-eminence, which the King hath, over and above all other persons, and out of the course of the common law, in right of his Royal dignity. It signifies ... something that is required or demanded before, or in preference to, all others.' (Blackstone, W., 1769, *Commentaries on the Laws of England*)

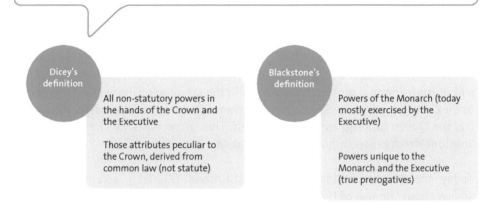

Dicey's definition

All non-statutory powers in the hands of the Crown and the Executive

Those attributes peculiar to the Crown, derived from common law (not statute)

Blackstone's definition

Powers of the Monarch (today mostly exercised by the Executive)

Powers unique to the Monarch and the Executive (true prerogatives)

Sources of Prerogative Powers

Case law dealing with the Royal Prerogative can be diverse and confusing, which means that the law in this area remains uncertain because we are dealing with an ancient power still applied in modern parliamentary times. It is therefore difficult to give a comprehensive catalogue of Prerogative Powers but below you will see the most common ones exercised only by the Monarch and those powers only used by Members of Parliament today. The most common Prerogative remaining today is **Crown Immunity** (also known as 'Sovereign Immunity').

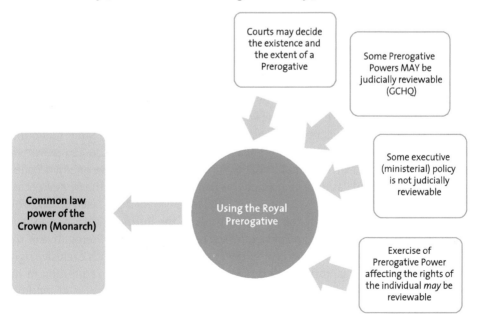

Courts may decide the existence and the extent of a Prerogative

Some Prerogative Powers MAY be judicially reviewable (GCHQ)

Some executive (ministerial) policy is not judicially reviewable

Common law power of the Crown (Monarch)

Using the Royal Prerogative

Exercise of Prerogative Power affecting the rights of the individual *may* be reviewable

Crown Immunity

There is a legal prerogative that still has modern constitutional significance, namely, the principle that the Crown (or the state) can do no wrong. This is known as **Crown (or Sovereign) Immunity**. The British constitutional monarchy is founded on the origin that the King is the authority who originally created the courts (i.e. King's or Queen's Bench Divisional Courts). Thus the courts have no power to compel the Monarch to be bound by the courts, as they were created by him for the protection of the King's (or Queen's) subjects. Crown Immunity remains a legal doctrine, part of the Royal Prerogative by which the Sovereign and his or her state representatives cannot commit a legal wrong; they are then immune from being sued in a civil law suit or from criminal prosecutions. Action in the criminal courts is taken 'on behalf of the Crown' (such as *R v Smith*). It would therefore be rather strange for the Crown (i.e. the Queen or King) to prosecute itself. This is the basis for the Crown being 'immune' from prosecution for criminal liability.

Today, the Queen (or King), as the constitutional Monarch, accepts ministerial advice about the use of the remaining Prerogative Powers, whether the Monarch personally agrees with that advice or not. Many of these legal prerogatives have been amended or substituted by legislation. While it is fair to assume that all core departments in the Civil Service enjoy Crown Immunity, it is possible that some government agencies are no longer protected in this way (such as contracted-out services in the National Health Service or private prisoner transport by security services). For example, the Crown is no longer 'immune' from the requirements of health and safety legislation. There are some prerogatives which Parliamentarians think are in urgent need of reform. It has been suggested that the Law Commission should review all Royal Prerogatives.

Conflict between legislation and Prerogative Powers

Blackstone said that Prerogative Powers were of an exclusive nature. So, what happens if there is legislation (an Act of Parliament) and a prerogative in place? Which one takes precedence over the other? This was first raised in the *De Keyser's Royal Hotel* case in the 1920s. The conflict arose over acquisition of land or property by the state during times of war. There existed the Royal Prerogative (also known as the 'scorched earth' policy) that there is no compensation to an individual if the state had either requested land or property, and there was no common law right to compensation from the state for battle or war damage or for damage done by the enemy to one's property or land. Lord Parmoor confirmed this Prerogative Power in the *De Keyser* case (see *Attorney-General v De Keyser's Royal Hotel Limited* [1920] AC 75) (see below). This principle was contradicted by the House of Lords in the *Burmah Oil* case in 1965 (a Scottish appeal case) when Lord Reid expressed concern about the Prerogative of the Crown in relation to the 'scorched earth' policy and the Government's exclusive right not to compensate a land or property owner for war damage or requisition of his property (see *Burmah Oil Company (Burma Trading) v Lord Advocate* [1965] AC 75). Both the *De Keyser* and the *Burmah Oil* cases concerned requisition of land and property by the state in times of war. The *Burmah Oil* case set a new precedent for compensation by the state to land and property owners for war damage (see also *Laker Airways v Department of Trade* [1977] 1 QB 643; *R v Secretary of State for the Home Department ex parte Fire Brigades Union and Others* [1995] 2 AC 513).

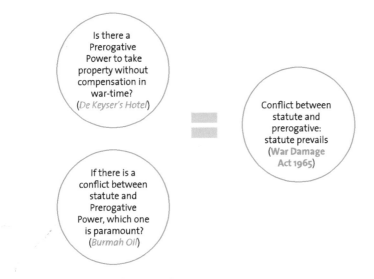

Conflict between statute and the Royal Prerogative

Case precedent – *Attorney-General v De Keyser's Royal Hotel Limited* [1920] AC 75 (HL)

Facts: A hotel owner claimed compensation under the Defence Act 1842 for occupation of the hotel by the armed forces during the First World War. The Government relied on the Royal Prerogative under which 'less compensation would be payable'. The House of Lords rejected the Government's reliance on the Prerogative and held that once a statute had been enacted, the Prerogative Powers 'fall into abeyance' (are no longer used) for the duration of the life of the statute unless Parliament creates a new statute or amends or modifies an existing one.

Principle: The House of Lords ruled that where an Act of Parliament covers the same scope as the Royal Prerogative, the Act of Parliament prevails. The prerogative, if not expressly abolished, is effectively suspended. Accordingly, the Government could not choose to use the prerogative to award a lesser amount of compensation for occupation of property in wartime than the amount provided for under the statute. *De Keyser* is the authority for the Royal Prerogative being placed in abeyance (suspended) when a statute provides a legal basis for an action.

Application: There is a general constitutional common law principle established in *De Keyser* that the Crown (or authorities of the state) is not entitled as of right by virtue of its Royal Prerogative to take possession of a subject's land or buildings for administrative purposes in connection with defence of the realm without paying compensation for that use.

Case precedent – *Burmah Oil Company (Burma Trading) v Lord Advocate* [1965] AC 75

Facts: The *Burmah Oil* case dealt with the destruction of oil fields in Burma by British forces during the Second World War. The sabotage was committed in order to prevent the plantations from falling into the hands of the advancing Japanese army. The House of Lords held, by majority, that although the damage was lawful, it was the equivalent of requisitioning the property altogether. Their Lordships held that *any* act of requisition was done for the good of the public, at the expense of the individual proprietor, and for that reason, the proprietor should be compensated in full from public funds. The result was that the pursuers (the party initiating a Scottish law suit), Burmah Oil Company and others, would receive compensation for their destroyed plantations.

Principle: Any act of requisition of either land or property 'done for the good of the public' in times of war at the expense of the individual proprietor or land owner, must be fully compensated from public funds (by the state). The House of Lords ruling meant that Burmah Oil and other companies were to receive compensation for their destroyed plantations from the state.

Application: The House of Lords in *Burmah Oil* established a legal right to full compensation to land and property owners, if the damage or requisition was caused during time of war. However, the result in *Burmah Oil* was subsequently frustrated (overruled) by the passing of a retrospective Act of Parliament, the War Damage Act 1965, which abolished any common law right to compensation in respect of damage to, or destruction of, property affected by, or on the authority of, the Crown during, or in contemplation of the outbreak of, war. This meant that the Crown was exempted from liability in respect of damage to land or property caused lawfully in the name of the Crown during time of war (see **Crown Immunity** above).

How effective is the Prerogative in law today?

There are **legal prerogatives** of the Crown (vested in the Crown) which are legal rather than constitutional in character. Some of these historical remnants are still in the Sovereign's hands today. These include the Crown's rights to sturgeon, certain swans, and whales, and the right to impress men into the Royal Navy. Another prerogative is the dissolution of Parliament, but the last time a Monarch dissolved

Parliament on his own initiative without his Prime Minister's advice was William IV in 1835. If the power exists at all today it is by Convention subject to the advice of the Prime Minister and possibly his or her Cabinet (see Chapter 2). If the Monarch ignored the Convention and dissolved Parliament regardless of advice, the consequence would be political rather than legal. The governing party would fight an election and seek a new mandate, which could include curtailing the Prerogative Power!

Today, this unique constitutional power of the Monarch ensures that ministers take responsibility for the use of these Prerogative Powers. The Monarch still has certain Prerogative Powers today, which are exclusive to him or her; these include the rights to advise, encourage and warn ministers in private; to appoint the Prime Minister and other ministers; to assent to legislation (Royal Assent); to prorogue or to dissolve Parliament; and (in grave constitutional crisis) to act contrary to or without ministerial advice. A **Royal Pardon** removes the penalty (i.e. sentence), not the conviction. Realistically today, the Monarch exercises this power on the advice of the departmental minister (i.e. Minister of Justice; before 2005, the Home Secretary). A decision not to grant a pardon can be challenged by Judicial Review (see *R v Secretary of State for the Home Department ex parte Bentley* [Derek] 1993 in the Divisional Court when the then Home Secretary, Kenneth Clarke, refused a pardon to Derek Bentley who was hanged for murdering PC Miles in 1953, aged 19).

Up for Debate

'Let him have it Chris' – those were the words spoken by 19-year-old Derek Bentley (1933–1953) to his accomplice, 16-year-old Christopher Craig, during the burglary of a warehouse in south London in November 1952, when confronted by Police Constable Sidney Miles. Bentley was sentenced to death for encouraging (so it was alleged) his friend Craig to shoot the policeman. The Bentley case created a cause célèbre and led to a 45-year-long campaign to award Derek Bentley a posthumous pardon. You may wish to research this legal case as well as the campaign to invoke this Royal Prerogative, which was eventually granted in 1998. While Craig was too young for the death penalty, Bentley was hanged in 1953. What is important to note, and should then be made clear by you in writing academically about the Derek Bentley case, is that a Royal Pardon removes the penalty, not the conviction. When the Monarch exercises her (or his) power on the advice of the departmental minister (such as the Home Secretary in the case of Derek Bentley, or now, the Secretary of State for Justice), the minister's decision can be challenged by Judicial Review (see *R v Secretary of State for the Home Department ex parte Bentley* [Derek] 1993 Div Ct). There is also a film called 'Let him have it' (1991, DVD), which dramatises the story of Derek Bentley, starring Christopher Eccleston as Derek Bentley, Tom Courtenay as William Bentley and Eileen Atkins as Lilian Bentley.

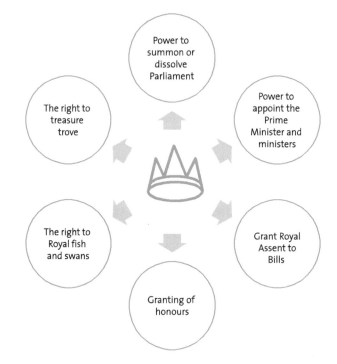

Prerogative Powers used by Monarch only

Prerogatives exercised by the Executive only

Prerogative executive powers (by Government) form the category of prerogatives which has been under review and is constantly changing with developing case law. Over time, ministers took responsibility for actions done **in the name of the Crown**, so these Prerogative Powers were, in effect, delegated to responsible ministers. But Parliament has not really been directly involved in that transfer of power over time. Today, some of these Prerogative Powers are effectively in the hands of ministers – though these powers are not strictly 'law'. The connection between these Prerogative Powers and the Crown (King or Queen) is now tenuous and the term Royal Prerogative could now mislead. For example, Members of Parliament are prevented from raising certain prerogatives in the House of Commons, such as the honours list. It would make more sense if these powers only now exercised by ministers could be referred to as the 'Ministerial Executive' (rather than the Royal Prerogative).

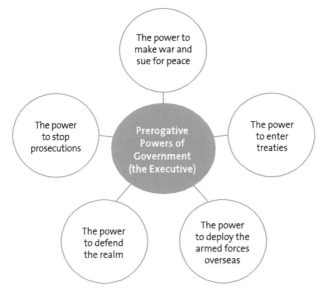

Prerogatives exercised by Government only

Prerogative Powers of ministers

These powers are among the most significant that any Government can possess. However, the ability of ministers to rely on Prerogative Powers continues to give rise to problems of accountability. Ministers regularly use the Royal Prerogative without any parliamentary approval or scrutiny.

The making and ratification of treaties

❖ **North Atlantic Treaty 1949.** The North Atlantic Treaty Organisation (NATO) is a security alliance of 28 North American and European states. NATO protects the freedom and security of its 28 Member States

Recognition of states; the appointment of Ambassadors and High Commissioners abroad

❖ **Overseas Interparliamentary Assemblies,** including Council of Europe, European Security and Defence Assembly, North Atlantic Treaty Organisation, Organisation for the Security and Cooperation in Europe

Governance of British Overseas Territories and Foreign Office

❖ **House of Commons Select Committee on Foreign Affairs** consists of 11 MPs from the three largest political parties; monitors policy, administration and expenditure of Foreign & Commonwealth Office

Deployment of armed forces overseas, including involvement in armed conflict, or the declaration of war	❖ Both Houses of Parliament look after the constitutional arrangements for British armed forces (e.g. Armed Forces Act 2006)
The use of the armed forces within the United Kingdom to maintain the peace in support of the police	❖ **Ministry of Defence** provides legal basis for the system of military law in the UK; introduces new measures relating to the armed forces outside the traditional sphere of Service discipline (e.g. Armed Forces Act 2011)
Prime Minister appoints ministers, judges, senior positions in Church of England and proposes Life Peers and honours	❖ The **Archbishops of Canterbury and York** get life peerages on retirement; **Judicial Appointments Commission** appoints on merit, respecting the constitutional principle of the independence of the judiciary
Recommendations for honours by the Foreign and Commonwealth Secretary and the Defence Secretary	❖ 118 members of the British armed forces received honours in the Queen's Honours List in March 2013 (e.g. Lance Corporal Ashworth, VC (killed in action); Air Commodore Wigston, CBE; Captain Higham, OBE)
Organisation of the Civil Service	❖ The **Public Administration Select Committee** (PASC) set up an inquiry into the future of the Civil Service in June 2013
Grant and revocation of passports	❖ In 2010 Home Secretary Theresa May revoked 16 UK passports of alleged militants and terrorists (e.g. Mohamed Sakr's citizenship was revoked in September 2010; 17 months later he was killed in a US drone strike in Somalia)
Royal Prerogative of Mercy (Grant of Pardon); Attorney-General's power to stop prosecutions	❖ Convicted loyalist murderer Robert Rodgers killed Catholic teenager Eileen Doherty in 1973. She was shot three times after her taxi was hijacked by gunmen in south Belfast. In February 2013, Rodgers applied to NI Secretary, Theresa Villiers, to be freed under the Royal Prerogative of Mercy

Ministerial executive powers under the Royal Prerogative

Up for Debate

In June 2013, Robert Rodgers (59) failed in his High Court bid to be freed under the Royal Prerogative of Mercy. He was imprisoned for the sectarian murder of a Catholic teenager, Eileen Doherty, in 1973. The 19-year-old was shot three times after her taxi was hijacked by gunmen in south Belfast. Despite being given a life sentence, Rodgers could have been freed under the **Royal Prerogative of Mercy** (RPM) under the **Good Friday Agreement of 1998**. Rodgers sought to judicially review Northern Ireland Secretary Theresa Villiers' decision to turn down his request for RPM. The judge said a pardon could lead to a form of amnesty for anybody who killed more than once during the Troubles in Northern Ireland.

Relationship between the state and Prerogative Powers

How are the Prerogative Powers controlled? This happens in two ways. First, there is political and statutory control by Parliament. Secondly, there is judicial control usually through Judicial Review proceedings (see below, *Judicial Review of Prerogative Powers*). It is now generally accepted that Parliament is not powerless in the face of some of these weighty prerogatives. Some of the Prerogative Powers have been put on a statutory footing, such as the Interception of Communications Act 1985, the Security Service Act 1989 and the Intelligence Services Act 1994. Some non-legal rules have been adopted so as to provide procedural safeguards, for instance in relation to the ratification of treaties, known as the **Ponsonby Rule**, which states that any treaty that requires ratification must be laid before Parliament 21 days before it is ratified, and the revocation of passports. Many public appointments, too, are now subject to regulation and monitoring by a Commissioner and are made in accordance with the **Nolan Rules**. These rules were established by a Committee on Standards in Public Life, chaired by Lord Nolan, a distinguished judge, in 1994 under Conservative Prime Minister, John Major, in the wake of the cash-for-questions scandal. The Nolan Committee specifically looked at the practices of those who serve the public, including MPs, civil servants and appointees to non-departmental public bodies such as the BBC.

Is there any statutory control to limit the Royal Prerogative?

In short, no. The basic rule established in the Bill of Rights 1689 has been that Parliament is sovereign and can abolish, amend or curtail Prerogative Powers. And we have already established that it is a fundamental principle of British constitutional law that no Parliament can bind its successors and that any statute can be repealed (see Chapter 3). The principle of Parliamentary Sovereignty means that the UK Parliament can enact *any* law whatsoever on any subject whatsoever (although there are now considerations of compatibility with European Union law, and it is arguable that the European Communities Act 1972 is 'semi-entrenched'; for as long as the UK remains a member of the EU, the 1972 Act cannot be repealed – see Chapter 8). Furthermore, changes in rules of UK constitutional law can be effected by ordinary legislation (unlike the situation, for example, in the United States of America, where changes can only be made by a complicated process of constitutional amendment). The courts do, however, draw the line where a Prerogative Power is used to defeat a Statutory Power (see *R v Secretary of State for the Home Department ex parte Fire Brigades Union* [1995]).

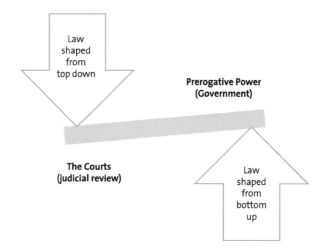

Why are people generally unaware of Prerogative Powers?

Not many people know (except public law students!) that the Royal Prerogative is concerned with several areas critical to the UK Government, including the conduct of foreign affairs, defence and national security. Today, the Monarchy has significantly less power in these matters (the true Royal Prerogative) and Prerogative Powers are largely in the hands of the Prime Minister and his or her Cabinet (the Executive). That said, ministers are accountable to Parliament for the **use** of Prerogative Powers, but they are only accountable **after** the event. This means that – constitutionally – the UK still permits its ministers to use certain powers without parliamentary approval under the Royal Prerogative.

Aim Higher

In February 2005, Labour Home Secretary Charles Clarke used the Royal Prerogative to stop two British men freed from Guantanamo Bay being issued with passports. The executive ministerial decision meant that Martin Mubanga and Feroz Abbasi were effectively confined to Britain, although their citizenship was not affected. Find out how many times ministers have used the Royal Prerogative since 1947.

Judicial Review of Prerogative Powers

The courts have traditionally been unwilling to subject **Prerogative Powers** to Judicial Review (see also Chapter 9). Historically, the Monarch's judges have been reluctant to question the exercise of the Sovereign's Prerogative Powers and this form of **judicial deference** continued well into the twentieth century. William Blackstone considered it appropriate, in certain circumstances, that the courts could review the legality of the use of **some** Prerogatives, although they do not have a remit over all of them, and the courts can only help the aggrieved citizen **after** the event. This generally included ministerial accountability and the Ministerial Code on patronage and public appointments as well as the Civil Service. With the approach of the twentieth century, it became clear that the Monarch was no longer involved in day-to-day Government and there was no meaningful distinction between a Government action based on statutory or Prerogative Power, thus this approach became anachronistic (i.e. old-fashioned and belonging to another era). Lord Denning pointed this out in the *Laker case* in the Court of Appeal in 1977 when he said: 'Seeing that the Prerogative is a discretionary power to be exercised for the public good, it follows that its exercise can be examined by the courts just as any other discretionary power that is vested in the executive.'

Until then, judges were only willing to state whether or not Prerogative Powers existed, not whether they had been used appropriately. They would merely apply the '***Wednesbury* reasonableness**' test and whether the prerogative was used *ultra vires* (illegally) (see Chapter 10). A year later Lord Denning was the dissenting judge in *Gouriet v H.M. Attorney-General* [1978] AC 435, when the majority in the Court of Appeal refused to review a decision of the Attorney-General not to commence '**relator proceedings**'. Relator proceedings (a Prerogative Power) enable the Attorney-General to initiate civil proceedings in defence of the public interest where an individual is either unable or unwilling to take action, in this case, to protect the public interest during the postal workers' strike by boycotting mail and telephone calls to and from South Africa in their protest against Apartheid. The Government had decided not to prosecute the postal workers. Major John Prendergast Gouriet (1935–2010) had asked the court for an injunction, with the backing from the 'National Association For Freedom', availing himself of the Post Office Act 1953 in his court action (the Act makes it illegal to impede mail). The Court of Appeal declined judgment. Lord Denning (dissenting) during the appeal in the House of Lords opined that it was about time the courts reviewed the Relator Prerogative, asking, 'are the courts to stand idly by'? But the House of Lords decided to stand idly by and **not interfere with the Royal Prerogative**. When the Attorney-General, Samuel Silkin, appeared in court, he insisted that the courts had power to examine his reasons for refusing Mr Gouriet an injunction.

Can a Royal Prerogative be subjected to Judicial Review?

The turning point came in 1985 when in the **GCHQ case** the House of Lords established that there could be Judicial Review of a Prerogative Power – in that case, the termination of the right of workers to belong to Unions at GCHQ by prerogative order (see *Council for Civil Service Unions v Minister for the Civil Service* [1985] AC 374).

Case precedent – *Council for Civil Service Unions v Minister for the Civil Service* [1985] AC 374

Facts: In 1984, the British Government under Prime Minister Margaret Thatcher decided that employees of the Government Communications Headquarters (GCHQ) would not be allowed to join any trade union for national security reasons. This was enforced through a Prerogative Power (an Order in Council). The Council for Civil Service Unions chose to bring this matter to court through Judicial Review. The High Court ruled that the Order was invalid. The Court of Appeal decided that reasons of national security should prevail. The House of Lords decided that exercises of the Royal Prerogative were generally subject to Judicial Review, with certain exceptions such as matters of national security. This was a significant break from previous common law decisions, which held that Prerogative Powers were not in any way subject to Judicial Review (see *Laker Airways* and *Gouriet*).

Principle: The Unions failed on the issue that their work related to national security and that aspect was **non-justiciable** (GCHQ monitors all radio and satellite transmissions of overseas countries). Any justiciability based on national security is a bar on Judicial Review, whether the origin of the power in question is statute or the prerogative.

Application: The *GCHQ* case served to identify that the application of Judicial Review would be dependent on the nature of the Government's powers, not their source.

In the *GCHQ* case, the House of Lords indicated the following matters are non-justiciable (i.e. not subject to Judicial Review):

Prerogative Powers that are non-justiciable (not subject to Judicial Review)				
Appointment of ministers	Dissolution of Parliament	The granting of honours	Making of treaties	Matters of national security

Which Prerogative Powers can be judicially reviewed?

Since the *GCHQ* case in 1985, the courts have agreed to review prerogatives, especially where they have little policy content and relate to individual rights or interests:

Prerogative Powers that are judicially reviewable			
Refusal of a passport (*R v Secretary of State for Foreign and Commonwealth Affairs ex parte Everett* [1989])	Expelling friendly aliens (*R v Home Secretary ex parte Beedassee* [1989])	Prerogative of Mercy (*R v Home Secretary ex parte Bentley* [1993])	Exclusion of members of the armed forces (e.g. on the ground of sexual orientation) (*R v Ministry of Defence ex parte Smith* [1996])

GCHQ established the principle that Prerogative Powers are *capable* of Judicial Review. Whenever a Prerogative Power is now challenged, this power must be recognised by the courts. As a result, the courts define the limits and ultimately decide the existence of any alleged Prerogative Power.

Aim Higher

You may wish to look at proposals by the Government to reform the Royal Prerogative. For this you would have to do some online research, but this would assist you in your conclusion to a discursive essay on the subject. In July 2007, the Government published a *Green Paper*, 'The Governance of Britain', which discussed reform of the Royal Prerogative. It proposed that 'in general the Prerogative Powers should be put onto a statutory basis'. This was followed by a *White Paper* (with a draft *Constitutional Reform Bill* included) in March 2008. The *White Paper* contained proposals for reform of the Attorney-General's powers, for placing the Civil Service on a statutory footing and for greater parliamentary control over deploying the armed forces abroad and ratifying treaties. The prerogative of issuing passports was to be placed on a statutory footing separately by future legislation. The **Constitutional Reform and Governance Act 2011** put the functions and duties of the Civil Service on a statutory footing, now allowing for parliamentary scrutiny of treaty ratification (in the form of a resolution of the House of Commons).

Putting it into practice

Essay questions are likely to relate to one of the following:

❖ Definition of the Royal Prerogative in British constitutional law
❖ Which Prerogative Powers lie only with the Monarch and which are now only exercised by Government Ministers

❖ Discussion and examples of Crown (Sovereign) Immunity
❖ Conflicting issues and case law concerning legislation (statutory provision) and Prerogative Powers
❖ The question of whether Prerogative Powers are judicially reviewable

Essay 1

The Royal Prerogative (i.e. Prerogative Powers) remains an important element of the UK Constitution. Should they be subject to judicial scrutiny? Discuss.

Feedback on putting it into practice

a) Note that the question has two parts. To gain the full marks allocated to this question, you must answer both elements: first, define the Royal Prerogative clearly, naming the main Prerogative Powers and, secondly, which ones are (now) judicially reviewable.

b) Introduction – this will be largely descriptive; you can mention the historical development of the special powers awarded to the King (Queen) and how these prerogatives came about.

c) Prerogative Powers are widely accepted as one of the many sources of the British Constitution (at this point you might briefly mention the other sources – see previous chapters).

d) You should then cite the powers that are specifically used only by the Monarch and those now used only by the Executive (Government Ministers); provide examples.

e) Next, highlight the change in the way the powers are executed as politics and the political system have developed; at this point, you will need to cite case law.

f) Now move into the area of Judicial Review; cite case law and its development, providing examples where the courts said they would not interfere with Judicial Review of the Royal Prerogative, followed by the precedent set in the *GCHQ* case (1985) (HL) (see also Chapters 8 and 9).

Essay 2

Are Royal Prerogative Powers judicially reviewable?

Feedback on putting it into practice

a) Similar to the introduction for Essay 1 above, define the Royal Prerogative, using legal writers' definitions such as those of Blackstone and Dicey.

a) Briefly describe the historical background and development of the various prerogatives and the role that they play within the UK Constitution (past and present) and how they impact on the workings of Government today.

b) As times have changed so too has the way in which Prerogative Powers are exercised (both by the Monarch and by the Executive); provide examples in case law.

c) Demonstrate the judicial mechanisms (judicial review – cite case law) that are used to scrutinise and control these discretionary powers (the Royal Prerogative) – particularly used by Government Ministers.

d) Conclude by introducing some of the reasons why greater scrutiny is desirable; most importantly you need to conclude and deduce whether greater scrutiny is actually required or is simply just preferred by Parliament and/or the Judiciary.

Chapter summary

❖ The Royal Prerogative is a body of customary authority, privilege and immunity, recognised in common law.

❖ Sources of Prerogative Powers as part of the UK Constitution.

❖ Legal writers' definitions of the Royal Prerogative.

❖ Prerogative Powers exercised only by the Monarch and those only by the Executive (Government Ministers).

❖ Prerogative Powers and Judicial Review.

❖ Prerogative Powers used by the Government in domestic and foreign matters.

❖ Are these powers judicially reviewable (justiciable)?

❖ Powers that have become either redundant or have been replaced by legislation.

❖ Reform of Prerogative Powers (Constitutional Reform and Govermance Act 2011).

Table of key cases referred to in this chapter

Case name	Area of law	Principle
Attorney-General v De Keyser's Royal Hotel Limited [1920]	Royal Prerogative	The Crown (or authorities of the state) is not entitled as of right by virtue of its Royal Prerogative to take possession of a subject's land or buildings for administrative purposes in connection with defence of the realm without paying compensation for that use

Case name	Area of law	Principle
Burmah Oil Company (Burma Trading) v Lord Advocate [1965]	Royal Prerogative and legislation (Prerogative of Government)	Established a legal right to full compensation by the state for damage caused to land or property during times of war
Gouriet v H.M. Attorney-General [1978]	Royal Prerogative (relator proceedings by the Attorney-General) and judicial review	House of Lords held it would be unconstitutional to judicially review the Attorney-General's Prerogative Power
Council for Civil Service Unions v Minister for the Civil Service [1985] (*GCHQ* case)	Prerogative Power (Government) and Judicial Review	In principle, a Royal Prerogative can be subject to Judicial Review. However, any justiciability based on national security is a bar on Judicial Review, whether the origin of the power in question is statute or the prerogative
R v Home Secretary ex parte Beedassee [1989]	Prerogative Power; Judicial Review	Expelling friendly aliens is judicially reviewable
R v Secretary of State for Foreign and Commonwealth Affairs ex parte Everett [1989]	Prerogative Power; Judicial Review	Refusal of a passport is judicially reviewable
R v Secretary of State for the Home Department ex parte Bentley [Derek] [1993]	Royal Prerogative of Mercy; Judicial Review	Royal Pardon (mercy) of convicted criminals is judicially reviewable
Laker Airways v Department of Trade [1977]	Royal Prerogative and EU law	Prerogative (here: treaty-making power) could not be used to defeat a right granted under an Act of Parliament

R v Secretary of State for the Home Department ex parte Fire Brigades Union and Others [1995]	Royal Prerogative and the use by ministers and the courts	The courts have no power to compel a minister to bring a statute into effect. But an alternative scheme devised by the Government (to statutory provision) is unlawful. While the Secretary of State (in this case the Home Secretary and the Criminal Injuries Compensation Scheme of 1988) is under no legally enforceable duty to bring the main provisions of an Act into force, he must consider when it is appropriate for him to do so and does not enjoy an absolute and unfettered discretion not to do so
R v Ministry of Defence ex parte Smith (1996)	Prerogative Power; Judicial Review	Exclusion of members of the armed forces (here: on the ground of sexual orientation) is judicially reviewable

@ **Visit the book's companion website to test your knowledge**

❖ Resources include a subject map, revision tip podcasts, downloadable diagrams, MCQ quizzes for each chapter, and a flashcard glossary

❖ www.routledge.com/cw/optimizelawrevision

5 Separation of Powers

Revision objectives

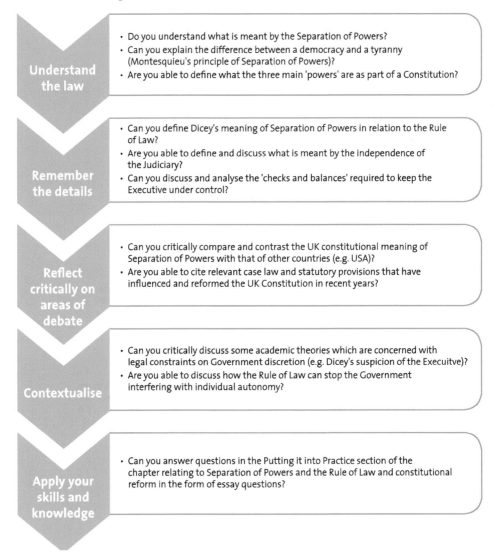

Understand the law
- Do you understand what is meant by the Separation of Powers?
- Can you explain the difference between a democracy and a tyranny (Montesquieu's principle of Separation of Powers)?
- Are you able to define what the three main 'powers' are as part of a Constitution?

Remember the details
- Can you define Dicey's meaning of Separation of Powers in relation to the Rule of Law?
- Are you able to define and discuss what is meant by the independence of the Judiciary?
- Can you discuss and analyse the 'checks and balances' required to keep the Executive under control?

Reflect critically on areas of debate
- Can you critically compare and contrast the UK constitutional meaning of Separation of Powers with that of other countries (e.g. USA)?
- Are you able to cite relevant case law and statutory provisions that have influenced and reformed the UK Constitution in recent years?

Contextualise
- Can you critically discuss some academic theories which are concerned with legal constraints on Government discretion (e.g. Dicey's suspicion of the Execuitve)?
- Are you able to discuss how the Rule of Law can stop the Government interfering with individual autonomy?

Apply your skills and knowledge
- Can you answer questions in the Putting it into Practice section of the chapter relating to Separation of Powers and the Rule of Law and constitutional reform in the form of essay questions?

Chapter Map

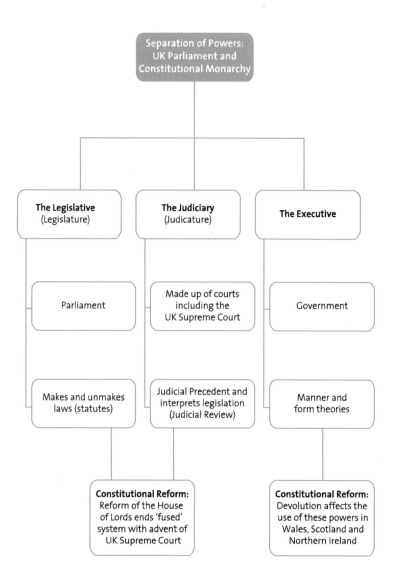

Separation of Powers:
UK Parliament and
Constitutional Monarchy

The Legislative
(Legislature)

The Judiciary
(Judicature)

The Executive

Parliament

Made up of courts
including the
UK Supreme Court

Government

Makes and unmakes
laws (statutes)

Judicial Precedent and
interprets legislation
(Judicial Review)

Manner and
form theories

Constitutional Reform:
Reform of the House
of Lords ends 'fused'
system with advent of
UK Supreme Court

Constitutional Reform:
Devolution affects the
use of these powers in
Wales, Scotland and
Northern Ireland

Introduction: what is meant by Separation of Powers?

In democracies, there are three sorts of power. The first is the **Legislative** (also known as the Legislature), which makes laws. The second is the **Executive** (Government), which makes peace or war, sends or receives embassies, establishes the public security, and provides against invasions in respect of things dependent on the law of nations; and the executive in regard to matters that depend on the civil law. The third is the **Judiciary** (or Judicature), which can punish criminals or determine disputes in civil law between individuals. In Chapter 1, you learnt about general constitutional principles and the **Rule of Law**. This will be used as a basis for your knowledge and you may wish to have another look at Chapter 1, which introduced you to the general principles of the Rule of Law and the Separation of Powers. This chapter will build on this knowledge, and focus on 'checks and balances' of the Executive by Parliament (the Legislature) and judicial control (the Judicature).

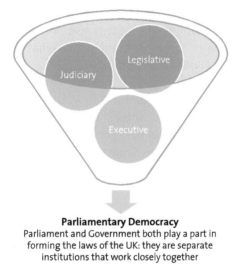

Parliamentary Democracy
Parliament and Government both play a part in
forming the laws of the UK: they are separate
institutions that work closely together

Montesquieu's pure theory of Separation of Powers

Charles Louis de Secondat, Baron de Montesquieu ('Montesquieu', 1689–1755), wrote about the 'pure' Separation of Powers, which, to him, was the basis for the Constitution of a democratic state. Where this was not the case, and the Executive was unchecked and randomly made laws at will, he warned that this might lead to a tyrannical state. In summary, Montesquieu's pure Separation of Powers refers to the idea that the major institutions of state should be functionally independent and that no individual should have powers that span these offices. The principal institutions are usually taken to be the Executive, the Legislature and the Judiciary.

'When legislative power is united with executive power in a single person or in a single body of the magistracy, there is no liberty, because one can fear that the same monarch or senate that makes tyrannical laws will execute them tyrannically.'

(Montesquieu, *De l'Esprit des Loix* ['The Spirit of the Laws'], 1748)

The UK and US Constitutions

The Separation of Powers forms an integral part of both the UK and American Constitutions. In the United States and other presidential systems, a strict separation is often a fundamental constitutional principle (also known as the 'pure' system as per Montesquieu). In the United Kingdom and other common law jurisdictions, however, the theory of separation is less clear. In the UK, the major offices and institutions have evolved to achieve balance between the Crown (and more recently the Government) and Parliament. The system resembles a balance of powers more than a formal separation of the three branches, or what Walter Bagehot called a 'fusion of powers' in *The English Constitution* (1867).

While the Separation of Powers is guaranteed in the American codified (written) model, it is not so clear and guaranteed in the British Constitution, which is uncodified and therefore the roles of the various parts of Government have merged. Montesquieu's pure theory of the Separation of Powers for truly democratic Government and its functions lies in three bodies:

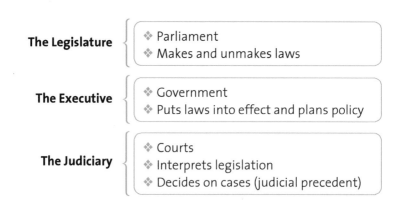

The Legislature
- ❖ Parliament
- ❖ Makes and unmakes laws

The Executive
- ❖ Government
- ❖ Puts laws into effect and plans policy

The Judiciary
- ❖ Courts
- ❖ Interprets legislation
- ❖ Decides on cases (judicial precedent)

The United States Constitution adheres closely to the Separation of Powers: all three branches (or powers) are systematically split between the Executive (the President), the Legislative (Congress) and the Judiciary (the Supreme Court). The President cannot serve in Congress and serving Congressmen cannot be a Supreme Court judge. Montesquieu's pure theory is then realised in American politics in that no branch becomes more powerful than the other two, so that a balance is achieved.

The American Constitution clearly states what the Executive, the Legislative and the Judiciary can do. Article I grants powers to the Legislature; Article II gives executive power to the President; and Article III creates an independent Judiciary. Congress is elected separately from the President, who does not sit as part of the Legislature. The Supreme Court can declare the acts of both Congress and President to be unconstitutional.

In **Britain** this is not so clear. The legislative aspect is Parliament where laws are made (remember Parliamentary Supremacy, in that the UK Parliament can make and unmake laws – see Chapter 3). The Executive (Government or 'the Cabinet') plans future legislation and formulates policy while the Judiciary is made up of all the UK courts, the UK Supreme Court and the Judicial Committee of the Privy Council, who have a final say on legal issues (added to which is the European Court of Justice – see Chapter 7). The Prime Minister is an active member of the Legislative. He or she can vote for or against a Bill in Parliament but nonetheless is also the leading member of the Executive. Reforms of the House of Lords and the introduction of the UK Supreme Court will be discussed later in this chapter. Members of the Cabinet (the Executive, i.e. Ministers with a Portfolio) are also members of the Legislative who have the right, as a Member of Parliament (MP), to vote on issues.

We therefore see a merging of roles in the British constitutional model where the Separation of Powers is not as clear and 'pure' as Montesquieu saw it. Supporters of the British model argue that this adds more flexibility to a constitutional model in support of a modern society and the freedom of the individual. Supporters of the American model claim that a written (codified) Constitution gives a Government the rights it has so that it cannot trespass onto power held by other parts of the political system or have its powers trespassed on by others. This is known as 'checks and balances'.

The American Constitution, then, prescribes very clear powers for the Executive (President's office), the Legislative (Congress) and the Judiciary (Supreme Court). Each section's powers is restricted and well defined and crossover between the three sectors of politics is avoided. This is not so clear in the United Kingdom. Therefore, checks and balances have to be in place, particularly of the Executive. In summary, the American constitutional model has separation as part of the American Constitution, which is less clear-cut in the United Kingdom.

Separation of Powers and the Rule of Law

The concept of the Rule of Law has already been discussed in detail in Chapter 1 (see the theories by Dicey, Raz and Allan, for example). We will therefore concentrate on the underlying principle of the Separation of Powers and the role the Rule of Law plays in this context. Montesquieu warned us if the three powers (Legislative,

Executive and Judiciary) are concentrated as one within a state, there will be tyranny (such as dictatorship under Adolf Hitler in the Third Reich in Germany, 1935–1945; or under the Fascist leader, 'Il Duce' Mussolini, who seized total power as dictator, ruling Italy from 1930 to 1943). Only when these branches of a state are separate, unique and equal, when there is a true Separation of Powers, can any potential harm to citizens within a state be averted or kept at bay. For Dicey, the Rule of Law is the primary tool as a check on the Crown (or the Executive) not to abuse its powers. This is commonly known as 'checks and balances' of the Executive. For Dicey, there could be no conflict between Parliamentary Sovereignty and the Rule of Law.

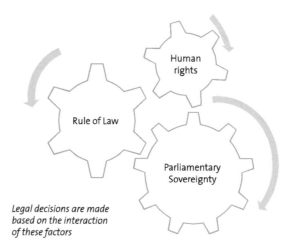

Legal decisions are made based on the interaction of these factors

Today, the **Rule of Law** has a broader meaning. With the impact of the Human Rights Act 1998 (HRA), incorporating the European Convention on Human Rights (ECHR), the Rule of Law includes basic recognition of human rights that should be acknowledged as part of a democratic Constitution of a liberal society. The Rule of Law, then, generally refers to legal authority and the influence of law in society, such as constraints on behaviour, including behaviour of the Executive (e.g. Government officials, the Civil Service, and Ministers of the Crown). Some senior judges have argued that the Human Rights Act 1998 has eroded the Sovereignty of Parliament, itself a construct of common law.

The *Jackson* case

The scope of the legislative supremacy of Parliament issue was considered by the Appellate Committee of the House of Lords in the case of *R (Jackson) v Attorney-General* [2005] UKHL 56. The case concerned a challenge to the constitutional validity of the Hunting Act 2004. The reason why the case is of such constitutional importance is that it was the first time the Law Lords declared (*obiter dicta*) that Parliament's ability to pass primary legislation was limited in substance. Lord Steyn, Lord Hope and Baroness Hale commented *obiter* that there might be limits to Parliamentary Sovereignty (although Lords Bingham and Carswell supported the orthodox view that there are no limits to Parliamentary Sovereignty). They suggested that in certain circumstances the courts had inherent powers to disapply legislation.

Lord Steyn declared (*obiter*) that the principle of the Sovereignty of Parliament, while still being the general principle of the UK Constitution, was:

> '. . . a construct of the common law. The judges created this principle. If that is so, it is not unthinkable that circumstances could arise where the courts may have to qualify a principle established on a different hypothesis of constitutionalism.'
>
> (Lord Steyn, in *Jackson v AG* [2005])

Lord Steyn's dicta in *Jackson* meant that, if the Government were to try to tamper with the fundamental principle of the Rule of Law, this would interfere with the fundamental principles of the UK Constitution. Meaning, the Rule of Law should triumph over Parliamentary Supremacy.

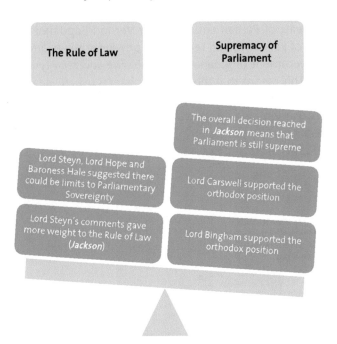

The House of Lords ruled in *Jackson* that there were no limits to the type of legislation that could be passed using the Parliament Acts 1911 and 1949, except for the express limitations contained in the legislation. The Parliament Act 1949 had therefore been validly made using the Parliament Act 1911; therefore, the Hunting Act 2004 was also held a valid Act of Parliament.

The relationship between the Legislative, the Executive and the Judiciary

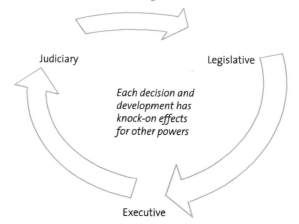

Each decision and development has knock-on effects for other powers

Judiciary

Legislative

Executive

Separation of Executive and Legislature

In the UK (and other common law jurisdictions), the Executive and Legislature are closely entwined. The Prime Minister and a majority of his or her ministers are Members of Parliament and sit in the House of Commons. The Executive is therefore present at the heart of Parliament. Professor Vernon Bogdanor believes that the UK's integration of Executive and Legislature provide stability and efficiency in the operation of Government (Bogdanor, V., 2006, *The Sovereignty of Parliament and the Rule of Law*). This means that the Prime Minister is usually head of the Executive branch of Government as well as leader of the majority party in the Legislature. Additionally, Parliament may delegate law-making powers to the Government through powers to draft secondary or delegated legislation (see Chapter 6). In conclusion, the Legislature and Executive in Britain are not strictly separate powers.

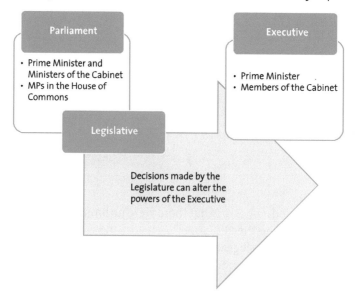

Parliament
- Prime Minister and Ministers of the Cabinet
- MPs in the House of Commons

Legislative

Executive
- Prime Minister
- Members of the Cabinet

Decisions made by the Legislature can alter the powers of the Executive

Checks and balances: who controls the Executive?

How, then, is the Executive kept in check? The UK Parliament can facilitate scrutiny provided by a number of procedures, including Prime Minister's Question Time, a powerful procedure for holding the Executive to account, whereby ministers have to answer weekly questions in Parliament (a public event) and are answerable to the Legislature. Then there are Select Committees, which scrutinise the work of the Executive.

What happens if there is a party majority in Government?

Where a Government has a large majority of seats in the House of Commons, the crucial issue is whether the Government (Executive) can dominate Parliament (Legislature) and ensure that its proposed legislation is enacted, or whether there are sufficient procedures in place to ensure that proposals are sufficiently scrutinised and either endorsed or rejected by Parliament.

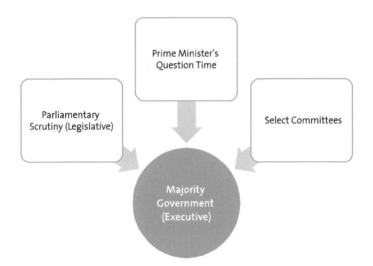

Checks and balances of the Executive

Another way of preventing the Executive from becoming too powerful (particularly in a party-majority Government) and thereby controlling Parliament is the House of Commons (Disqualification) Act 1975, which created limits on the number of salaried (Cabinet) ministers sitting in the House of Commons. The legislative branch of Government also retains the formal power to dismiss executive officers from office. The Convention of **Collective Ministerial Responsibility** established the accountability of Government to Parliament. In 2011, the Public Administration Select Committee examined the role and responsibilities of ministers, following the Parliamentary expenses scandal in 2009. This resulted in the Parliamentary Voting System and Constituencies Act 2011, which cut the number of MPs in the House of Commons from 650 to 600.

Aim Higher

You may wish to look into the Parliamentary expenses scandal, uncovered largely by *The Daily Telegraph* from 2008 onwards, and first instigated by journalist Heather Brooke via the **Freedom of Information Act 2000** (FOIA) from January 2005 (when the FOIA came into force). In January 2008, the House of Commons was ordered by the Information Commissioner to release a detailed breakdown of expenses claimed by six MPs including Prime Minister Gordon Brown and his predecessor Tony Blair. This was followed, in March 2008, by the *Telegraph* publication of the so-called 'John Lewis list', revealing that MPs were allowed to claim up to £10,000 for a new kitchen, more than £6000 for a bathroom and £750 for a television on Parliamentary allowances. In March 2009, Sir Christopher Kelly, the Chairman of the Parliamentary Scrutiny Committee on Standards in Public Life, announced an inquiry into MPs' expenses. From May 2009 onwards, *The Daily Telegraph* printed a series of extracts from leaked computer discs containing the Commons' authority's documentation of MPs' second home claims. Over the next few weeks, daily reports in the paper put the spotlight on dozens of MPs, revealing practices such as 'flipping' homes to maximise claims and the avoidance of capital gains tax by changing the designation of second homes. The Speaker of the House of Commons, Mr Martin, announced on 19 May 2009 that he would stand down after telling the Commons that he was 'profoundly sorry' about misusing parliamentary expenses and that the public had been let down 'very badly indeed'.

The independence of the Judiciary

The second element of the Separation of Powers is separation between Legislature and Judiciary. The independence of the Judiciary manifests itself in many forms in the UK. For example, judges are prohibited from standing for election to Parliament under the House of Commons (Disqualification) Act 1975. Judges are expected to interpret legislation in line with the intention of Parliament and are responsible for the development of common law (judge-made or case law). Judges in the higher courts have life tenure (retirement age is 75), which protects their independence, and a resolution of both Houses of Parliament is needed to remove a High Court judge from office, while judges at the lower levels can only be removed after disciplinary proceedings. Judges are also protected by immunity from legal action in relation to judicial functions and absolute privilege in court proceedings.

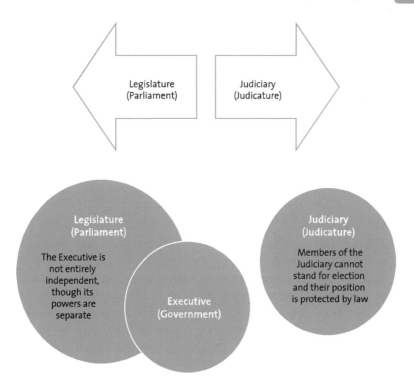

Independence of the UK Judiciary

In practice, the Separation of Powers means that citizens must be able to challenge the legitimacy of executive action before an **independent Judiciary**. This is because it is the Executive that exercises the power of the state and because it is the Executive, in one form or another, that is the most frequent litigator in the courts (see Chapter 8). Constitutionally, judges are subordinate to Parliament and may not challenge the validity of Acts of Parliament (see *Pickin v British Railways Board* [1974] AC 765). However, judges interpret legislation, which leads us to ask the popular question, do judges make law?

Up for Debate

Do judges make law? Hilaire Barnett argues that there is an element of judicial law-making in the evolution of common law (see *Constitutional and Administrative Law*, 10th edn., 2013). Lord Reid said in his lecture, 'The Judge as Lawmaker' (1972), that while it was once 'thought almost indecent' to suggest that judges make law, the notion that judges only declare the law was outdated. Lord Scarman argued that 'the objective of judges is the formulation of principles; policy is the prerogative of Parliament' (see *McLoughlin v O'Brian* [1983] 1 AC 410 – where the House of Lords gave judgment in favour of the claimant in relation to nervous shock). You may also wish to look at the *Jackson* case (2005) on the application of the **Parliament Acts 1911** and **1949** to the **Hunting Act 2004**, which prompted *obiter dicta* (remarks said by the way) from their Lordships. They questioned the relationship between Parliamentary Sovereignty and the Rule of Law in a novel manner, suggesting that there were limits to Parliamentary Sovereignty where constitutional fundamentals were at risk. You may well argue that there are elements of judicial law-making in the evolution of common law. On the other hand, you may agree with Lord Scarman.

The Executive and Judiciary

The third element of separation is between the Executive and the Judiciary. The judicial scrutiny function of the Executive should ensure that any delegated legislation (e.g. Statutory Instruments) is consistent with the scope of power granted by Parliament and to ensure the legality of Government action and the actions of other public bodies. This is done by way of **Judicial Review**. By contrast, following the principle of Parliamentary Supremacy, primary legislation is not usually subject to Judicial Review (see Chapter 9). On the application of an individual, Judicial Review is a procedure in the administrative courts which may question the lawfulness of actions or decisions by public bodies (doctrine of *ultra vires*). This requires judges to be independent of governmental and parliamentary influence.

Generally, judges have tended to exercise self-restraint (known as 'deference') in this area of administrative law. Some have used the **Royal Prerogative**, when issues of 'high policy' are involved, such as the appointment of ministers, the allocation of financial resources, national security, the signing of treaties and defence matters (see Chapter 4). In these cases, judges do not generally interfere in matters of policy (see *Council of Civil Service Unions v Minister for the Civil Service* [1985] AC 374 – the *GCHQ* case). In *A and others v Secretary of State for the Home Department* [2004] UKHL 56 (also known as the 'Belmarsh Prisoners case') concerning the detention without charge of suspected international terrorists in Belmarsh Prison, the Attorney-General argued that 'these were matters of a political character calling for an exercise of political and not judicial judgment' and that 'it was not for the courts to usurp authority properly belonging elsewhere'. However, Lord Bingham, who gave the leading judgment in the *Belmarsh* case, rejected this argument, concluding that 'the function of independent judges charged to interpret and apply the law is universally recognised as a cardinal function of the modern democratic state' and that the Attorney-General was 'wrong to stigmatise judicial decision-making as in some way undemocratic'.

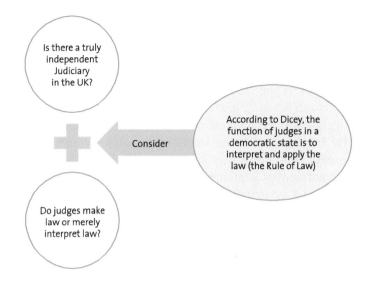

Constitutional reform in the United Kingdom

Constitutional reform in the UK has brought about certain limitations to the powers of the Executive (Government). The Parliament Act 1911, for example, weakened the power of the House of Lords by removing entirely the power of the Lords to amend or reject a Money Bill, replacing its absolute veto with a delaying power on Non-Monetary Bills for three sessions. Dicey described this Act as the last and greatest triumph of party government (Dicey, A.V., 1915, *Law of the Constitution*). We have seen that the British Constitution is founded on legal principles and various sources of law and Conventions (see Chapter 2). Whereas many continental codified Constitutions, such as those of Germany, Belgium, France or Spain, are based on a legislative act, the UK Constitution is based on general principles and particular decisions and pronouncements by the courts. Continental codified Constitutions usually contain fundamental individual rights contained in the first ten or so Articles.

Over the last two decades, the concept of **Separation of Powers** has undergone a number of policy reforms and initiatives. The Labour Government (1997–2010), under Prime Ministers Tony Blair and Gordon Brown, suggested two major reforms, the reform of the House of Lords and that of the Judiciary in the Constitutional Reform Act 2005. This reform formally moved the UK Constitution towards a clearer Separation of Powers: the creation of an independent **Supreme Court** in 2009 (UKSC) and dismantling of the many-faceted office of the Lord Chancellor. The Lord Chief Justice replaced the Lord Chancellor as head of the Judiciary in England and Wales. It also placed a statutory duty on ministers to uphold judicial independence – all of which clearly separated the Executive and judicial fusion of powers.

Until 2009, the Lords of Appeal in Ordinary (the Law Lords) sat in the Legislature as well as acting as the highest appeal court in the UK. However, the Constitutional Reform Act 2005 created a separate Supreme Court, separating out the judicial role from the Upper House. From 2009, the 'Law Lords' (now Justices of the Supreme Court) no longer sat in the House of Lords during the legislative process. The Constitutional Reform Act 2005 also changed the way judicial appointments were made. The legislation established an independent **Judicial Appointments Commission** for England and Wales. The Commission recommends candidates to the Lord Chancellor, who has a very limited power of veto. Separate procedures apply to the appointment of Supreme Court judges, which take account of the fact that the Court has a UK-wide remit.

Furthermore, life peerages (created in 1958) were discontinued in 2005; these are now discontinued when the holder dies (unlike hereditary peerages). The number of hereditary Peers was cut to 92, leaving the House of Lords to elect among themselves which of their number should get a seat when one of them dies.

The Human Rights Act 1998 (which came into force in October 2000) now requires all judges to consider the European Convention on Human Rights (ECHR) in their decision-making process and reasons have to be given at sentencing stage. Judicial decisions of the European Court of Human Rights in Strasbourg (ECtHR) have also influenced the Judiciary. More recently, the proposed changes and review of the Parliamentary Privilege and MPs' involvement in superinjunctions have also raised issues of the interaction of the institutions of state in relation to Separation of Powers.

A further limitation to Parliamentary Sovereignty has been the incorporation of European Community (EU) law into UK domestic law. In *Factortame (No. 2)*, Lord Bridge interpreted the European Communities Act 1972 to mean that UK statute would not apply where it conflicted with European law, a significant departure from the principle of Parliamentary Sovereignty (see *R v Secretary of State for Transport ex parte Factortame Ltd (No. 2)* [1990] 2 AC 85). Furthermore, under s 4 of the Human Rights Act 1998, a court can declare a statute to be incompatible with the European Convention on Human Rights and the Government is then obliged by the Convention to rectify the inconsistency.

Up for Debate

Recently, the question of Separation of Powers has arisen in relation to the use of court injunctions. Find out a little more about the meaning of an injunction (a court order requiring a party to do or refrain from doing certain acts). There have also been so-called superinjunctions which tend to be used by celebrities who increasingly use the courts to provide privacy for them, such as footballers John Terry, Rio Ferdinand or Ryan Giggs. In some of these cases (which are difficult to find, because they are usually only known by letters of the alphabet, such as LNS (John Terry)), superinjunctions have provided total anonymity and a prohibition on publishing or disclosing the very existence of the order. Would you agree that superinjunctions have created a new kind of procedure for an entirely new legal process conducted in private and out of the public's view? In April 2011, Prime Minister David Cameron said that he felt 'uneasy' about superinjunctions and that judges were developing a privacy law without Parliamentary approval. What do you think he meant? And does the **Human Rights Act 1998** not impose a duty on the judges to interpret legislation 'as far as possible' in a manner to make it compatible with the European Convention on Human Rights?

Putting it into practice

Essay questions are likely to relate to one of the following:

- ❖ Montesquieu's definition of the Separation of Powers intended to guard against tyranny and preserve liberty
- ❖ A comparison between the US and the UK constitutional systems and the way powers are separated
- ❖ The three main institutions of state: the Legislature, the Executive and the Judiciary
- ❖ Separation of Executive and Legislature
- ❖ The independence of the Judiciary
- ❖ Whether judges make laws?
- ❖ The *Jackson* case (2005) on the application of the Parliament Acts 1911 and 1949 to the Hunting Act 2004, questioning the relationship between Parliamentary Sovereignty and the Rule of Law
- ❖ Limitations to Parliamentary Sovereignty by the Human Rights Act 1998 (European Convention on Human Rights) and EU Law (*Factortame* case)
- ❖ Judicial scrutiny functions of the Executive
- ❖ Constitutional reform (Constitutional Reform Act 2005) and its implications for the Separation of Powers

Essay 1

'There is no such thing as Separation of Powers in the United Kingdom.' Discuss this statement by a US Congressman and compare the UK constitutional set-up with that of the USA.

Feedback on putting it into practice

a) Note that this question is divided into two parts: in the first part of the essay, discuss what is meant by Separation of Powers, and give examples. In the second part, look at how the American Constitution varies from that of the UK – and it is worth citing some learned academic writers like Montesquieu and his definition of a true democracy versus tyranny (where a state's powers are not separate).

b) Your introduction should include that the British Constitution is founded on statutory and common law rules, made up of Conventions, common law (judicial precedent), legislation (Acts of Parliament) and EU law; you should then compare the uncodified UK Constitution with the American Constitution with its strictly separate powers.

c) Define the Separation of Powers as referred to by Montesquieu, and his version of the three main institutions of state: Legislative, Executive and Judiciary. Explain how these manifest themselves in the United Kingdom and the USA.

d) Discuss the UK's common law jurisdiction and that the Executive and Legislature are closely entwined (e.g. the role of the Prime Minister, his ministers, the fact that they are both Members of Parliament and sit in the House of Commons and are part of the Executive (the Cabinet)).

e) Then compare and contrast the UK interlinked powers with the USA, where powers of state are strictly separated, enshrined in the codified Constitution (e.g. the President may not be a member of the Legislature (Congress), and is elected separately from congressional elections).

f) Discuss why the UK constitutional set-up might be seen as a positive element, i.e. the integration of Executive and Legislature can provide stability and efficiency in the operation of government.

Essay 2

Explain the 'checks and balances' which the UK Parliament can effectively provide on the Executive. Have there been any constitutional changes over the past decade?

Feedback on putting it into practice

a) Note that this question is divided into two parts: the first part of your essay should deal with the various checks and balances provided by the House of Commons and the House of Lords and the various Select Committees; the second part should deal with constitutional reform, for example the House of Lords and the Judiciary. For high marks you must answer *all* elements of the question. If you answer only one part of the question, you will be marked down.

b) Discuss the role of Select Committees of the House of Commons.
c) Discuss the role of 'Prime Minister's Question Time' and debates in the House of Commons as providing 'checks and balances' of the Executive.
d) Explain the scrutiny role of the House of Lords and the way its veto powers have been curtailed by the Parliament Acts 1911 and 1949.
e) You should discuss the *Jackson* case (2005) and the application of the Parliament Acts 1911 and 1949 and cite the *obiter dicta* remarks by the Appeal Committee of the House of Lords which questioned the relationship between Parliamentary Sovereignty and the Rule of Law, suggesting that there were limits to Sovereignty where constitutional fundamentals were at risk.
f) The second part of the essay should focus on constitutional reform under the Constitutional Reform Act 2005, including:
g) reform of the House of Lords,
h) the creation of the UK Supreme Court (2009), and
i) devolution to Scotland, Northern Ireland and Wales.

Chapter summary

❖ Definition of the Separation of Powers.
❖ The relationship between the Legislative, the Executive and the Judiciary in the UK.
❖ Checks and balances of the Executive.
❖ The independence of the Judiciary.
❖ The relationship between the Executive and the Judiciary.
❖ Constitutional reform in the United Kingdom.

Table of key cases referred to in this chapter

Case name	Area of law	Principle
R (Jackson) v Attorney-General [2005]	Rule of Law; Parliamentary Sovereignty	There are limits to Parliamentary Sovereignty (e.g. EU Law; Human Rights Act 1998)
Pickin v British Railways Board [1974]	Separation of Powers; the Judiciary and Parliament (Legislature)	Judges are subordinate to Parliament and may not challenge Acts of Parliament; the courts interpret Acts of Parliament
McLoughlin v O'Brian [1983] ('nervous shock case')	The Judiciary (do judges make law?)	The objective of judges is the formulation of principles; policy is the prerogative of Parliament

Case name	Area of law	Principle
R v Secretary of State for Transport ex parte Factortame Ltd (No. 2) [1990]	Supremacy of EU law; Parliamentary Sovereignty	UK statute does not apply where it conflicts with Community Law (significant departure from Parliamentary Sovereignty)
A and others v Secretary of State for the Home Department [2004] ('Belmarsh Prisoners case')	The Executive and the Judiciary (judicial independence)	The function of independent judges is to interpret and apply the law (Lord Bingham)

@ **Visit the book's companion website to test your knowledge**

❖ Resources include a subject map, revision tip podcasts, downloadable diagrams, MCQ quizzes for each chapter, and a flashcard glossary

❖ www.routledge.com/cw/optimizelawrevision

The Law-making Process

Revision objectives

Understand the law
- Can you provide details on how laws are made in the UK Parliament?
- Can you explain why a Bill might start in the House of Commons or the House of Lords?
- Are you able to discuss reform of the House of Lords since 1999 and how this has affected the law-making process?
- Can you explain whether Devolution has made a difference to the law-making process as part of the UK Constitution?

Remember the details
- Can you characterise the different functions of the bi-cameral parliamentary system in the UK (i.e. both Houses of Parliament)?
- Are you able to discuss how the Lords' legislative function has been curtailed over the years?
- How have constitutional reforms impacted on the law-making powers of Parliament?

Reflect critically on areas of debate
- Can you critically discuss the passage of legislation and debates in both Houses of Parliament?
- Are you able to elaborate on the passage of legislation and meaning of delegated legislation?
- Can you cite relevant case law and statutory provisions that have influenced and reformed the UK Constitution and Parliament in recent years?

Contextualise
- Are you able to discuss the Parliament Acts 1911 and 1949 in relation to the legislative power of the House of Lords (Upper House)?
- Can you discuss some of the recent legislative proposals to reform the Upper House of Parliament?
- Can you argue legislation and case law relating to Devolution in the UK?

Apply your skills and knowledge
- Can you answer questions in the Putting it into Practice section of the chapter relating to the legislatve powers of the Westminster Parliament and devolved powers to the Scottish, Welsh and Northern Ireland institutions and constitutional reform in the UK?

Chapter Map

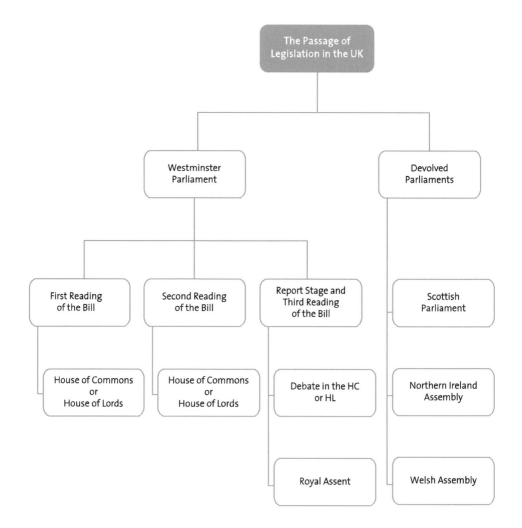

Introduction: how laws are made

In previous chapters, we have looked at how one of the duties of the Legislature (Parliament) is to examine what the Executive (Government) is doing and to keep the Executive in check ('checks and balances' – see Chapter 5). Another main function of Parliament is making new laws (Bills in Parliament).

The House of Commons and House of Lords each play an important role in Parliament's legislative work. Green is the principal colour for furnishings and fabrics throughout the accommodation used by the House of Commons, and from 1981, volumes of **Hansard** were issued in green for the first time. In the House of Lords, red is similarly employed in upholstery, notepaper, Hansard, etc. The use of red relates to the King's or Queen's Royal colour.

Together with the House of Commons and the House of Lords, the Crown is an integral part of the institution of Parliament. The Queen (or King) plays a constitutional role in opening and dissolving Parliament and approving Bills before they become law, known as Royal Assent. The Crown informs Parliament of the Government's policy ideas and plans for new legislation in a speech delivered from the throne in the House of Lords (known as the Queen's or King's Speech). Although the Queen or King makes the speech, the Government draws up the content. When a Bill has been approved by majorities in both Houses, it is formally agreed to by the Crown. This is known as the **Royal Assent**. This turns a Bill into an Act of Parliament (or statute), allowing it to become law in the UK.

The Westminster Parliament

The business of Parliament takes place in two Houses: the **House of Commons** and the **House of Lords** – also known as a **bi-cameral system**. Their work is similar: making laws (the Legislature), checking the work of the Government (scrutiny or 'checks and balances'), and debating current issues. The House of Commons is also responsible for granting money to the Government through approving Bills that raise taxes. Generally, the decisions made in one House have to be approved by the other. In this way, the two-chamber (bi-cameral) system acts as a check and balance for both Houses. Parliament is responsible for approving new laws (legislation). The Government (Executive) introduces most plans for new laws, or changes to existing laws – but they can originate from an MP, a Lord or even a member of the public or a private group. Before they can become law, both the House of Commons and the House of Lords must debate and vote on the proposals (usually in the form of a Green or White Paper).

Parliamentary debates

Parliamentary debates are an important opportunity for MPs and the Lords to discuss Government policy, proposed new laws and current issues. It allows MPs to voice the concerns and interests of their constituents, and members of the House of Lords can speak about issues brought to their attention by the public. Debates can result in Informed Decision on a subject and members of both Houses can vote for or against – called a 'Division'.

Early day motions

Early day motions (EDMs) are formal motions submitted for debate in the House of Commons. However, very few are actually debated. Early day motions allow MPs to draw attention to an event or cause. MPs register their support by signing individual motions. An example of a recent EDM is set out below.

House of Commons

The House of Commons (also known as the 'Commons') is publicly elected. The party with the largest number of members in the Commons forms the Government. The UK public now elects 600 Members of Parliament (MPs) in a General Election (usually every five years). MPs represent their constituencies' interests and concerns in the House of Commons. MPs consider and propose new laws, and can scrutinise Government policies by asking ministers questions during Prime Minister's Question Time about current issues either in the Commons Chamber or in **Select Committees**. Members of the Commons (MPs) debate the big political issues of the day and proposals for new laws. It is one of the key places where Government ministers, like the Prime Minister and the Chancellor, and the principal figures of the main political parties work (the Executive). The House of Commons alone is responsible for making decisions on Financial Bills, such as proposed new taxes. Commons debates are known to be noisy affairs, with MPs intervening in each other's speeches to support or challenge what they are saying. The Speaker of the House of Commons makes sure that every MP is heard, adhering to strict rules and Parliamentary conventions on unparliamentary language and time-limits (guillotine).

House of Lords

The House of Lords (or Upper Chamber) is the second chamber of the UK Parliament; it complements the work of the House of Commons. It makes laws, holds Government to account and investigates policy issues. Its membership is mostly appointed and includes experts in many fields. The main role of the House of Lords is to debate and revise major legislation. The Lords regulate themselves and the order of business in the House, which means there is greater flexibility among its members to examine an issue for longer than is typical in the House of Commons. The Lords can consider Bills before Parliament but cannot block or amend them.

Since the removal of the majority of the hereditary peers as a result of the House of Lords Act 1999, the 'second stage' of House of Lords reform (see below) has suffered a number of false starts. Attempts to determine the shape of a future second chamber by a previous parliamentary Joint Committee ended in failure, when the House of Commons rejected all its options for composition. The House of Lords Reform Bill announced in the 2003 Queen's Speech was never published. This means there are presently 825 members in the House of Lords, known as 'Peers'. Since 2005, most of them are appointed on the recommendation of the Prime Minister or other party leaders (Constitutional Reform Act 2005). This is usually along party lines, although some are non-political experts in their fields, such as eminent scientists and generals. Twenty-six Peers are senior Church of England Bishops. Another 92 are hereditary Peers, the remnants of the group who once made up the entire membership.

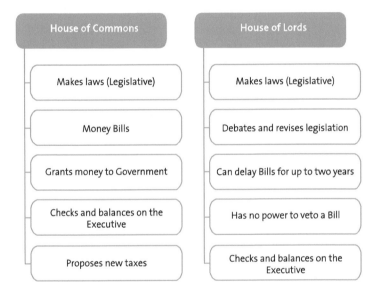

The bi-cameral system of the UK Parliament

Conventions on the relationship between the House of Commons and the House of Lords

Chapter 2 introduced you to Conventions, and you now know that these are an integral part of the UK Constitution. The force of Conventions relies on those involved observing the rules, and for a common understanding of the **Rule of Law**. You also learnt that the nature of Conventions is that they are not necessarily closely defined and change over time. There are a number of Conventions and statutes, which, together, enshrine the primacy of the elected chamber of the UK Parliament at Westminster, that is the House of Commons over the House of Lords. The composition of the House of Lords has changed since the Constitutional Reform Act 2005, which means that some of the Conventions have come under pressure. Reform of the House of Lords has been further tested by the creation of the first coalition Government (2010) in peacetime since the 1930s. Other Conventions have been challenged by new legislation, such as the Parliamentary Voting System and Constituencies Act 2011. In 2006 a Joint Committee of both Houses of Parliament was established to consider 'the practicality of codifying the Conventions on the relationship between the two Houses of Parliament which affect the consideration of legislation'.

The Salisbury-Addison Convention (1945) (Bills implementing manifesto commitments)

Convention that the House of Lords does not usually object to secondary legislation

Convention that the Government should get its business done in 'reasonable time'

Financial privilege of the House of Commons

Exchange of amendments between both Houses of Parliament

Conventions on the relationship between the House of Commons and House of Lords

The Parliament Acts

The Parliament Act 1911

Until the early years of the twentieth century, the House of Lords had the power to veto (stop) legislation. However, this arrangement was put under pressure during a constitutional crisis, when the Conservative-dominated House of Lords refused to pass the Liberal Government's 'people budget' of 1909 (championed by David Lloyd-George). In the two General Elections that followed in 1910, the issue of the House of Lords dominated debate. The Parliament Bill of 1911 sought to remove the power of the House of Lords to reject Money Bills, and to replace the Lords' veto over other

Public Bills with the power of delay. In addition, it was proposed to reduce the maximum duration of a Parliament from seven years to five. The Parliament Act 1911 was passed only under the threat of the creation of a large number of Liberal Peers (the Bill was passed in the House of Lords by a 131 to 114 vote in August 1911). The Act did nothing to alter the Conservative-dominated composition of the Upper House, but pointed the way towards future constitutional reform by hinting that attention would turn shortly to the question of restructuring the House of Lords. However, the pressure of other issues, followed by the upheaval of the First World War, meant that it would be some years before the matter was looked at again. The Parliament Act 1911 had a profound constitutional effect well into the twenty-first century.

The 1911 Act ensured that a **Money Bill** could receive Royal Assent without the approval of the House of Lords, if not passed by the Lords without amendment within one month. The 1911 Act also provided that any other **Public Bill** (except one extending the life of a Parliament) would receive Royal Assent without the consent of the House of Lords, if it had been passed by the House of Commons in three successive sessions, as long as two years had elapsed between its second reading in the first session and its final passage in the Commons. The Act also shortened the maximum length of a Parliament from seven to five years.

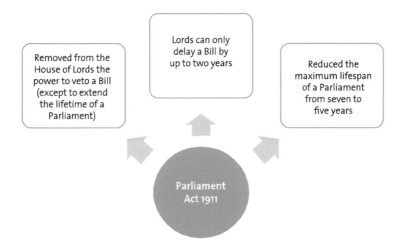

Lords can only delay a Bill by up to two years

Removed from the House of Lords the power to veto a Bill (except to extend the lifetime of a Parliament)

Reduced the maximum lifespan of a Parliament from seven to five years

Parliament Act 1911

The Parliament Act 1949

Although the Parliament Act 1911 was seen as a battle between the House of Lords and the Liberal Party, the Parliament Act 1949 saw the Labour Party, elected in 1945, take on the Upper House of Parliament. The contentious issue was Clement Attlee's post Second World War Government nationalisation programme. In particular, Labour feared that the Lords would reject the Iron and Steel Bill. Labour sought to reduce the Lords' power further, by reducing the time that the House of Lords could delay Bills from three sessions over two years to two sessions over one year. The House of Commons passed the Parliament Bill in 1947, but it took until December

1949 for the law to be given Royal Assent under the provisions of the Parliament Act 1911. In recent times, the validity of the 1949 Act has been questioned based on the legal principle of *delegatus non potest delegare* (a delegate cannot enlarge on his own power) (see *R (Jackson) v Attorney-General* [2005] UKHL 56).

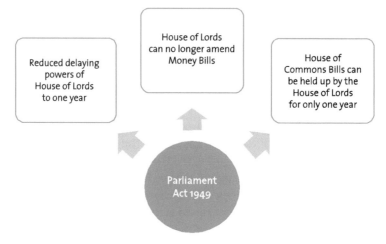

Application of the Parliament Acts

The Parliament Act 1911 as amended by the Parliament Act 1949 (known jointly as the Parliament Acts) sets out conditions under which Bills that have been passed by the House of Commons may acquire the force of law without being passed by the House of Lords.

The Parliament Acts do **not** apply to:

❖ Bills originating in the House of Lords;
❖ Bills to extend the maximum life of Parliament beyond five years;
❖ Provisional Order Bills;
❖ Private Bills; or
❖ delegated legislation (Statutory Instruments).

> Bills extending the life of a Parliament beyond five years

> Private and Provisional Order Bills

> Bills sent up to the Lords less than a month before the end of a session

> Bills which start in the House of Lords

> Delegated legislation (Statutory Instruments)

Bills not subject to the Parliament Acts 1911 and 1949

The passage of a Bill

Bills normally introduce new laws. A Bill is a draft law; it becomes an **Act of Parliament** (statute or legislation) if it is approved by majorities in the House of Commons and House of Lords, and formally agreed to by the reigning Monarch (Royal Assent). An Act of Parliament is primary legislation (also known as 'black letter law'), enforced in all areas of the UK where it is applicable. Bills that deal with more political or controversial issues usually begin in the House of Commons. To become law the text of a Bill must be agreed by both Houses. Either House can vote down a Bill, in which case it will normally not become law – but there are exceptions. The House of Commons can pass the same Bill in two successive years, in which case it can become law without the agreement of the House of Lords. Bills that are only about money (raising taxes or authorising government expenditure – so-called 'Money Bills') are not opposed in the Lords and may only be delayed for a month. Once a Bill has received Royal Assent, it is then the responsibility of the relevant Government Department to implement that legislation (e.g. the Home Office will deal with new statutes relating to immigration).

Once presented, the Bill goes through the following stages in each House in turn:

First Reading (House of Commons or House of Lords)	❖ Formal introduction of the Bill, which is held without debate
Second Reading (House of Commons or House of Lords)	❖ Normally approved formally unless a Member wishes to have a debate on the Bill. In the Commons the motion may be repeatedly blocked, which can delay progress indefinitely
Committee Stage	❖ Bills which have outstanding petitions against are considered by an Opposed Bill Committee, whereas Bills not petitioned against go to an Unopposed Bill Committee
Report Stage	❖ Only available in House of Commons; last chance for MPs to amend the Bill (in the House of Lords, Private Bills do not have a report stage after they have left committee)

Third Reading (House of Commons or House of Lords)	❖ Principles of the Bill are debated. It is the opportunity for the House to reject the Bill. It is also the last chance for MPs and Lords to debate or block a Private Bill. In the House of Lords, the Bill can be amended on third reading
Royal Assent	❖ When a Bill has completed all its parliamentary stages in both Houses, it must have Royal Assent before it can become an Act of Parliament. Royal Assent is the Monarch's agreement to make the Bill into an Act and is a formality. There is no set time period between the consideration of amendments to the Bill and Royal Assent.

Passage of a Bill

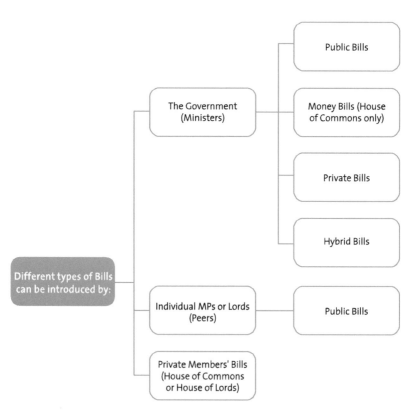

Different types of Bills before Parliament

Public Bills

Public Bills change the law as it applies to the general population and are the most common type of Bill introduced in Parliament. Public Bills are introduced in either House and go through a number of set stages that generally involve Members of both Houses examining the Bill. The majority of Public Bills are introduced by Government Ministers; those put forward by other MPs or Lords are known as Private Members' Bills. Bills that are largely financial, or involve public money – like new taxes or public spending – are always introduced in the House of Commons. If members of the public want to voice their objections to Public Bills, they can:

❖ write to their MP or a Lord
❖ write to the Government Department responsible for the Bill
❖ lobby Parliament
❖ submit evidence to the relevant Public Bill Committee

Age of Criminal Responsibility Bill [HL] 2013–14	❖ A Bill to raise the age of criminal responsibility from 10 to 12
Assisted Dying Bill [HL] 2013–14	❖ A Bill to enable competent adults who are terminally ill to be provided at their request with specified assistance to end their own life
Voting Age (Comprehensive Reduction) Bill [HL] 2013–14	❖ A Bill to extend the franchise for parliamentary and other elections, and for referendums, to all citizens over the age of 16 years

Examples of Public Bills

Money Bills

Money Bills are Bills designed to raise money through taxes or spend public money. A Money Bill starts in the **House of Commons** and must receive Royal Assent no later than one month after being introduced in the House of Lords, even if the Lords has not passed it. The Lords cannot amend a Money Bill.

Private Members' Bills

Private Members' Bills are Public Bills introduced by MPs and Lords who are **not** Government Ministers. As with other Public Bills their purpose is to change the law as it applies to the general population. A minority of Private Members' Bills become law but, by creating publicity around an issue, they may affect legislation indirectly. (e.g. Prisoners Earnings Act 1997 introduced by Conservative MP Hartley Booth as a

Private Member's Bill in 1995). Like other Public Bills, Private Members' Bills can be introduced in either House and must go through the same set stages. To introduce this type of Bill, a Member needs to provide its short title (by which it is known) and its long title (which describes briefly what it does). Private Members' Bills introduced in the House of Lords go through the same stages as any other Public Bill.

Other Private Bills

A Private Bill is a proposal to confer particular powers or benefits on any person or body of persons – including individuals, local authorities, companies, or corporations – in excess of or in conflict with the general law. Historically, Private Bills concerned 'turnpiking' a road or the railways (e.g. Great Northern Railway Bill of 1845–46). Private Bills can start in either House. Today, Private Bills are usually promoted by organisations to give themselves powers beyond, or in conflict with, the general law (e.g. The Crossrail project – the Crossrail Bill 2007).

Hybrid Bills

Hybrid Bills mix the characteristics of Public and Private Bills. The changes to the law proposed by a Hybrid Bill would affect the general public but would also have a significant impact for specific individuals or groups. Hybrid Bills often propose works of national importance but in a specific area of the UK (e.g. the Channel Tunnel Bills passed in the 1970s and 1980s). Both Houses debate Hybrid Bills and they go through a longer parliamentary process than Public Bills. In 2013 Parliament debated two Hybrid Bills, one on the second phase of the High Speed rail link (HS2) and the other on the national significance of nuclear power stations (Hinkley C).

The House of Lords and delegated legislation

Unlike most primary legislation, the House of Lords is able to exercise a veto over delegated (or secondary) legislation (such as Statutory Instruments) (see also Chapter 2). This means the Parliament Acts do not apply to delegated legislation. So delegated legislation rejected by the Lords cannot have effect even if the House of Commons has approved it. Neither House of Parliament has the power to amend delegated legislation. The House has only occasionally rejected delegated legislation and affirmed its 'unfettered freedom' to vote on any subordinate legislation submitted for its consideration. Delegated legislation may be debated in Grand Committee, but must return to the floor of the House if a formal decision is required.

Legislation that reformed the House of Lords

When the New Labour Government came to power in 1997, Prime Minister Tony Blair made it clear that the House of Lords was to be abolished (Labour Party Manifesto, 1997). 1999 saw the first significant constitutional reform by removing the right of the majority of the hereditary Peers to sit and vote by reducing their number in the House of Lords to 92. The Constitutional Reform Act 2005 brought about the new **Supreme Court** (see Chapter 5) and reduced the number of Peers in the House of

Lords from 826 to 700. This meant the 'reformed' House of Lords has Peers from a variety of professional backgrounds, including politics, education, sport, science and the arts. This is seen as a positive step, since this knowledge helps the understanding and passing of legislation. When the Coalition Government came to power in May 2010 (Conservatives and Liberal Democrats), Deputy Prime Minister Nick Clegg (Liberal Democrat) introduced a Reform Bill in 2012 that proposed a mainly elected Upper Chamber of Parliament on the basis of proportional representation. The Bill also proposed to reduce the number of Peers in the House of Lords to 450. But the Bill did not achieve much support in the House of Commons, and in August 2012 Prime Minister David Cameron shelved the Bill until the next General Election in 2015.

Aim Higher

When you are discussing delegated legislation in a piece of coursework or an exam question, you should provide examples of instances where the House of Lords rejected a Statutory Instrument. Here are some examples which you could cite for higher marks:

❖ 18 June 1968: Southern Rhodesia (United Nations Sanctions) Order 1968;

❖ 22 February 2000: Greater London Authority (Election Expenses) Order 2000;

❖ 28 March 2007: Gambling (Geographical Distribution of Casino Premises Licences) Order 2007.

See House of Lords, *Companion to the Standing Orders and Guide to the Proceedings of the House of Lords*, 2010 at: http://www.publications.parliament.uk/pa/ld/ldcomp/compso2010/compso.pdf

Devolution and Executive power: the *AXA* case

In Chapter 1, you were introduced to Devolution. The Scottish Parliament and the Welsh and Northern Ireland Assemblies now execute some legislative powers. The leading case which questioned whether devolved legislation is subject to Judicial Review is *AXA General Insurance Limited and others v The Lord Advocate* [2011] (see below). *AXA* is of great constitutional importance because it considers the devolved role of the Scottish Parliament (and therefore all other devolved legislations). *AXA* challenged the law-making role of the Scottish Parliament under the Scotland Act 1998, and alleged incompatibility with the European Convention (ECHR) and whether Scottish legislation was judicially reviewable. Most importantly, *AXA* explored the distinctions between the status of the Westminster and the other devolved Parliaments and contributed to the understanding of reviewability (Judicial Review) (see also Chapter 9).

Case precedent – *AXA General Insurance Limited and others v The Lord Advocate* [2011] UKSC 46 (On appeal from the Scottish Court of Session [2011] CSIH 31) (UK Supreme Court)

Facts: AXA and four other insurance companies issued a petition for Judicial Review, claiming that the Damages (Asbestos-related Conditions) (Scotland) Act 2009 was outside the legislative competence of the Scottish Parliament. The 2009 Act provides for personal injury claims to asbestos-related diseases (known as 'pleural plaques'), actionable under Scottish law (the Act substituted common law in *Rothwell v Chemical & Insulating Co Ltd* [2007] UKHL 29). The insurance companies further alleged that the 2009 Act violated human rights legislation (Article 1 of the first Protocol ECHR – 'right to peaceful enjoyment of their possessions'). The respondent, the Lord Advocate for Scotland, refused the claim, stating that AXA and others did not have standing in Judicial Review and were not 'victims' under Article 34 ECHR. The appellants challenged the validity of the 2009 Act, that it was not 'proper' law and outside the legislative competence of the Scottish Parliament and also incompatible with the ECHR.

Principle: The UK Supreme Court dismissed the appeal by AXA. It held that the Scottish Parliament passed the Scottish 'Asbestos' Act 2009 with a 'legitimate aim', i.e. addressing social policy; and that the Act did **not** contravene the ECHR. The UKSC declared the 2009 Act valid, that a reasonably proportionate and legitimate aim had been pursued. The leading judgments were given by Lord Hope and Lord Reed. This means that Acts of the Scottish Parliament are subject to Judicial Review (though not grounds of irrationality, unreasonableness or arbitrariness).

Application: *AXA* is important because the UKSC held that devolved legislation (Scotland, Wales, Northern Ireland) is subject to Judicial Review (unless it can be shown to be manifestly unreasonable).

Aim Higher

When writing a piece of coursework on devolved legislation and the law-making powers of the devolved Parliaments (Scotland, Wales, Northern Ireland), you should use the *AXA* case as an example (remember to read the whole case!). This case challenged the principle of Separation of Powers, i.e. how truly independent are the devolved Parliaments? Is devolved legislation judicially reviewable? And how far did the UK Supreme Court go in ruling that devolved law is subject to Judicial Review? You should further debate the Scottish Referendum on Scottish independence (2014) and what this would mean to future Scottish legislation. The UKSC held in *AXA* that the Scottish Parliament, as a devolved legislature, was **not** sovereign. How would the balance of law-making powers change if Scotland became an independent country in 2017? Would the Scottish legislation still be judicially reviewable?

Putting it into practice

Essay questions are likely to relate to one of the following:

- ❖ The constitutional make-up of the Westminster Parliament
- ❖ The Parliament Acts 1911 and 1949 (the 'Parliament Acts') and the limitations put on the legislative procedure in the House of Lords
- ❖ Constitutional change in respect of the House of Lords (reform of the House of Lords)
- ❖ The decision in *AXA* [2011] and devolved legislation in relation to Judicial Review

Essay 1

Would you agree that the House of Lords is redundant when it comes to law-making in Parliament? Discuss.

Feedback on putting it into practice

a) Your introduction should include a brief discussion of the set-up of the Westminster Parliament (House of Commons and House of Lords) and the doctrine of Separation of Powers.

b) Go straight on to law-making and describe how, until the early years of the twentieth century, the House of Lords had the power to veto (stop) legislation; this arrangement changed under the Parliament Acts 1911 and 1949 (the 'Parliament Acts').

c) Explain the scrutiny role of the House of Lords and the way its veto-powers have been curtailed by the Parliament Acts.

d) Extra marks will be given if you critically discuss the Salisbury Convention and that the Lords can veto secondary legislation.

e) Discuss the Supremacy of Parliament and illustrate the Government's (Executive's) omnipotence by using practical examples of Bills that have passed through Parliament without the Lords' consent.

f) Highlight when the Parliament Acts have been used to provide a framework and a means of solving disagreement between the Commons and Lords (i.e. to pass legislation in spite of a veto from the House of Lords – where the Lords did not consent to a Bill), e.g. War Crimes Act 1991, European Parliamentary Elections Act 1999, Sexual Offences (Amendment) Act 2000, Hunting Act 2004.

g) Discuss the case of *Jackson* and the dicta in this case (you **must** read this case properly by using Westlaw or LexisNexis).

Essay 2

'*Reform of the UK's Constitution has been historically preoccupied with reform of the House of Lords. As a consequence other demands for reform have been ignored.*' Discuss this introductory statement by Jack Straw MP, then Labour Leader of the House of Commons and Lord Privy Seal, in his White Paper 2007, 'The House of Lords Reform' (Cm 7027).

Feedback on putting it into practice

a)   Since this could be a typical coursework (rather than an examination) essay,
     you should really undertake a great deal of background research, i.e. read and
     analyse the Government White Paper of 2007 (see http://www.official-
     documents.gov.uk/document/cm70/7027/7027.pdf). A well structured and
     researched answer will gain you high marks.
b)   When studying the White Paper of 2007, you will note that no agreement was
     reached between the cross-party working group on parliamentary reform of
     the Upper House of Parliament at the time.
c)   Comment on the various pieces of legislation (and draft Bills) that emerged
     from 1999 onwards, and how Prime Minister David Cameron (Conservative)
     shelved reform of the House of Lords in August 2012 until the next General
     Election in 2015.
d)   Additionally, you should look up relevant legal journal articles by academic
     commentators (legal writers) on the topic of 'House of Lords' reform – which
     has by no means finished.
e)   You will be given credit for recognising the impact of the Parliament Acts 1911
     and 1949 and the way the legislation reduced the powers of the Lords.
f)   Although you should spend the majority of your time providing a detailed
     discussion of the various reforms of the House of Lords, additional credit will
     be given if you provide some comments on some other major constitutional
     reforms from the following list:
     ❖   European Communities Act 1972
     ❖   Devolution – Scotland Act 1998/Government of Wales Act 1998/Good
         Friday Agreement 1998 (Northern Ireland)
     ❖   Human Rights Act 1998
     ❖   Constitutional Reform Act 2005.
g)   You can also discuss the House of Lords Draft Reform Bill 2011, which can be
     accessed here: https://www.gov.uk/government/uploads/system/uploads/
     attachment_data/file/61215/house-of-lords-reform-draft-bill.pdf.
h)   Additional credit will be given if you discuss either the *Jackson* or the *AXA* case
     to make your point.

Common Pitfalls

The most common problem in an essay or coursework question on the set-up
of the Westminster Parliament is that students tend to be too descriptive when
writing about the House of Commons and the House of Lords. Since there is
not very much case law in this area of constitutional law, answers need to be
structured properly, showing the historical development of legislation. Students
should focus mainly on the Parliament Acts and constitutional changes affecting
the law-making power of the House of Lords.

Chapter summary

❖ Definition of the set-up of the Westminster Parliament.

❖ Role and work of the House of Commons and the House of Lords (control of the Executive).

❖ How a Bill passes through Parliament and the most common Bills.

❖ Definition of the Parliament Acts 1911 and 1949.

❖ When and how the Parliament Acts 1911 and 1949 have been used to curtail the Lords' veto powers and pass legislation in the House of Commons.

❖ What the consequences were of the House of Lords Act 1999.

❖ What the constitutional reforms were following the Constitutional Reform Act 2005.

❖ What, if any, further reforms are planned to change the Upper House of Parliament.

❖ Definition of Devolution and law-making powers of the devolved parliaments (Scotland, Wales, Northern Ireland)

Table of key cases referred to in this chapter

Case name	Area of law	Principle
R (Jackson) v Attorney-General [2005]	Rule of Law; Parliamentary Sovereignty	There are limits to Parliamentary Sovereignty (e.g. EU law; Human Rights Act 1998)
AXA General Insurance Ltd v Lord Advocate [2011] (UKSC)	Scottish law; Devolution	Acts of the Scottish Parliament must adhere to human rights law (ECHR) and are subject to Judicial Review

@ Visit the book's companion website to test your knowledge

❖ Resources include a subject map, revision tip podcasts, downloadable diagrams, MCQ quizzes for each chapter, and a flashcard glossary

❖ www.routledge.com/cw/optimizelawrevision

7 The European Convention on Human Rights and the Human Rights Act 1998

Revision objectives

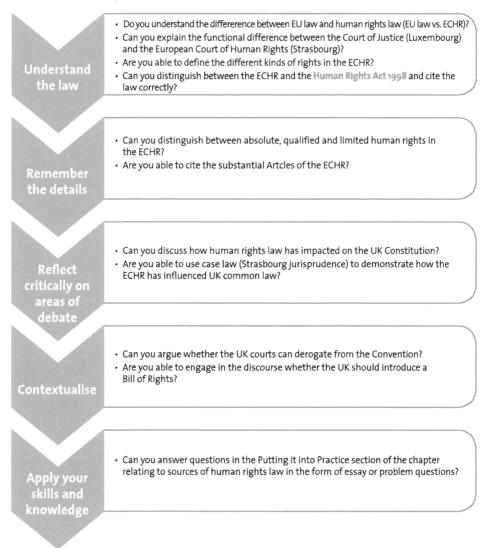

Understand the law
- Do you understand the differerence between EU law and human rights law (EU law vs. ECHR)?
- Can you explain the functional difference between the Court of Justice (Luxembourg) and the European Court of Human Rights (Strasbourg)?
- Are you able to define the different kinds of rights in the ECHR?
- Can you distinguish between the ECHR and the Human Rights Act 1998 and cite the law correctly?

Remember the details
- Can you distinguish between absolute, qualified and limited human rights in the ECHR?
- Are you able to cite the substantial Artcles of the ECHR?

Reflect critically on areas of debate
- Can you discuss how human rights law has impacted on the UK Constitution?
- Are you able to use case law (Strasbourg jurisprudence) to demonstrate how the ECHR has influenced UK common law?

Contextualise
- Can you argue whether the UK courts can derogate from the Convention?
- Are you able to engage in the discourse whether the UK should introduce a Bill of Rights?

Apply your skills and knowledge
- Can you answer questions in the Putting it into Practice section of the chapter relating to sources of human rights law in the form of essay or problem questions?

Chapter Map

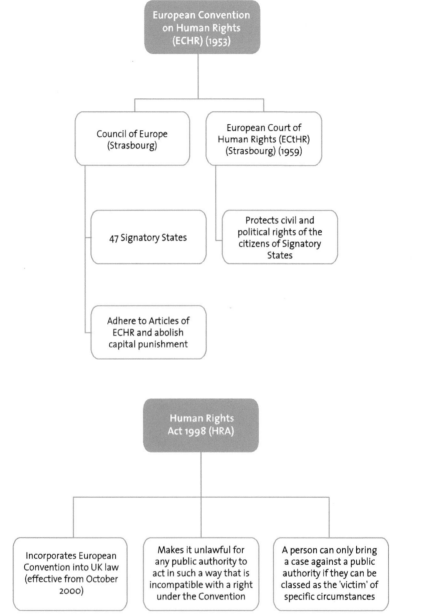

The Council of Europe and the European Convention on Human Rights

The Council of Europe is an international organisation in Strasbourg that represents 47 countries of 'greater' Europe. It was set up to promote democracy and protect human rights and the Rule of Law in Europe. The founding fathers of the Council of Europe in 1949–1950 were Winston Churchill (Prime Minister, UK), Konrad Adenauer (Chancellor, West Germany), Robert Schuman (Minister for Foreign Affairs, France), Paul-Henri Spaak (Prime Minister, Belgium), Alcide de Gasperi (Prime Minister, Italy) and Ernest Bevin (Foreign Secretary, UK). These leaders lived through two world wars and had first-hand experience of a number of European cultures. Their ultimate aim was peace in Europe. The present 47 signatory states to the ECHR are members of the Council of Europe, ranging from Albania to Azerbaijan, Liechtenstein to Serbia (see http://www.coe.int).

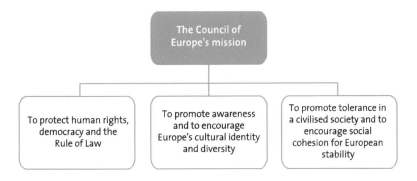

The death penalty

The Council of Europe made abolition of the death penalty a prerequisite for membership. All 47 members and signatory countries to the human rights Convention had to either abolish capital punishment or institute a moratorium on executions. This is reflected in Protocol No. 6 to the European Convention on Human Rights (ECHR). In 2002, Protocol No. 13 ECHR abolished capital punishment in all circumstances, even for acts committed in time of war. As a result, no execution has taken place on the territory of the organisation's Member States since 1997.

The European Convention on Human Rights and Fundamental Freedoms (ECHR)

The European Convention on Human Rights is the founding legislation of the Council of Europe and aims to protect human rights (officially known as 'Convention for the Protection of Human Rights and Fundamental Freedoms', as amended by Protocols Nos. 11 and 14, signed in Rome, 4 November 1950). The Convention came into force in 1953 and its ratification is a prerequisite for joining the Council of

Europe. The European Convention on Human Rights (ECHR or 'Convention') sets out a number of fundamental rights and freedoms:

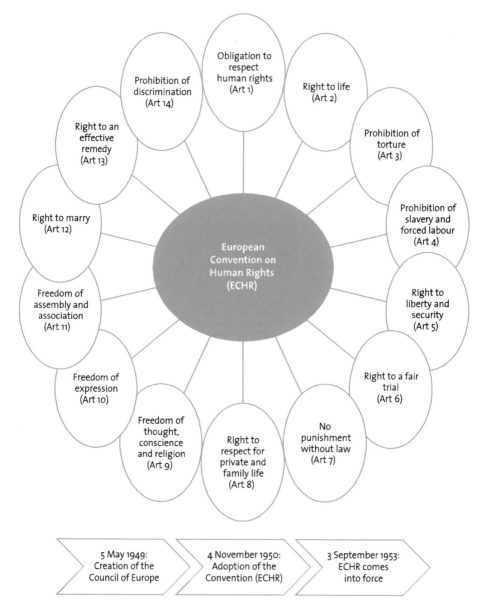

Key dates: timeline

What is a Protocol to the Convention?

A Protocol to the Convention is a text that adds one or more rights to the original Convention or amends certain of its provisions. Protocols that add rights to the Convention are binding only on those states that have signed and ratified them; a state that has merely signed a Protocol without ratifying it is not bound by its provisions. The right to property is not embodied in the Convention, but was added in the First Protocol to the Convention (Art 1 of Protocol 1 [1954] ECHR). Protocol No. 13 concerns the Abolition of the Death Penalty (2005). Some 14 additional Protocols have been adopted to date. This means that the Convention constantly evolves by means of its case law, i.e. the interpretation of the ECtHR (see http://www.conventions.coe.int).

Main Convention Articles and interpretation of Convention rights

The following lists some of the main rights and Articles of the Convention (ECHR), plus some examples, which you can use in your essays or problem questions. Article 1 ECHR covers the general obligation to respect human rights.

THE MAIN CONVENTION ARTICLES

Article 2 ECHR – Right to Life ('Everyone's right to life shall be protected by law')

Example: Protecting prisoners. States must take the necessary steps to protect the life of those detained in prison. In 2008, the Court found that there had been a violation of Art 2 ECHR in the case of *Renolde v France* (Application no. 5608/05) (2008) ECHR 1085. Hélène Renolde complained that the French authorities had not taken the necessary measures to protect the life of her brother, who hanged himself in July 2000 in his cell in Bois-d'Arcy Prison, where he was in pre-trial detention. The Court observed, among other things, that prisoners known to be suffering from a serious mental disturbance and to pose a suicide risk required special measures geared to their condition.

Article 3 ECHR – Prohibition of Torture ('No one shall be subjected to torture or to inhuman or degrading treatment or punishment in all circumstances')

Example: Police brutality during interrogation. In 2007, the Court found that there had been a violation of Art 3 in the case of *Mammadov (Jalaloglu) v Azerbaijan* (Application no. 34445/04) (2007). Sardor Jalaloglu Mammadov, Secretary General of the Democratic Party of Azerbaijan (one of the opposition parties that considered the results of the October 2003 presidential elections to be illegitimate), was arrested and taken into police custody on 18 October 2003. Several masked police officers, armed with machine guns, had forced their way into the applicant's home, arrested him and took him to a temporary detention facility in order to interrogate him in connection with a demonstration two days earlier. The demonstration had taken place in the Azadliq Square in the centre of Baku to protest against the results of the elections and had turned violent. The ECtHR found that Mr Mammadov had been tortured while in police custody and that the authorities had not carried out an effective investigation into his allegations of torture.

Example: Extradition and deportation. In 2008, the Court found that there had been a violation of Art 3 in the case of *Saadi v Italy* (Application no. 37201/06) (2008). The case concerned the possible deportation of Nassim Saadi to Tunisia, where he claimed to have been sentenced in 2005, in his absence, to 20 years' imprisonment for membership of a terrorist organisation acting abroad in peacetime and for incitement to terrorism. The ECtHR held that if the decision to deport the applicant to Tunisia were to be enforced, there would be a violation of Art 3.

Article 4 ECHR – Prohibition of Slavery and Forced Labour ('No-one shall be held in slavery or . . . required to perform forced or compulsory labour')

Example: Protection of domestic employees. In 2005, the ECtHR found that there had been a violation of Art 4 in the case of *Siliadin v France* (Application no. 73316/01) (2005). Siwa-Akofa Siliadin complained that French criminal law had not afforded her sufficient and effective protection against the 'servitude' in which she had been held, or at the very least against the 'forced and compulsory' labour she had been required to perform, which in practice had made her a domestic slave. The Court considered that the French criminal legislation in force at the relevant time had not afforded the applicant specific and effective protection against the actions of which she had been a victim.

Example: Human trafficking. In January 2010, the Court found that there had been a violation of Art 4 in the case of *Rantsev v Cyprus and Russia* (Application no. 25965/04)(2010), holding that the Cypriot and Russian authorities had failed to protect a 20-year-old Russian cabaret artist from human trafficking.

Article 5 ECHR – Right to Freedom and Security ('right to liberty and security')

Example: Unlawful or arbitrary detention. In 2004, the ECtHR found that there had been a violation of Art 5 in the case of *Frommelt v Liechtenstein* (Application no. 49158/99) (2004). Peter Frommelt was placed in pre-trial detention in 1997 on suspicion of offences including embezzlement and fraud. He alleged that there had been procedural shortcomings in the review of his pre-trial detention.

Example: In April 2004, the ECtHR found that there had been a violation of Art 5 in *Assanidze v Georgia* (Application no. 71503/01) (2004). Tengiz Assanidze, formerly the mayor of the Black Sea port of Batumi, Georgia, was arrested in October 1993 for illegal financial dealings in the Batumi Tobacco Manufacturing Company and for the unlawful possession and handling of firearms. He was convicted in November 1994 and sentenced to eight years' imprisonment. The applicant had been held in detention for more than three years after his acquittal by the Supreme Court of Georgia in 2001. The Court found that the applicant had been arbitrarily detained and held that the Georgian State had to secure his release at the earliest possible date. The Court also awarded the applicant monetary damages of €150,000 plus costs and interest.

Article 6 ECHR – Right to a Fair Trial ('Everyone is entitled to a fair public hearing within a reasonable time by an independent, impartial tribunal. All persons charged with an offence shall be presumed innocent until proven guilty.') This article is one of the pillars of what is generally known as the Rule of Law. To encourage the full application of Art 6, the Council of Europe has established a Consultative Council of European Judges (CCJE) composed exclusively of judges from the organisation's 47 member countries. The role of the CCJE is to strengthen the independence, impartiality and competence of judges. The Consultative Council has no equivalent in any other international organisation. Its activities are matched by those of the European Commission for the Efficiency of Justice, or CEPEJ, which has a more general remit to develop the standards of judicial systems and public justice services (see also the European Convention for the Prevention of Torture and Inhuman or Degrading Treatment or Punishment, Strasbourg, 26 November 1987).

Article 8 ECHR – Right to Respect for Private and Family Life ('Everyone has the right to respect for his private and family life, his home and his correspondence')

Example: Privacy and media intrusion. In 2004, the ECtHR found that there had been a violation of Art 8 in the case of *von Hannover v Germany* (Application no. 59320/00) (2004). Princess Caroline von Hannover had on several occasions unsuccessfully applied to the German courts for an injunction preventing any further publication of a series of photographs which had appeared in German magazines in the 1990s, claiming that they infringed her right to protection of her private life and her right to control the use of her image. The Court said that everyone, including people known to the public, had to have a 'legitimate expectation' that his or her private life would be protected.

Article 9 ECHR – Freedom of Thought, Conscience and Religion ('Everyone has the right to freedom of thought, conscience and religion')

Example: States must uphold the Article 9 right. In 1993, the Court found that there had been a violation of Art 9 in *Kokkinakis v Greece* (Application no. 14307/88) (1993). Mr Minos Kokkinakis, a retired businessman of Greek nationality, was born into an Orthodox family at Sitia (Crete) in 1919. After becoming a Jehovah's Witness in 1936, he was arrested more than sixty times for proselytism. He was also interned and imprisoned on several occasions.

Example: In 2000, the ECtHR found that there had been a violation of Art 9 in the case of *Hasan and Chaush v Bulgaria* (Application no. 30985/96) (2000) 24 EHRR 55. The applicants, a former Chief Mufti of the Bulgarian Muslims and a teacher of Islam, complained about the Bulgarian authorities' decision to change the leadership and statute of the Muslim community. The Court found that there had been interference with the internal organisation of the Muslim community and the applicants' freedom of religion.

Article 10 ECHR – Freedom of Expression ('Everyone has the right to freedom of expression and to receive and impart information. This right also covers the freedom of the press')

Example: Freedom of the press and broadcasting media. Without a free and diverse press there can be no democratic society. The freedom of expression guaranteed by Art 10 is also applicable to 'information' or 'ideas' that offend, shock or disturb the state or any sector of the population. States have a duty to uphold this right. In 2000, the Court found that there had been a violation of

Art 10 in the case of *Lopes Gomes da Silva v Portugal* (Application no. 37698/97) (2000). Vicente Jorge Lopes Gomes da Silva, who at the relevant time was manager of the daily newspaper *Público*, was convicted of libel. The Court stated in particular that freedom of expression was of particular importance with regard to the press, the limits of acceptable criticism being wider with regard to a politician acting in his public capacity.

Example: In 2009, in *Times Newspapers Ltd v the United Kingdom* (Nos. 1 and 2) (Application nos. 3002/03 and 23676/0) (2009) EMLR 14, The Times retained two articles in its internet archive after a libel action brought by GL in respect of the hardcopy publication of those articles. GL then brought a second claim in respect of the internet publications. The Times argued that the internet publication rule on re-publication restricted its ability to maintain an archive and exposed the Times to ceaseless liability, and there should not be any obligation to publish qualifications until litigation had been resolved. The ECtHR concluded that the newspaper's conviction for the publication of libellous articles archived on the Internet did not constitute a violation of the Convention.

Article 14 ECHR – Prohibition from Discrimination ('Everyone must enjoy the rights enshrined in the European Convention on Human Rights regardless of skin colour, sex, language, political or religious beliefs or origin')

Example: Discrimination based on sexual orientation. In 2003, the Court found that there had been a violation of Art 14 in the case of *Karner v Austria* (Application no. 40016/98) (3003). Siegmund Karner complained about the Austrian courts' decision that the statutory right of a family member to succeed to a tenancy did not apply to homosexual couples.

Example: Discrimination based on origin. In 2007, the Court found a violation of Art 14 in the case of *D.H. v the Czech Republic* (Application no. 57325/00) (2007). The case was brought by 18 Roma students from the Ostrava region in the Czech Republic. During 1996 and 1999, all the applicants had been assigned to special schools for children with learning difficulties where they received inferior education based on a diluted curriculum. In 2000, the applicants complained to the European Court of Human Rights arguing that their treatment amounted to discrimination in violation of Art 14 in conjunction with Art 2 of Protocol 1 ECHR, as their right to education had been denied. The Grand Chamber of the ECtHR made a landmark decision ruling in favour of the applicants and found that the applicants had suffered discrimination when denied their right to education.

Example: Discrimination based on descent. In 2004, the Court found that there had been a violation of Art 14 in the case of *Pla and Puncernau v Andorra* (Application no. 69498/01) (2004). Antoni Pla Puncernau was an adopted child who had been excluded from his grandmother's estate under the terms of the will on account of his adoptive status in 1939. The domestic courts found that the applicant could not be considered 'a child of a lawful and canonical marriage' and could not, therefore, inherit the estate in question. The court ordered the applicants to hand over the property to the other beneficiaries, the great-granddaughters of the testatrix, deemed to be her rightful heirs. The applicant complained that the court decisions finding that he could not inherit his grandmother's estate were discriminatory. The ECtHR found an Art 14 discrimination by the state of Andorra (in conjunction with Art 8 ECHR). This demonstrates the horizontal effect of the Convention in action. The domestic courts had applied national testamentary provision incorrectly and public authorities have to adhere to Convention rights.

Human Rights Act 1998

The Human Rights Act 1998 (HRA) introduced the European Convention on Human Rights (ECHR) into British law. When citing the Articles of the Convention, use 'ECHR' (not HRA) in your citations (e.g. Art 8 ECHR 'right to privacy'). What this means in practice is that people who wish to bring cases where they believe their human rights have been violated, are able to do so through the British courts since the HRA came into force on 2 October 2000. The Act makes it unlawful for any public authority to act in such a way that is incompatible with a right under the Convention (s 6 HRA 1998). A person can only bring a case against a public authority if they can be classed as the 'victim' in a specific circumstance (see Chapter 10).

Fundamental principles of the Human Rights Act 1998

This means that the rights are subject to a limited amount of interference by the state in certain legally defined circumstances that benefit society as a whole rather than just the individual. For example, the Convention protects somebody from arbitrary detention, i.e. no one can be imprisoned or detained against their will in accordance with a procedure prescribed in law.

Proportionality

This means that exercising the rights and their protection by the courts have to be in a way that is proportional to the needs of society (also referred to as a 'pressing social need for interference'). This offers the individual a shield against the state interfering with one's liberty or the state overriding an individual's right through disproportionate action. For example, a privacy law would disproportionately curtail press freedom, i.e. the freedom of expression (Art 10 ECHR). But at the same time, case law formed from the Convention (Strasbourg jurisprudence) can provide adequate protection of privacy from disproportionate media intrusion (Art 8 ECHR).

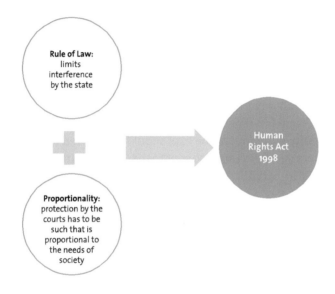

European Court of Human Rights (ECtHR) (Strasbourg)

The number of judges of the Court is the same as that of the States Parties to the Convention (47 at present). The Parliamentary Assembly of the **Council of Europe** elects the judges from lists of three candidates proposed by each state. They are elected for a non-renewable term of nine years. Judges hear cases as individuals and do not represent any state. They are totally independent and have to judge impartially. Cases are heard by one of four main formations. The Court has five sections in which **Chambers** are formed. Each section has a President, a Vice-President and a number of other judges. A Chamber is composed of the President of the Section to which the case was assigned, the 'national judge' (the judge elected in respect of the state against which the application was lodged) and five other judges designated by the Section President in rotation. A three-judge Committee may rule by a unanimous vote on the admissibility and merits of cases that are already covered by well-established case law of the ECtHR (also known as 'Strasbourg jurisprudence'). An application may also be assigned to a seven-judge Chamber that rules by a majority vote, mostly on the admissibility and merits of a case.

The Grand Chamber

The Grand Chamber of 17 judges hears cases referred to it either after relinquishment of jurisdiction by a (lower) Chamber or when a request for referral has been accepted. The Grand Chamber is made up of the Court's President and Vice-Presidents, the Section Presidents and the national judge, together with other judges selected by drawing of lots. When it hears a case on referral, it does not include any judges who previously sat in the Chamber which first examined the case. Proceedings before the Grand Chamber take two different forms:

❖ Referral
❖ Relinquishment.

After a Chamber judgment has been delivered, the parties may request referral of the case to the Grand Chamber (this is exceptional). A panel of judges of the Grand Chamber decides whether or not the case should be referred to the Grand Chamber for fresh consideration. Cases are also sent to the Grand Chamber when relinquished by a Chamber (also exceptional). The Chamber to which a case is assigned can relinquish it to the Grand Chamber if the case raises a serious question affecting the interpretation of the Convention or if there is a risk of inconsistency with a previous judgment of the Court.

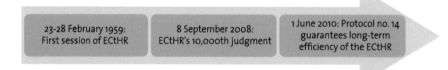

23-28 February 1959: First session of ECtHR

8 September 2008: ECtHR's 10,000th judgment

1 June 2010: Protocol no. 14 guarantees long-term efficiency of the ECtHR

How are cases brought before the European Court of Human Rights?

Cases can be brought directly by individuals and the assistance of a lawyer is not necessary at the start of the proceedings. Cases can only be brought against one or more states that have ratified the Convention. Since the Court was established, almost all applications have been lodged by individuals who have brought their cases directly to the Court, alleging one or more violations of the Convention.

The Convention makes a distinction between two types of application:

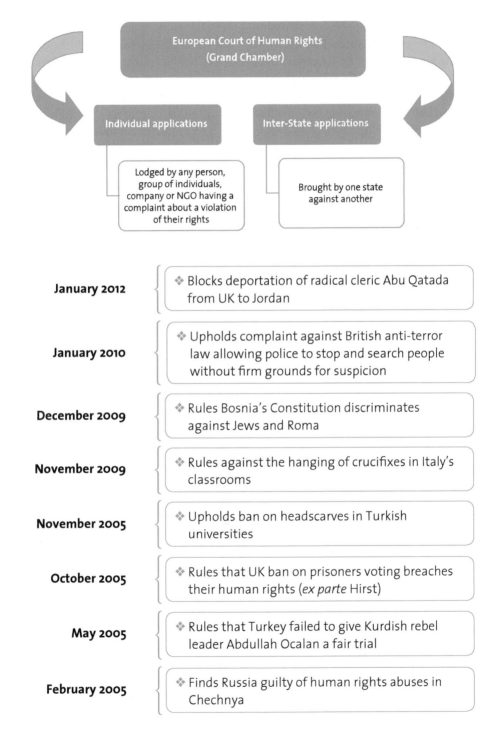

January 2012	❖ Blocks deportation of radical cleric Abu Qatada from UK to Jordan
January 2010	❖ Upholds complaint against British anti-terror law allowing police to stop and search people without firm grounds for suspicion
December 2009	❖ Rules Bosnia's Constitution discriminates against Jews and Roma
November 2009	❖ Rules against the hanging of crucifixes in Italy's classrooms
November 2005	❖ Upholds ban on headscarves in Turkish universities
October 2005	❖ Rules that UK ban on prisoners voting breaches their human rights (*ex parte* Hirst)
May 2005	❖ Rules that Turkey failed to give Kurdish rebel leader Abdullah Ocalan a fair trial
February 2005	❖ Finds Russia guilty of human rights abuses in Chechnya

Grand Chamber rulings

Relationship between the European Court of Human Rights and domestic courts

The Convention is applicable at national level. It has been incorporated into the legislation of the **States Parties**, which have undertaken to protect the rights defined in the Convention. Domestic courts therefore have to apply the Convention. This is achieved in the UK by way of the HRA 1998. If a state contravenes the Convention, the European Court of Human Rights (ECtHR) will find against the state in the event of complaints by individuals about failure to protect their rights. The Court cannot take up cases of its own motion. It has jurisdiction to hear allegations of violations of the ECHR and does so on receiving individual or inter-state applications.

Up for Debate

Speaking in March 2013 at a conference, Conservative Home Secretary Theresa May said that by the next General Election her party would legislate to 'opt out' from the European Convention. Mrs May asked: 'When Strasbourg constantly moves the goalposts and prevents the deportation of dangerous men like Abu Qatada, we have to ask ourselves to what end are we signatories to the Convention?' But the UK Supreme Court had ruled that Abu Qatada, suspected of terrorism, could not be tried on evidence obtained through torturing his co-defendants. In an essay on the topic of the influence of the European Convention on UK constitutional law, you need to engage with the basic principles of any democracy and the Rule of Law. Would you agree that a UK pullout from the ECHR (and therein the Council of Europe) would be a disaster? The President of the Strasbourg Human Rights Court (ECtHR), Judge Dean Spielmann, warned in July 2013 that renouncing the Convention would result in the UK losing global credibility on human rights grounds. Do you agree?

Public versus private bodies

Section 6 of the Human Rights Act 1998 (HRA) makes it clear that every public authority must adhere to Convention Articles (ECHR). However, case law shows us that it is often not clear when we are dealing with 'hybrid' authorities (usually those which were once public authorities, such as the health service, housing associations, prisoner authorities) and which are now privatised but still seemingly perform public functions. Each case will then have to be taken on its own merit and will have to be proved in the UK administrative courts (see more on Judicial Review in Chapter 9).

Case precedent – *Aston Cantlow and Wilmcote and Billesley Paroch Council v Wallbank* [2004] HL ('Chancel repair case')

Facts: Mrs and Mr Wallbank were joint owners of Glebe Farm and Mrs Wallbank was lay rector of St John the Baptist on the ancient Saxon site of the farm. Notice was served by the Parochial Church Council (the PCC) on 12 September 1994 that under s 2(2) Chancel Repairs Act 1932 Mrs Wallbank had to pay for the repair of the chancel (estimated at £95,260.84). She disputed liability, so the PCC brought proceedings against her under the 1932 Act. The Wallbanks believed they had no defence to the claim made against them by the PCC, except under s 6 HRA 1998 (it is unlawful for a public authority to act incompatibly with a Convention right). The courts had to decide whether the HRA applied in this case, and whether the PCC was a public authority for the purposes of the HRA. The House of Lords overturned the Court of Appeal's ruling, and held that the PCC was **not** a 'core public authority' and not performing public functions either.

Principle: The problem highlighted in this case is that the HRA 1998 does not define what is meant by public authority. Sections 6(3)(a) and (b) and 6(5) HRA 1998 give no real definition of 'public authority'. A Parochial Church Council has no obligation to act compatibly with the ECHR. A non-governmental organisation should not be regarded as a 'core public authority' for the purpose of the Convention (ECHR).

Application: This case concerned the arcane and unsatisfactory areas of UK property law–here, the liability of a lay rector for the repair of the chancel of a church, i.e. defendants Mrs and Mr Wallbank were under a common law duty to repair the chancel of the parish church. The House of Lords (by reversing the Court of Appeal's decision) held that a PCC is not a public authority. Therefore, the duty of liability to repair the chancel of the church lay with the rector, Mrs Wallbank. The PCC did not fall within the remit of s 6 HRA 1998 (public authority) (see also *R (A) v Partnership in Care Limited* [2002] 1 WLR 2610 – private psychiatric care; *Poplar Housing & Regeneration Community Association v Donoghue* [2001]; *YL v Birmingham City Council* [2007] UKHL 27 ('Southern Cross Care Home case').

Case precedent – *Hirst v United Kingdom* (No. 2) (Application no. 74025/01 (2005) Grand Chamber (ECtHR)

Facts: John Hirst (born 1950) pleaded guilty to murdering his landlady in February 1980 on the ground of diminished responsibility. He was sentenced to life imprisonment. Though his tariff expired in June 1994, he was denied parole due to his being 'high risk' and dangerous to the public. Under s 3 Representation of the People Act 1983, prisoners in the UK are barred from voting in parliamentary and local elections. During his time in prison, Hirst began his campaign to change the law on prisoners' voting rights. As part of Judicial Review proceedings, he sought a declaration under s 4 HRA 1998 seeking incompatibility of the 1983 Act with the European Convention (ECHR) in 2001 (Hirst No. 1). The application was dismissed. However, in 2005, he was successful, relying on Art 3 of Protocol No. 1 ECHR, which provides for universal suffrage and voting rights to all 'contracting parties' to the Convention. The Grand Chamber of the ECtHR found that the exclusion from voting imposed on convicted prisoners in detention in the UK was disproportionate. This meant the UK stripped a large group of people of the vote; that it applied automatically irrespective of the length of the sentence or the gravity of the offence. The Court also noted that disqualifying convicted prisoners from voting amounted to an additional punishment for which there was no logical justification. And in Hirst's case the disqualification from voting in elections was particularly irrational since the applicant had completed the part of his sentence relating to punishment and deterrence. The ECtHR ruled that Hirst's human rights had fundamentally been violated.

Principle: While the Grand Chamber did not state that all prisoners in the UK should be given voting rights, it held that if the disenfranchisement (barring prisoners to vote) was to be removed, then the measure needed to be compatible with Art 3 of the First Protocol of the Convention. This meant that the ECtHR placed the onus on the UK Parliament to justify its departure from the principle of universal suffrage.

Application: The UK Parliament was asked by the ECtHR to address prisoners' voting rights by August 2012, either by formulating new legislation or amending or explaining the current measures which did or did not permit prisoners to vote. The Voting Eligibility (Prisoners) Draft Bill was before Parliament in 2013.

Aim Higher

In an exam essay or piece of coursework, you will be asked to discuss the implied limitations of the European Convention. You need to cite specific case law (both UK and Strasbourg jurisprudence). High marks will be awarded if you discuss the application of Convention Articles (ECHR) by domestic courts, i.e. the 47 signatory states to the Convention. How does a domestic court, such as a UK court, actually apply the margin of appreciation in its sphere of public law? You could discuss the ECtHR ruling in *Hirst v UK* (No. 2) (2005), for example, in relation to prisoner voting rights. Your discussion should then lead on to: how absolute are the individual human rights articles? Discuss how the Grand Chamber (ECtHR) in *Hirst* ruled that the UK should bestow voting rights on its convicted prisoners. You will gain high marks if you say that Art 3 of Protocol No. 1 ECHR does not bestow absolute rights on individuals. How, then, did the UK resolve this issue? Clearly, the UK Parliament did not (yet) legislate on prisoner voting rights. Your discussion should lead on to the 'punishment' powers of the Strasbourg human rights court (ECtHR). What penalties are there for the ECtHR to enforce its rulings? Clearly, the Strasbourg human rights court does not have the powers of judicial enforcement which the Court of Justice (ECJ) has in relation to EU law and its strict enforcement penalties on the 28 members of the EU. The judgment in *Hirst* is useful: if you look at the case, you will find plenty of other human rights case law to cite in your coursework or examination (e.g. *Mathieu-Mohin and Clerfayt v Belgium* [1987]). Further marks will be awarded for recent judgments by the UK Supreme Court in relation to challenges by convicted murderers, Peter Chester and George McGeoch, who lost their appeal when challenging prisoners' right to vote in June 2013.

Putting it into practice:

Essay questions are likely to relate to one of the following:

❖ Implied limitations of the ECHR (the Convention)
❖ Detailed knowledge of the main Convention Articles
❖ The role and function of the Human Rights Act 1998 (HRA) (see also Chapter 10)
❖ Strasbourg jurisprudence (comparative case law and application in domestic courts)
❖ The influence of Strasbourg jurisprudence on the UK Constitution
❖ The impact of the Convention on public authorities: s 6 HRA 1998 created a new type of illegality in the UK courts ('breach of Convention rights') (see also Chapter 9)
❖ The 'victim' status of individuals in Judicial Review proceedings, i.e. individuals can rely directly on the ECHR (see also Chapter 10)
❖ The difference between public and private functions of public authorities under s 6(3)(b) HRA 1998 (e.g. the National Health Service; HM Prison Service; the Police; or hybrid authorities such as public/private health authorities and care homes; privately run prisons and prisoner transport) (see *Aston Cantlow and Wilmcote and Billesley Parochial Church Council v Wallbank* [2004] 1 AC 546 (HL))
❖ Functions performed by public authorities of a purely public nature under s 6 (5) HRA 1998 (see *R (Heather) v Leonard Cheshire Foundation* [2002] 2 All ER 936; *Poplar Housing & Regeneration Community Association v Donoghue* [2001] 3 WLR 183).

Problem questions tend to include the following themes; in your answers, you should concentrate on the following:

❖ There will usually be a given scenario in which it is **alleged** an individual's (or a group's) human rights have been breached. You are to assess whether that person (persons or group) can bring a claim for breach of a Convention right (or rights) under the Human Rights Act 1998 (see also Chapters 9 and 10).

❖ Look at the factual situation and identify which Convention right(s) are engaged and will be invoked by the applicant(s) (e.g. Art 8 ECHR 'right to privacy'; Art 10 ECHR 'freedom of expression').

❖ If a number of Convention rights are allegedly violated, take a step-by-step approach and identify precisely each right at stake, protected by a particular Article of the ECHR (you need to point out that this will take the form of Judicial Review in the UK, citing relevant case law, such as *Hirst*).

❖ 'Victims' of human rights violations must invoke s 7(1) HRA 1998, i.e. only a person directly affected by a decision of a public authority can bring an action in either the domestic court or the ECtHR and rely on Convention right(s) ('...only if he is (or would be) a victim of the unlawful act'); this is known as 'victim status' in Judicial Review proceedings (see *Pretty v DPP* [2001] UKHL 61).

Essay

Are human rights absolute? Discuss with reference to Article 8 ECHR 'the right to privacy' and Article 10 ECHR 'the freedom of expression' and Strasbourg jurisprudence.

Feedback on putting it into practice

a) Note that this essay question is divided into three parts: (1) human rights are not always absolute, (2) discuss Art 8 ECHR + case law, (3) discuss Art 10 ECHR + case law. For high marks, you must answer all elements of the question. If you answer only one part of the question, you will be marked down.

b) Discuss the enforceability in law and the distinction between laws (Acts of Parliament) and Convention rights (+ case law); you can cite cases where the courts upheld UK statutory provision and where the Strasbourg court ruled differently (e.g. prisoner votes).

c) Discuss the different viewpoints by legal writers in relation to Supremacy of Parliament (e.g. Dicey, Jennings) and how the European Convention has influenced the UK Constitution.

Problem question

Shabana Akhtar (age 15) attends a high school in Milton Keynes. The school, which has a Muslim headmistress, has modified its school uniform policy, to accommodate Muslim dress for all its pupils. As part of the girls' uniform, Muslim girls are allowed to wear the shalwar kameez (a sleeveless smock). While Shabana has worn the shalwar kameez since she joined the school, aged 12, her father now wants her to wear the full jilbab (a coat-like garment), explaining to the headmistress that this is appropriate for maturing girls. The headmistress does not allow this dress and says that the shalwar kameez is perfectly adequate. Since Shabana refuses to comply with the school's uniform policy, she is excluded from attending the school. At the same time, Anil Singh, a Sikh schoolboy (age 16) is told by the headmistress that he cannot wear his religious wrist bangle to school. Anil is also excluded from school. Advise both pupils whether they have a claim against the school on human rights grounds.

Feedback on putting it into practice

a) In this problem question you need to apply your legal knowledge. There are two issues here, Shabana's religious dress and Anil's religious emblem (the wrist bangle). There is no clear answer here and you need to argue both the pupils' side (human rights law) and that of the school. Identify the areas of law and argue the case clearly. Do not waffle and concentrate on the problem(s) and areas of law (here human rights law, i.e. ECHR and HRA and case law).

b) There are potentially several inherent human rights claims that both pupils can invoke.

c) You are advised to deal with each 'problem' (i.e. each pupil) separately; therefore, you should start with Shabana, argue her case, and then move on to Anil. In court (or at the school hearing before the school governors), they would most likely have their own lawyers.

d) Both Shabana and Anil will invoke Art 2 of the First Protocol of the Convention (ECHR) ('right to education'), and

e) Art 9 ECHR ('freedom of religion and beliefs').

f) This may well provide both pupils with the necessary 'victim' status under the HRA 1998; if the school continues to exclude Shabana and Anil, both pupils could apply for Judicial Review against the school governors.

g) The case that most closely resembles Shabana's case is *R (Begum) v Denbigh High School* [2006] UKHL 15 (also known as the 'Denbigh High School case'). You should argue the facts of this case but only if you have READ the *Denbigh High School* case, demonstrating particular judgments in your answer – then applying the facts to Shabana's case.

h) Both pupils would invoke Art 2 ECHR First Protocol and Art 9 ECHR, contending that their exclusion from school contravenes their right to education as well as their right to exercise religious freedom.

i) You need to argue both sides, i.e. the school governors will argue that they have adapted the school's uniform policy to accommodate all faiths, that Shabana and Anil are unreasonable and, since they do not comply with the school uniform policy, they must be excluded; you need to flag up whether the school has a jewellery policy (e.g. no jewellery on the premises, no jewellery during PE).

j) Has the school contravened Shabana's rights under Art 2 First Protocol and Art 9 ECHR? It was held in the *Denbigh High School* case that the school in Luton did **not** violate Shabina Begum's rights. Denbigh High School's refusal to exclude a pupil for wearing the Jilbab at school did **not** interfere with her right to manifest her religious beliefs under Art 9 of the Convention, nor did it deny her access to education in violation of Art 2 of the First Protocol to the Convention.

k) It seems that on the facts the school in Milton Keynes in our problem question has fully justified its actions by way of its school uniform policy, i.e. the governors and headmistress have taken immense pains to devise a uniform policy that respected Muslim (and other) beliefs in the school. Shabana would probably not succeed in her human rights claim (in terms of Judicial Review, she would most likely not be successful at the 'standing' (*locus standi*) stage).

l) You could argue that the school rules have been inclusive, unthreatening and uncompetitive (take a look at the *Denbigh High School* judgment and ratio).

m) In relation to Anil, you might argue differently, if the school uniform policy does not say anything about pupils wearing jewellery. If only he is excluded for wearing a Sikh bangle, then the exclusion would be rather discriminatory and senseless, disturbing the school's harmony.

n) Anil's case most likely resembles the case of *Eweida and Others v UK* [2013] ECHR 37 (ECtHR) 15 January 2013, which also concerned the wearing of a religious object (i.e. a religious cross as a necklace).

o) Have Anil's human rights been breached (i.e. Art 9 ECHR)?

p) It is unclear from the facts in our problem question what the school's policy is on the wearing of jewellery. And because you are not told about this fact, you need to argue both ways. The Human Rights Court (ECtHR) judgment in *Eweida* will assist you, since not all three applicants were granted their Art 9 right (just Ms Eweida).

q) The ECtHR granted Ms Nadia Eweida the right to wear her religious cross around her neck (she worked for British Airways) but not Ms Shirley Chaplin (as nurse) who was not permitted to wear her cross during her work; this was held by the Strasbourg Court as non-discriminatory.

r) Turning to Anil's case, you need to argue the school's possible policy on jewellery and/or the wearing of religious objects during school time. If Anil is granted standing and the administrative court would consider his case at Judicial Review, the court would adopt the proportionality approach and judge his case objectively against the school's policy.

s) The court will have to consider the proportionality of the school's decision and consider its interference with Anil's Art 9 right to manifest his religious belief (cite the *Eweida* judgment in Ms Chaplin's case, which was heard as a conjoined case with Eweida at the ECtHR hearing).

t) You may therefore argue that the school's policy on jewellery is correct, i.e. no jewellery to be worn during school time; in which case, **all** pupils will have to adhere to that policy.

u) If the school's jewellery policy is clear and precise, Anil would not succeed in his claim of being a 'victim' in human rights terms and would not have a claim in Judicial Review (no victim status).

v) You need to argue that Art 9 ECHR is not an absolute right that was affirmed in *Eweida*; this means that Art 9 does not provide Shabana and Anil with an absolute right to wear religious dress or symbols at school.

w) It does, however, require schools (and employers) to be particularly cautious in denying pupils (and employees) the wearing of either religious dress or symbols depending on the type of school policy (e.g. during PE or food preparation lessons).

x) Conclusion: On the facts before us – the school might well be fully justified in acting as it has done, i.e. it has taken immense pains to devise a school uniform/jewellery policy that respects all beliefs; but on health and safety grounds, has forbidden **any** jewellery to be worn at school. The rules are written in an inclusive, unthreatening and uncompetitive way. The rules contribute to the school's period of harmony and success (refer to the *Denbigh High School* and *Eweida* judgments).

Common Pitfalls

Make sure you do not confuse EU Law with human rights law (ECHR). Remember these are two different sources of law, and there are two completely separate courts of law: the Court of Justice (or 'European Court of Justice – ECJ) in Luxembourg stands for EU Law. The European Court of Human Rights (ECtHR) in Strasbourg, France, enforces human rights law in the form of the European Convention on Human Rights (ECHR). EU law is supreme to all 28 Member States of the European Union (the EU). The European Convention on Human Rights (ECHR or 'Convention') covers all 47 signatory countries under the Council of Europe.

Chapter summary

❖ Historical background to the Council of Europe and its signatory countries.

❖ The principal aims and objectives of the European Convention on Human Rights (ECHR) and the main Articles of the Convention.

❖ The jurisdiction and role of the European Court of Human Rights (ECtHR) in Strasbourg.
❖ ECtHR judgments and how they have influenced UK decisions.

Table of key cases referred to in this chapter

Case name	Area of law	Principle
Renolde v France (2008)	Art 2 ECHR 'right to life'	Prisoners known to be suffering from a serious mental disturbance and to pose a suicide risk require special measures and protection in prison or police custody
Mammadov (Jalaloglu) v Azerbaijan (2007)	Art 3 ECHR 'prevention from torture, inhuman and degrading treatment'	Human dignity and respect must be observed in detention
Poplar Housing & Regeneration Community Association v Donoghue [2001]	s 6(3)(b) HRA 1998 'Hybrid authorities' (public vs. private function)	Registered social landlord (Poplar Housing) was 'hybrid', as the company had retained close control of publicly funded housing; provided a public function
Aston Cantlow and Wilmcote and Billesley Parochial Church Council v Wallbank [2004]	s 6(3)(b) HRA 1998 'Hybrid authorities' (public and private functions fulfilling dual functions)	A non-governmental organisation should not be regarded as a 'core public authority' for the purpose of the Convention (ECHR)
R (Heather) v Leonard Cheshire Foundation [2002]	s 6(3) and s 6(5) HRA 1998 (what is a public authority and its functions)	Charity providing home for disabled children on behalf of local authority not held to provide a service

---

@ **Visit the book's companion website to test your knowledge**

❖ Resources include a subject map, revision tip podcasts, downloadable diagrams, MCQ quizzes for each chapter, and a flashcard glossary
❖ www.routledge.com/cw/optimizelawrevision

8

Administrative Law: General Principles of Judicial Review

Revision objectives

Understand the law
- Do you understand what is meant by Judicial Review and what type of decisions can be challenged?
- Can you explain the different ways in which a decision can be challenged?

Remember the details
- Can you explain and define how Judicial Review works?
- Are you able to describe and define what is meant by 'standing' (or locus standi)?
- Are you able to discuss the 'victim' status under the Human Rights Act 1998 (HRA)?
- Can you define a public authority's duty under the HRA?

Reflect critically on areas of debate
- Can you discuss the leave stage as part of a Judicial Review application?
- Can you define the relevant sections in the HRA which apply to public bodies?
- Do you know which courts JR is heard in?

Contextualise
- Are you familiar with the procedure in cases of Judicial Review?
- Can you discuss the various remedies available to the courts if the application for Judicial Review is successful?
- Do you know which courts JR is heard in?

Apply your skills and knowledge
- Can you answer questions in the Putting it into Practice section of the chapter relating to the public law procedure of Judicial Review in the form of essay and problem questions?

Chapter Map

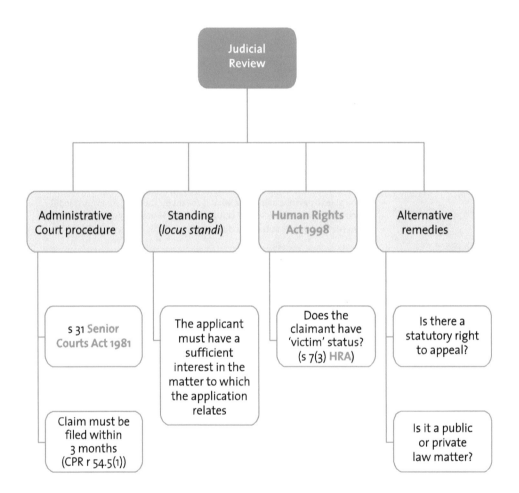

Judicial Review

- Administrative Court procedure
  - s 31 Senior Courts Act 1981
  - Claim must be filed within 3 months (CPR r 54.5(1))
- Standing (*locus standi*)
  - The applicant must have a sufficient interest in the matter to which the application relates
- Human Rights Act 1998
  - Does the claimant have 'victim' status? (s 7(3) HRA)
- Alternative remedies
  - Is there a statutory right to appeal?
  - Is it a public or private law matter?

What is Judicial Review?

Administrative law generally concentrates on the control of the **Executive**, i.e. Government, and public authorities. This area of your Public Law syllabus involves a set of constitutional legal principles that govern the exercise of judicial control over the power of public bodies. If, for example, a public body, such as your local authority, the education department or your local housing authority makes a decision that might potentially be in breach of any public law principle, then that decision may be challenged by you in the Administrative Court by way of **Judicial Review**. Reasons (or grounds) for this legal challenge will be dealt with in more detail in Chapter 9.

The purpose of Judicial Review

Judicial Review (JR) is dealt with in the Administrative Court (see below) and proceedings are initially paper-based, held in the judge's chambers. A single judge reviews the lawfulness of a decision or action made by a public body. Judicial Review can be defined as a means by which the **Judiciary** controls the **Executive** (i.e. the exercise of Governmental powers). The Administrative Court examines the way in which a decision by a public body was made and the claimant may allege that the decision (usually affecting his or her life) was unlawful, improper, irrational or disproportionate (see Chapter 9). Judicial Review allows individuals, organisations, businesses and other interest or pressure groups (also known in JR as 'surrogate' groups) to challenge the lawfulness of decisions made by Ministers, Government Departments, local authorities and other public bodies. Judicial Review is a type of court proceeding in which a (single) judge reviews the lawfulness of a decision or action made by a public body. The court will not look at the decision itself to find out if any powers have been abused. It will just look at the procedure and the way in which the decision was arrived at. This means the Administrative Court is not concerned with the merits of the decision under review but simply looks at whether an authority or public body has acted outside its legal powers (called *ultra vires*) (see *R v Somerset County Council ex parte Fewings* [1995] 1 All ER 513 (QBD)).

In the name of the Crown: Judicial Review applications

Judicial Review proceedings are brought in the name of the Crown, with the Crown as the first-named party: *R (on the application of A) v B*. The citation 'in the name of the Crown' (i.e. Regina or Rex) in JR is a formality that reflects the fact that the court is dealing with what are essentially issues of public law (formerly known as **exparte** hearings).

What is a public authority?

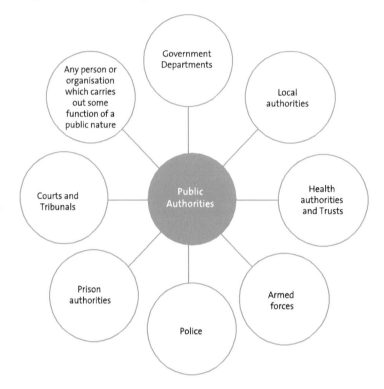

Aim Higher

Make sure you cite JR cases properly when writing in an examination, but particularly for your coursework. Before 2001, JR case names were cited: the Crown (*R*) against the public body under review, on behalf of (expressed as *ex parte*) (for example, *R v Lord Chancellor ex parte Witham* [1998] QB 575). For cases from 2001 onwards, the following is used: *R (on the application of Roberts) v Parole Board* [2004] EWCA Civ 1031. In both cases, you can write any subsequent citations as *Witham* or *Roberts* in your text or in a footnote.

The role of the Administrative Court

The work of the Administrative Court is varied, consisting of the administrative law jurisdiction of England and Wales as well as a supervisory jurisdiction over inferior courts and tribunals.

The leave stage

How does an individual or pressure group apply for Judicial Review? In practice, JR is an application to the judge in chambers (single judge hearing) of the Administrative

Court. The judge in chambers assesses an action or decision made by a public body on a point of public law. A particular decision may be found to be in breach of natural justice or have been made *ultra vires*, that is, beyond the scope of the powers of the public authority.

Judicial Review proceedings are commenced by filing a claim form at court, setting out the matter the claimant wants the court to decide and the remedy sought. This is known as the 'leave' or 'permission' stage. The claim must be submitted promptly and in any event within three months of the grounds giving rise to the claim. The claim form must be served on the defendant and any other interested party (unless the court directs otherwise) within seven days of issue. If the other parties wish to take part in the proceedings, they are required to file an 'Acknowledgement of Service' within 21 days of the service on them of the claim form. The Administrative Court's permission is required for a claim for JR to proceed.

Decisions on permission are normally considered by a single judge or 'Master' on a review of the papers filed. Permission may be granted in full, or limited to certain grounds set out in the claim (see below). In cases where the court refuses permission (either in full or in part), it will set out the reasons and serve them on the claimant and the other parties to proceedings. The claimant may request that the decision be reconsidered at a hearing (an 'oral renewal'). A request for an oral renewal must be filed within seven days of service of the reasons for refusing permission.

Note! Any applications for permission to apply for JR lodged on or after 1 July 2013 do not have a right to renew the application at an oral hearing if refused and identified as totally without merit (*Civil Procedure Rules* r 54.12(7) (2013)).

Types of Judicial Review case

Over the last decade, there has been a significant growth in the use of Judicial Review to challenge decisions of public authorities. In 1974, there were 1609 applications for JR, but by 2000 this had risen to nearly 4250, and by 2011 had reached over 11,000 (see *Judicial and Court Statistics 2011*, Ministry of Justice, June 2012). This growing area of law was criticised by Prime Minister David Cameron in 2013 who called many JR applications 'completely pointless'. Mr Cameron planned a broad clampdown on Judicial Review rights in order to 'speed up Government', particularly on the right to seek JR of asylum, immigration and environmental decisions. The Prime Minister sought to persuade Parliament to introduce legislation that would raise fees and impose tighter time limits for JR applications (see Prime Minister David Cameron's Speech to the CBI, video at about 9.20 minutes into the video recording online: http://www.cbi.org.uk/media-centre/videos/2012/11/david-cameron-cbi-annual-conference-speech.

Up for Debate

You are asked to write an essay on the purpose of Judicial Review. How will you go about it? How will you discuss the role of the courts in relation to JR? First, you should make the point at the start of your essay that JR is about the exercise of the court's inherent power at common law to determine whether an action or a decision by a local authority or Government Minister has been lawful or not. Secondly, make the point that it is the court's duty (Administrative Court at JR) to uphold the Rule of Law. You will then support your discussion with relevant case law, such as *R v Judicial Committee ex parte Vijayatunga* [1988] 1 QB 322.

The following diagram shows you some examples of decisions in common law of Judicial Review:

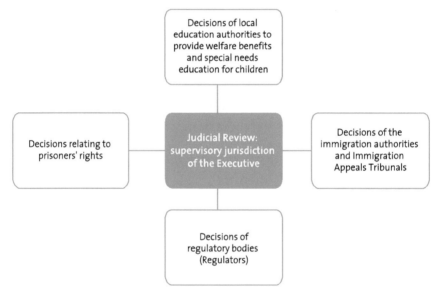

Examples of the types of Judicial Review decisions

Standing (*locus standi*)

Traditionally, to bring a Judicial Review challenge, an applicant had to show a **sufficient interest** in the decision to be reviewed, a test with a statutory basis in s 31(3) Senior Courts Act 1981 (formerly the Supreme Court Act 1981). One landmark case that helped establish the possibility of public interest challenges to administrative decisions was *R v Inspectorate of Pollution ex parte Greenpeace Ltd (No. 2), R v Ministry of Agriculture, Fisheries and Food ex parte Greenpeace Ltd* [1994] 4 ALL ER 329. The application concerned the thermal oxide reprocessing plant (THORP) which had been constructed by British Nuclear Fuels at Sellafield (formerly

Windscale) in Cumbria. Greenpeace was permitted to challenge a decision regarding the disposal of radioactive waste and was granted 'standing'. The reason was that the environmental pressure group is regarded as an organisation with relevant experience and real concern for the environment. Secondly, the fact that Greenpeace had 2500 supporters living in the region and were directly affected by the decision also gave the body standing. Furthermore, Greenpeace had been consulted as part of the Government consultation process leading to the decision.

Today, the majority of applications considered by the Administrative Court seeking permission to bring JR proceedings are refused. Of the 7600 applications for permission considered by the court in 2011, only around one in six (or 1200) was granted. Of the applications that were granted permission, 300 were granted following an oral renewal (out of around 2000 renewed applications that year) (see *Judicial and Court Statistics 2011*, Ministry of Justice, June 2012).

To be entitled to apply for JR of a decision, an individual or representative group must have **'sufficient interest'** (or **standing** – formerly known as *locus standi*). This means that the matter in question must be of sufficient public interest. It is well established that interested groups and trade associations, for example, may bring claims concerned without their sphere of interest (see list of cases below).

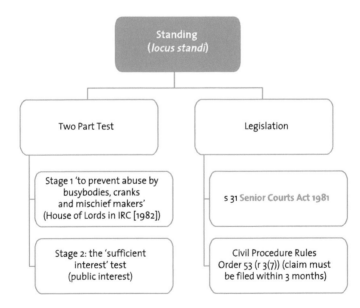

The test for standing in Judicial Review

Two separate routes for standing

There are **two separate tests** when an applicant is at leave stage (applying) for JR. Standing (*locus standi*) marks the eligibility of an individual or group who wishes to challenge a decision by a public authority or Government Department at JR in the Administrative Court. The individual can either take the traditional JR route (see Route 1 below) or rely on the 'victim' route under the Human Rights Act 1998 (see Table 2 below).

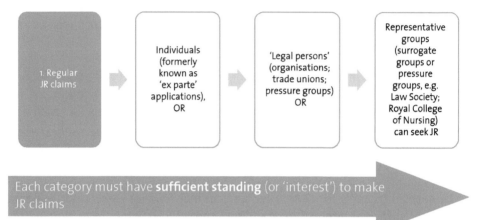

Route 1

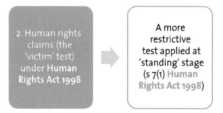

Route 2

Standing or no standing

Case name	Facts	Standing?
R v SOS for Environment ex p Ward (1984)	Gypsy required Council to provide appropriate caravan site	**Standing**: interest of individual
Gillick v Wisbech Area Health Authority (1986)	Policy relating to contraception for under-age girls	**Standing**: interest of individual
R v Liverpool Corp. ex p Liverpool Taxi Fleet (1972)	Council wanted to increase cab licences	**Standing**: interest of groups
Royal College of Nursing v Department for Health and Social Security (1981)	Role of nurses in abortions	**Standing**: interest of groups
R v SOS Environment ex p Greenpeace (No. 2) (1994)	THORP nuclear plant at Sellafield	**Standing**: Interest of groups – 400,000 signatories
Inland Revenue Commissioners v National Federation of Self-Employed and Small Businesses (1982) ('IRC')	Federation represented casual workers in newspaper industry (Fleet Street). Case concerned tax evasion	**No standing**: Federation had not sufficient interest
R v SOS for Environment ex p Rose Theatre Trust (1990)	Remains of the Rose Theatre (built 1587) were discovered in 1989 during excavations for a new Sainsbury's supermarket. Members of the public formed a campaign to 'Save the Rose' and protect it from redevelopment	**No standing**: not sufficient interest. 'No ordinary member of the public, nor even a very large number of members of the public who have joined together for that very purpose, has any standing to challenge a decision by the Secretary of State for the Environment' (Schiemann J).

Aim Higher

You may be asked in an essay or problem question whether an individual or surrogate group has sufficient standing (*locus standi*). Ample case law will assist you here. The court usually decides on the facts of the case, the importance of the issue, whether there is sufficient public interest and whether the individual is personally affected by the public body's decision. In *R v Inspectorate of Pollution ex parte Greenpeace (No. 2)* [1994] 4 All ER 329, the court ruled that the issue of whether an interest group or other body had sufficient standing should be decided on the facts of each case as a matter of discretion (see also *Campaign for Nuclear Disarmament v Prime Minister of the United Kingdom* [2002] EWHC 2777). In coursework, extra marks will be awarded if you cite judges' opinions in leading JR cases (you must quote correctly from the relevant law report). For example, Lord Justice Pill stated in *Al-Haq v Foreign Secretary* [2009] EWHC 1910 that, 'standing should not be treated as a preliminary issue but must be taken in the legal and factual context of the whole'. Slade LJ stated in *R v HM Treasury ex parte Smedley* [1985] 1 QB 657 that citizens would only be granted standing in JR on the basis of a 'serious question'. The *IRC* decision remains binding authority that taxpayers with genuine concerns do not necessarily have standing, even if the issues they raise are constitutionally important (see *Independent Revenue Commission v National Federation of Self-Employed and Small Businesses Ltd* [1982] AC 617 ('IRC').

The meaning of '*ultra vires*'

Judicial Review is not concerned with the 'merits' of a decision or whether the public body has made the 'right' decision. This means that the Administrative Court does not decide or rule in a particular case. The only question before the court is whether the public body has acted lawfully or outside its powers. Traditionally, the court would only intervene where a public body had used a power for a purpose not allowed by legislation (acting '*ultra vires*') or in circumstances where, when using its powers, the body had acted in a manner that was obviously **unreasonable** or **irrational** (see Chapter 9). Increasingly, where there is real unfairness, the courts are now more willing to intervene where the public body has made a serious factual error in reaching its decision (see *E v Secretary of State for the Home Department* [2004] EWCA Civ 49).

What types of decision can be challenged?

Judicial Review is, in principle, available in respect of most decisions by Government Departments, regulators and other public authorities (including local authorities). You need to point out in your essay or problem question answers that JR is a **remedy of last resort**, and that other appeals mechanisms usually have to be exhausted first before JR is granted 'standing'.

What kind of administrative decision may be unlawful?

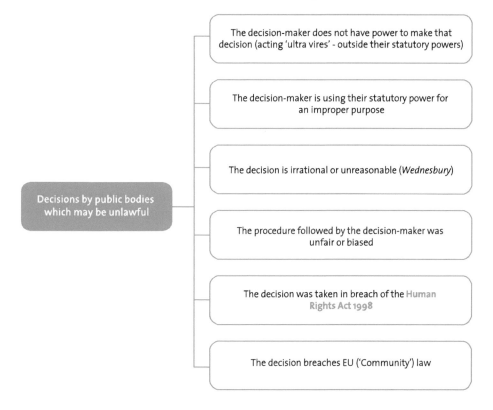

Decisions by public bodies which may be unlawful

- The decision-maker does not have power to make that decision (acting 'ultra vires' - outside their statutory powers)
- The decision-maker is using their statutory power for an improper purpose
- The decision is irrational or unreasonable (*Wednesbury*)
- The procedure followed by the decision-maker was unfair or biased
- The decision was taken in breach of the Human Rights Act 1998
- The decision breaches EU ('Community') law

Aim Higher

When answering an essay or problem question about the leave stage and standing (i.e. the initial procedural stage of a claimant's application for JR), you need to make it clear that JR is a remedy of last resort. The Administrative Court has made this crystal clear. Not everyone is granted leave to apply; this means not every applicant (including those in your problem questions) will have 'standing' ('*locus standi*'). You need to give reasons for this: as common law developed over the past decade and the caseload in JR applications has increased dramatically, the Administrative Court (usually the Master in Chambers) has refused JR applications because the applicant did not exhaust other remedies first before making a claim. These can include statutory appeals, private law remedies (e.g. breach of contract) or appeals tribunals (e.g. in immigration cases) (see *R v Sandwell Metropolitan Borough Council ex parte Wilkinson* (1998) 31 HLR 22; *R v Law Society ex parte Kingsley* [1996] COD 59).

Some decisions can be challenged but there are also those which, in law, cannot be challenged at JR.

'The subject matter of every Judicial Review is a decision made by some person (or body of persons) whom I shall call the "decision maker" or else a refusal by him to make a decision.' (Lord Diplock in *GCHQ*, 1985)

Have a look at the diagram below, which shows you the kind of administrative **decisions that *can* be challenged** (these often appear as problem questions in the exam):

Decision by a regulator to declare a person or business not fit to practise (e.g. Financial Services Authority or Financial Conduct Authority)

Decision by a local council to compulsorily acquire land (High Speed Rail network – HS2) see also: High Speed Rail (preparation) Bill.

Decision by a minister not to make a statutory grant (e.g. local council grant to artists or flood victims)

Decision to impose conditions on a pub or gambling licence

The following are examples of decisions that *cannot* be challenged at JR:

Legislative decisions (e.g. the validity of an Act of Parliament – except if it conflicts with a binding principle of EU law)

Acts of Devolved Parliaments on the grounds of irrationality, unreason-ableness or arbitrariness (see *AXA v HM Advocate* [2011] UKSC 46)

Decisions taken under Royal Prerogative (e.g. decision to enter into a Treaty with a foreign state)

Employment decisions (e.g. to dismiss an employee)

Contractual matters (e.g. decisions by Government Department to privatise certain parts of the HM Prison Service, such as kitchens or laundries)

What constitutes a public body?

The case of *O'Reilly v Mackman* [1983] 2 AC 237 gives us the general rule when claiming against a public body that Judicial Review should be used. The House of Lords held in *O'Reilly v Mackman* (see below) that it is an abuse of process to bring a public law challenge otherwise than by way of an application for JR. The four plaintiffs, prisoners in Hull Prison, were charged with disciplinary offences before the Board of Visitors to the prison. The Board of Visitors at that time imposed penalties on all four prisoners, three of whom brought actions by writ in the Queen's Bench against the board alleging that the Board of Visitors had acted in breach of the Prison Rules. The House of Lords dismissed the prisoners' appeals stating they should have obtained remedies for the infringement of their rights (to natural justice) by way of Judicial Review. Lord Diplock further defined a 'public body' in the *GCHQ* case, in that it normally derives its powers from common law or statute (see case of *Council of Civil Service Unions v Minister for the Civil Service* [1985] AC 374 (the *GCHQ* case)).

The *O'Reilly v Mackman* rule:

When a decision is contrary to public policy and the complainant alleges that a public authority has infringed his or her public law rights, they must seek redress by way of Judicial Review in the Administrative Court.

Aim Higher

At times it can be difficult to decide in a problem question whether you are dealing with a public or private authority (who has made an adverse decision against the claimant). The definition of a 'core public body' can then be found in case law where the courts have identified which public bodies fall within the scope of section 6(1) **Human Rights Act 1998**, as 'pure' or 'core' public authority. Under s 6(1) **HRA**, 'pure' public authorities include all Government Departments, local authorities, police and prison authorities. They are required to comply with Convention rights in all their activities, both when discharging intrinsically public functions and when performing functions that could be done by any private body or 'hybrid' authority. You would then refer to the *Aston Cantlow* case where the House of Lords concluded that a Parochial Church Council is not a 'core' public authority.

Case precedent – *O'Reilly v Mackman* [1983] 2 AC 237 (HL)

Facts: Four prisoners challenged the prison's Board of Visitors over their loss of remission after being found guilty at the adjudication of offences inside Hull Prison. They filed a court action by means of a writ, rather than by an action for Judicial Review (JR). The House of Lords held that since this was a public law matter they were wrong to do so; they should have applied by JR. Their Lordships held that the forfeiture of remission for a prisoner was a public law matter (including loss of liberty and privileges in prison). Lord Diplock said that this matter was public policy and should have been dealt with by JR.

Principle: Matters concerning a public body's decision must be challenged in a JR action. The purpose of this requirement is to protect the public administration against false, frivolous or late challenges to official action.

Application: The House of Lords ruling in *O'Reilly v Mackman* [1983] provides the general rule for claiming against a public body. Lord Diplock described this action in JR as the 'exclusivity principle'.

What is a private body?

Privatisation has made the courts increasingly willing to accept jurisdiction where the decision in question impacts on matters of business and commerce. City regulatory bodies, even those that are non-statutory and non-mandatory, may now be reviewable (see *R v Panel on Takeovers and Mergers ex parte Datafin plc* [1987] QB 815; *R v Advertising Standards Authority Ltd ex parte Insurance Service plc* [1989] 133 Sol Jo 1545; *R v Code of Practice Committee of the Association of the British Pharmaceutical Industry ex parte Professional Counselling Aids Ltd* [1990] 10 BMLR 21;

R (on the application of Ford) v The Press Complaints Commission [2001] EWHC Admin 683).

The general rule is that a private body can only be judicially reviewable where such bodies have been *'woven into the fabric of public regulation'* (as per Sir Thomas Bingham MR in *R v Disciplinary Committee of the Jockey Club ex parte The Aga Khan* [1992] EWCA Civ 7). Decisions of private organisations contracted to carry out a public body's statutory functions may also be reviewable; for example, the managers of a private psychiatric hospital were held to be a public authority when making decisions about the 'focus' of wards in their hospital (see *R (A) v Partnerships in Care Ltd* [2002] 1 WLR 2610). There is considerable legal debate about whether commercial bodies are challengeable by way of JR, particularly relating to their involvement and procurement with public bodies. Some authorities suggest that such decisions will only be challengeable where:

❖ There is a suggestion of 'fraud, corruption or bad faith' (see *Mercury Energy Ltd v Electricity Corporation of New Zealand* [1994] 1 WLR 521).
❖ Irrationality (see *R (on the application of Gamesa Energy UK Ltd) v National Assembly for Wales* [2006] EWHC 2167 (Admin) (see also Chapter 9).
❖ A failure to follow a statutory process (see *R (Cookson and Clegg) v Ministry of Defence* [2005] EWCA Civ 811).

Remedies

What remedies are available? If the applicant has been successful in challenging a Government or public authority's decision or piece of legislation at JR, the court may grant the following remedies (but is not forced to do so). You need to point out that **remedies in JR are discretionary**.

Up for Debate

The Government wants to cut legal aid for JR cases and introduce a residence test. It says the effects of these cuts can be mitigated by exceptional funding, and that this will protect the public's right to access to justice. Do you agree? Study the following legislation in respect of changes to legal aid funding: **The Legal Aid, Sentencing and Punishment of Offenders Act 2012** and the Government's consultation paper: 'Judicial Review: proposals for reform'. The Government Response April 2013. Cm 8611.

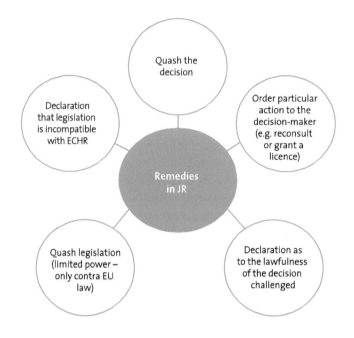

Aim Higher

What happens if legislation is challenged? This question goes to the heart of 'do judges make law' and you will gain high marks if you can discuss this in the exam or your coursework. This question leads you into discussing the Separation of Powers and the duty of the judiciary to review and apply the law, but not to 'make' laws. In relation to JR challenging primary legislation (Acts of Parliament), the court's powers are limited. In JR, the Administrative Court may only quash legislation if it is found to be contrary to EU law. If it is contrary to the European Convention on Human Rights (ECHR) the only remedy available is to make a declaration of incompatibility. When discussing such a claim in a problem question, you should always think about the remedies available to the court and the possibilities for the claimant. In practice, suggest either a declaration of unlawfulness or how the public authority (or Government Department) should remedy (or review) its decision. The public body should be expected to remedy the unlawfulness. Damages are, as a general rule, not available in JR proceedings. However, compensation or other forms of financial redress may naturally flow out of a successful challenge, particularly in human rights claims (see below).

The Human Rights Act 1998 and Judicial Review

Before the Human Rights Act 1998 (HRA) came into force (2 October 2000), the UK could only rely on the traditional common law approach to civil liberties, based on the idea that our liberty would be protected within the regular law and that there was no need for a separate law on human rights. Although the courts and Parliament had developed and created a number of constitutional rights, certain rights and liberties were left largely unprotected. For example, before the 'right to life' guaranteed under Art 2 **European Convention on Human Rights** (ECHR), there was no right to access for family members involved in an inquest when their relative or loved-one had died in custody. Or if a vulnerable adult who had been left unprotected by a local council from being beaten-up by a gang, would receive compensation from the local authority under Art 3 ECHR ('freedom from inhuman and degrading treatment').

The HRA has had a substantial impact on Judicial Review and individuals' claims against public bodies. Under s 3 HRA 1998 all legislation, whenever enacted, must be interpreted ('so far as it is possible') for compatibility with Convention rights. However, if this is not 'possible', UK legislation remains valid. Section 6 HRA 1998 imposes a duty upon public authorities to act compatibly with Convention rights (ECHR). This then provides a rights-based ground of challenge to public decisions adding a powerful string to the bow of a vast number of applicants for JR. The HRA has provided a constitutional change in legislative decision-making. There now exists a **legitimate expectation** that the Executive must abide by the terms of a ratified Treaty (namely the European Convention) (see *R v Home Secretary ex parte Ahmed and Patel* [1999] Imm AR 22; *R v Director of Public Prosecutions ex parte Kebilene* [2000] 2 AC 326).

'Victim' status under the Human Rights Act 1998

So far, we have established that Judicial Review allows people with a **sufficient interest** (standing) in a decision or action by a public body to ask a judge to review the lawfulness of that decision, action or failure to act in relation to the exercise of a public function (see also Chapter 9). Judicial Review may then only be used where there is no right of appeal or where all avenues of appeal have been exhausted.

The HRA created the so-called 'victim' status for those seeking JR against a public body as 'grounds' for standing (see above). For example, in April 2013, lawyers acting for ten disabled individuals were granted standing on human rights grounds, seeking urgent JR, following the Government's controversial introduction of the 'bedroom tax'. As part of the standing application, the lawyers cited breach of the Equality Act 2010 and the Human Rights Act 1998, as well as the UN Convention on the Rights of Persons with Disabilities (UNCRPD). The 'bedroom tax' meant cutting housing benefit for those judged to be 'over-occupying' their social housing.

However, the courts made clear that the definition of 'standing' when bringing a human rights claim under the HRA is much narrower, compared with traditional grounds for review (such as illegality, irrationality and procedural impropriety – see Chapter 9). Article 34 **European Convention on Human Rights** (ECHR) sets out how to bring a 'victim' claim.

Article 34 ECHR: Individual applications

The Court may receive applications from any person, non-governmental organisation or group of individuals claiming **to be the victim of a violation** by one of the High Contracting Parties of the rights set forth in the Convention or the Protocols thereto. The High Contracting Parties undertake not to hinder in any way the effective exercise of this right.

> **Case precedent – ex parte Smith (*R v Ministry of Defence ex parte Smith;**
> ***R v Admiralty Board of the Defence Council ex parte Lustig-Prean;***
> ***R v Admiralty Board of the Defence Council ex parte Beckett;***
> ***R v Ministry of Defence ex parte Grady* [1996] QB 517 (HL))**

Facts: Smith and three others, a lesbian and three gay men, appealed against the dismissal of their application for Judicial Review of the Ministry of Defence (MoD) policy which stated that homosexuality was incompatible with service in the armed forces. The policy had led to them being discharged. Smith argued that the MoD policy was irrational and contrary to the Equal Treatment Directive in EU law (Council Directive 76/207) and also to the **European Convention on Human Rights** (ECHR). The House of Lords dismissed the appeal, stating that the question of whether the MoD policy was contrary to the ECHR should be decided by the Strasbourg European Court of Human Rights (ECtHR). Also, the MoD policy was supported by both Houses of Parliament and the EU Directive did not apply to discrimination on the grounds of sexual orientation.

Principle: In *ex parte Smith* the House of Lords ruled that the dismissal of homosexuals from the armed forces was **not** unlawful (**Note**: When the case was appealed to the Strasbourg ECtHR, the opposite result was reached). Sir Thomas Bingham MR emphasised that any decisions involving human rights will have substantial policy implications.

Application: Generally, courts may not interfere with the exercise of an administrative discretion on substantive grounds, except where the decision is unreasonable (see *Wednesbury* unreasonableness). But the human rights context is important: the more substantial the interference with human rights, the more the court will require justification for the public authority's decision and whether it was 'reasonable'. The public body's decision must be rational and politically uncontroversial (see *Associated Provincial Picture Houses v Wednesbury Corporation* [1948] 1 KB 223).

Putting it into practice

Essay questions are likely to relate to one of the following:

❖ The scope of Judicial Review (JR) in relation to an administrative decision taken under statutory powers by a public body (see *A-G v Fulham Corporation* [1921] 1 Ch 440 where a local authority purporting to act under the authority of Victorian public health legislation was given a power to establish baths, wash-houses and open bathing places)

❖ 'Standing' (*locus standi*), which varies from case to case (consult case law where the courts have/have not awarded standing to someone or a group)

❖ Human Rights Act 1998 (HRA) and JR claims

❖ HRA 1998 standing test, laid down in s 7 of the Act (called the 'victim' test)

❖ Only victims can bring a claim in JR that a public authority has breached their rights under the **European Convention on Human Rights** (ECHR)

❖ The definition of a core public body under s 6(1) HRA 1998

❖ The function of a 'hybrid' public body under s 6 (3) HRA 1998 (including a court or tribunal, and 'any person certain of whose functions are functions of a public nature') (see *Poplar Housing and Regeneration Community Association v Donoghue* [2001] EWCA Civ 595)

❖ Remedies available to the courts

Problem questions are likely to involve the following issues:

❖ The claimant will need to rely on specific human rights violations which you will have to identify and specify within the ECHR

❖ He or she will have to prove their victim status under the HRA 1998 in order to challenge a decision by either a Government official, Government Department or public authority on the grounds that the decision was unlawful

❖ The challenge is then made by way of Judicial Review (JR) of an administrative action

❖ You need to show in your answer that you have considered the following:
  ❖ Is the body or authority making the decision susceptible to JR (justiciable)?
  ❖ Is there a public law issue or are you dealing with a mere 'busybody'?
  ❖ Does the claimant have standing?
  ❖ What are the grounds for review and are they arguable? (this will be dealt with in Chapter 9)
  ❖ Is the claim brought in time, i.e. within 3 months from the date of the decision?
  ❖ Has the claimant exhausted alternative remedies? (e.g. appeal? contract law remedies?)

❖ It is worth pointing out that JR is concerned with whether an administrative decision is lawful. It is **not** concerned with whether the public body's decision was correct

❖ The courts will not interfere with the 'merits' of the decision, but whether the decision was lawfully made or *ultra vires*

❖ The claimant's challenge in JR will be either on the grounds that the decision is unlawful or on human rights grounds ('victim status')
❖ A decision may be unlawful (*ultra vires*) if it is not authorised by statute or it violates the **European Convention on Human Rights** (ECHR)
❖ Suggest any available remedies

Essay

'In modern-day Britain, the real threat is seen as coming from an increasingly powerful judiciary'. Would you agree that the judiciary has been 'greatly empowered' as a result of the European Communities Act 1972 and the Human Rights Act 1998? Discuss.

Feedback on putting it into practice

a) This question is complex and multi-faceted. For high marks you must answer all elements of the question. If you answer only one part of the question, you will be marked down. Make sure you structure your answer well, including:

b) Begin your essay by introducing the constitutional theory of Parliamentary Supremacy and that the powers of the UK Parliament are unlimited (see Chapter 3).

c) Do judges make law? Cite the example of some leading Judicial Review case, such as *AXA* or *Jackson* (see also Chapters 5–7).

d) The main body of your essay should include that the Judiciary has already been 'greatly empowered' by EU law and the various Treaties, resulting from accession to the EC in 1972 (European Communities Act 1972). The Act allows the courts to override other legislation. Discuss the Supremacy of EU law.

e) You should then discuss the incorporation of the **European Convention on Human Rights** (ECHR) into UK law by way of the Human Rights Act 1998, which permits the courts to declare legislation incompatible with the ECHR.

f) While the answer to the question 'do judges make law' is 'no' (the courts, of course, will not override or overrule Acts of Parliament), they do decide whether or not the Executive (Government and public bodies) has followed the Rule of Law, has adhered to correct and fair procedures when making decisions, and whether any minister has been in contempt for breaching any lawful procedure? This is done by way of Judicial Review (JR).

g) What the judges have decided in certain cases (e.g. *Jackson* or *AXA*) is the next thread of your argument relating to the scope of Parliamentary Privilege. It is the judges (House of Lords) who ruled in *Jackson* that the Hunting Act 2004 was lawful under the **Parliament Acts**. It was the UK Supreme Court that ruled that devolved legislation is subject to JR (*AXA*).

h) You may well conclude that there has been a slow constitutional change as common law by the judges has developed and evolved, allowing for a gradual evolution to meet changing needs of both Houses of Parliament.

i) In spite of common law rulings in JR cases, the UK still does not have legislation that recognises all fundamental human rights as part of a (written) codified Constitution or Bill of Rights (such as a right to privacy).

j) This means that the UK Constitution is dominated by Parliamentary Sovereignty, which means that the human rights system is dependent on the goodwill of Parliament and the ingenuity of the courts in controlling executive power by way of JR, resulting in the fact that rights of minorities are overlooked (e.g. prisoners' voting rights – *Hirst v UK* [2005]; *R v Secretary of State for the Home Department ex parte O'Brien and Simms* [1998] 2 All ER 491, *Golder v UK* (1975) 1 EHRR 524, *Silver v UK* (1983) 5 EHRR 347 – right of access to courts and rights of free speech; *Hamer v UK* (1979) 24 DR 5 – private and family life; *Golder v UK* (1975), *Silver v UK* (1983), *Campbell v UK* (1992) 15 EHRR 137 – correspondence; *Weeks v UK* (1987) 10 EHRR 293, *Thynne, Wilson and Gunnell v UK* (1990) 13 EHRR 666, *Hussain and Singh v UK* (1996) 21 EHRR 1, *V and T v UK* (2000) 30 EHRR 11, *Stafford v UK* (2002) 35 EHRR 32 – liberty and security of the person).

Problem question

Wolsey County Council provided residential care for disabled young people (to the age of 21) at the Kelder Forest Lodge. Howard, a 19-year-old paraplegic following a motorbike accident, moved into 'Kelder' in 2011, after his parents read the Council brochure which promised, 'Our aim is to provide for all young disabled persons' needs, either for severely brain damaged or physically disabled conditions for life.' Howard (and his parents) did not have to pay for accommodation and food at the lodge. Unfortunately, Wolsey County Council's public policy changed under a new Liberal/Labour leadership. The Council decided in 2013 to contract its disabled services out to a private contractor under a Public–Private Finance partnership for the next 25 years. 'Caring for the Community plc' (CFC) are now running the Kelder home for profit. CFC is proposing to move all residents to its new facility some 100 miles away and to charge a fee for board and lodging. Howard will argue that moving him violates his human rights. Discuss.

Feedback on putting it into practice

a) Howard (H) will argue that the new disabled home provider for young persons, CFC, has violated his rights under Art 8 **European Convention on Human Rights** (ECHR) ('right to respect for home life') and argue victim status, the second limb under JR application.

b) H has standing because he is directly affected by the decision (100 miles away from his parents; having to pay for his board and lodging in future).

c) H has legitimate expectation (see Chapter 9).

d) **But:** Buxton LJ in the *Leonard Cheshire* case held that a resident of a privately operated care home **did not** have rights under the HRA 1998 against the owners of the home even though the resident was supported by the local authority under an 'arrangement' made between the local authority and the owners of the home under ss 21 and 26 of the National Assistance Act 1948 (see *R (Heather) v Leonard Cheshire Foundation* [2002] 2 All ER 936).

e) CA *YL* ruled that a private charity was not performing a public function under s 6(3)(b) Human Rights Act 1998 (HRA) when delivering residential care services on behalf of a local authority (see *YL (by her litigation friend the Official Solicitor) v Birmingham City Council and Others* [2007] UKHL 27).

f) You need to address the fact that CFC is a private provider (a plc) – but not a charity. H will argue that CFC is a hybrid public authority because it performs public duties and is therefore subject to JR.

g) Refer to both cases, *Leonard Cheshire* and *YL*, which dealt with a contracted-out care home operator, accused in court of violating the right to respect for home life under Art 8 ECHR by seeking to evict a resident; the providers' defence was as a hybrid public authority they could advance their own Convention rights to respect for property under Art 1 of the First Protocol of the ECHR in order to justify their behaviour.

h) Following *YL*, there now exists a precedent that a private, for-profit care home is not exercising public functions for the purposes of the HRA in relation to a resident supported by the local authority.

i) H will argue that CVC falls under s 6(3)(b) HRA, where 'a private company' certain of whose functions are functions of a public nature becomes a hybrid public authority.

j) Looking at existing case law, you may well conclude that CFC is not required to comply with the HRA.

k) H will argue that CFC (though a private plc) is undertaking a public act (providing for disabled young persons on behalf of the local council) (see *R v Panel on Take-overs and Mergers ex parte Datafin plc* [1987] QB 815).

l) CFC will rely on s 7 HRA, which states that a hybrid public authority can rely on its own Convention rights in domestic law, even during the performance of its public functions under s 6(3)(b) HRA unless it would be considered by Strasbourg jurisprudence as a governmental organisation under Art 34 ECHR.

m) Does H have a legitimate expectation to remain in a care home (or similar lodge) provided for without having to pay for board and lodging for life (as the council brochure stated)? Can he be evicted? Can he be expected to pay for his new accommodation and keep? After all, he has lived at the Kelder Lodge since 2011. So, probably not.

n) You must have a look at the leading judgment by Lord Woolf CJ in the *Leonard Cheshire* case. This is worth quoting and this will give you a sound conclusion to this problem question.

o) You should then have a look at the judgment in *YL*, which left much to be desired (see the judgments by Lords Mance and Neuberger) and a rather negative judgment by Buxton LJ. This will not assist Howard in his victim status.

p) You may well conclude that this area of law is confusing, especially since Strasbourg jurisprudence has not (yet) set a clear precedent in this area (i.e. care homes).

q) You need to suggest a remedy, especially if the Administrative Court may not come to a satisfactory solution for Howard. The court may suggest that Parliament enact new legislation, as was the case following the negative rulings in *YL* [2007] and *Leonard Cheshire* [2002] when Parliament enacted the Health and Social Care Act 2008 (HSCA) (s 145 HSCA provides for the application of s 6(3)(b) HRA to the provision of residential care services by private providers acting on behalf of local authorities).

r) This means that H could rely on statute as an alternative remedy – in which case he would not have standing because he has not exhausted alternative remedies.

Chapter summary

❖ Process of Judicial Review (JR).
❖ *Ultra vires* decisions.
❖ Application for JR and 'standing' (*locus standi*).
❖ What bodies and decisions can be challenged at JR.
❖ Remedies available to the Administrative Court.

Table of key cases referred to in this chapter

Case name	Area of law	Principle
R v Chief Constable of Merseyside Police ex parte Calveley [1986]	Standing; alternative remedies	Permission will not be granted for JR if alternative remedies are available
Al-Haq v Foreign Secretary [2009]	Standing (*locus standi*)	Standing must not be treated as a preliminary issue but must be taken in the legal and factual context of the whole
Independent Revenue Commission v National Federation of Self-Employed and Small Businesses Ltd [1982] AC 617 ('IRC').	Standing (*locus standi*)	Taxpayers with genuine concerns do not necessarily have standing, even if the issues they raise are constitutionally important
R v HM Treasury ex parte Smedley [1985]	Standing (*locus standi*)	Citizens will only be granted standing on the basis of a *'serious question'*

Case name	Area of law	Principle
O'Reilly v Mackman [1983]	Public v Private Law	When claiming against a public body, JR should be used
R v Disciplinary Committee of the Jockey Club ex parte The Aga Khan [1992]	Standing of private bodies	A private body can only be judicially reviewable where it has been 'woven into the fabric of public regulation' (Sir Thomas Bingham MR)
R v Home Secretary ex parte Ahmed and Patel [1999]	Human rights (HRA 1998); standing and 'victim' status in JR	There exists a legitimate expectation that the Executive must abide by the terms of the European Convention (ECHR)
R v Ministry of Defence ex parte Smith; R v Admiralty Board of the Defence Council ex parte Lustig-Prean; R v Admiralty Board of the Defence Council ex parte Beckett; R v Ministry of Defence ex parte Grady [1996] ('ex parte Smith')	Human rights (HRA 1998); standing and 'victim' status in JR	Collective ministerial responsibility cannot be enforced by the courts indefinitely
Associated Provincial Picture Houses v Wednesbury Corporation [1948]	Grounds for JR: irrationality (*Wednesbury* 'unreasonableness')	Courts may not interfere with the exercise of an administrative discretion on substantive grounds, except where the decision is unreasonable

Table 1 Cases on 'Standing' (Individual Applicants)

Type of standing	Case law	Notes
Direct interest	*Ridge v Baldwin* [1964] AC 40	**Standing:** Chief Constable had 'sufficient interest' as he was directly affected by decision to take away his pension
	R (Edwards) v Environment Agency [2004] 3 All ER 21	**Standing:** Although E did not take part in the application process, had standing as his health might be directly affected by the proposed operation

	R v N Somerset DC ex parte Garnett [1998] Env LR 91	**No standing:** The fact that G had used park for walking and kite-flying was **not sufficient public interest**
Consultation rights	*R v HMIP ex parte Greenpeace (No. 2)* [1994] 4 All ER 329 (THORP)	**Standing:** Greenpeace took part in the consultation process on nuclear power station
	R (Edwards) v Environment Agency [2004] 3 All ER 21	**Standing:** No need to take part in consultation process to have standing if directly affected. If legislation recognised individual right to be consulted, there is 'sufficient interest', regardless of whether individual/group exercise their consultation rights
	R v SOS for Environment ex parte Rose Theatre Trust [1990] 1 QB 504	**No standing:** Merely writing a letter to the decision-maker expressing an interest in the subject-matter is insufficient to give a person/organisation standing
Rate payers/ council tax payers	*Arsenal FC v Ende* [1979] AC 1	**Standing:** Sufficient interest. Rate payer will be affected if local authority spends rate payers' monies illegally or wastefully
	R v IRC ex parte National Federation of Small Businesses [1982] AC 617	**No standing:** Taxpayers could not challenge decisions relating to other taxpayers (unless extreme illegality)
Expertise of individual	*R v SOS for Foreign and Commonwealth Affairs ex parte Rees-Mogg* [1994] 2 WLR 115	**Standing:** Former chairman of Press Council had the right to challenge UK's signing of Maastricht Treaty as he had a known interest in politics/ public affairs

Table 2 Cases on 'Standing' (Group Applicants)

Type of standing	Case law	Notes
Representative standing ('standing on behalf of members of group')	*R v IRC ex parte National Federation of Small Businesses* [1982] AC 617	**Standing:** 'National Federation' represented interests of small businesses; had 'sufficient interest' to challenge any Government decision likely to affect its members
	R v HMIP ex parte Greenpeace (No. 2) [1994] 4 All ER 329 (THORP)	**Standing:** Greenpeace had 'sufficient interest' because 2500 paid-up supporters lived in the immediate vicinity of the proposed nuclear power station and their health could be directly affected by the operation of the plant
	R v SOS for Environment ex parte Rose Theatre Trust [1990] 1 QB 504	**No standing:** No member of the group had individual standing and the 'fact thousands of people join together and assert that they have an interest does not create an interest if the individuals do not have an interest'
Surrogate standing ('standing on behalf of those who cannot represent themselves')	*Sierra Club v Morton,* 405 US 727 (1972)	**No standing:** SC argued that trees have interests but cannot represent themselves. Environmental groups must be able to represent individuals' interests
	R v SOS for Social Services, ex parte Child Poverty Action Group (CPAG) [1990] 2 QB 540	**Standing:** CPAG was the 'poor people's champion' because they were advocates for people unable to bring legal action themselves
Group recognition	*R v HMIP ex parte Greenpeace (No. 2)* [1994] 4 All ER 329 (THORP)	**Standing:** Greenpeace's expertise is recognised by international bodies
	R v SOS for Foreign and Commonwealth Affairs ex parte World Development Movement [1995] 1 WLR 386 ('WDM')	**Standing:** WDM had consultative status at UNESCO, promoted international conferences and organised development groups at OECD

Group expertise	*R v HMIP ex parte Greenpeace (No. 2)* [1994] 4 All ER 329 (THORP)	**Standing:** Interest in environmental matters meant the pressure group was able to present a case more effectively than individual protesters
	R v SOS for Foreign and Commonwealth Affairs ex parte World Development Movement [1995] 1 WLR 386 ('WDM')	**Standing:** For over 20 years established interest in overseas development
	R v SOS for Environment ex parte Rose Theatre Trust [1990] 1 QB 504	**No standing:** Recently established group; not sufficient interest, despite members individually had expertise related to issue

Table 3 Cases on 'Standing' (Other Issues – Statutory Applicants)

Type of standing	Case law	Notes
Statutory setting	*R v SOS for Employment ex p Equal Opportunities Commission (EOC) and others* [1995] 1 AC 1	**Standing:** EOC could challenge Regulations concerning part-time working as organisation had been established to ensure equal pay. Regulations would be detrimental to females as more females were part-timers. **But:** Local authorities who had not been given this role did **not have standing** even though affected women in their areas
	R v SOS for Environment ex parte Rose Theatre Trust [1990] 1 QB 504	**No standing:** The Ancient Monuments and Archaeological Areas Act 1979 gave SOS exclusive power to determine which ruins should be preserved in national interest. No one could challenge decision

Type of standing	Case law	Notes
Public interest standing ('Everyone can bring an action where a public body acts unlawfully to vindicate the rule of law')	*R v IRC ex parte National Federation of Small Businesses* [1982] AC 617	**Standing:** Where serious illegality is alleged, anyone has standing to 'vindicate rule of law' (Lord Diplock)
	R v SOS for Foreign and Commonwealth Affairs ex parte World Development Movement [1995] 1 WLR 386 ('WDM')	**Standing:** Large-scale misuse of public funds alleged; in public interest to bring the Government to account

Table 4 Cases involving Local Government

Nottinghamshire County Council v Secretary of State for the Environment [1986] AC 240 – the Labour County Council challenged the Conservative Minister for having set targets for expenditure and thus grant distribution that discriminated in particular against a small number of authorities, including Nottinghamshire. The challenge was upheld by the Court of Administration in a decision that would have overturned the Government's whole target-based local finance policy, but was overturned when the Minister appealed to the House of Lords.
Wheeler v Leicester City Council [1985] 1 AC 1054 – the City Council banned Leicester Rugby Club from using a council-owned pitch, claiming the club had not fully supported the Council's anti-apartheid policy and its opposition to any sporting contacts with South Africa. Peter Wheeler (then club captain, later its Chief Executive) challenged the Council's decision, but was unsuccessful in the Court of Administration. But the House of Lords upheld his appeal and declared the Council's action 'unreasonable' (*Wednesbury*).
Bromley LBC v Greater London Council [1983] 1 AC 768 – the Labour-controlled Greater London Council, then led by Ken Livingstone, introduced a 'Fares Fair' scheme of subsidised fares on London Transport, financed partly through additional rates (local taxes) raised from the London boroughs, including Bromley, Conservative-controlled and without any underground station. Bromley's challenge, on behalf of its ratepayers, was dismissed in the lower Divisional Court, but upheld in the Court of Administration, and affirmed by the House of Lords. This meant that the power of councils was limited to provide grants 'as an object of social or transport policy'.

Table 5 Cases involving Ministers

Secretary of State for Education v Tameside MBC [1977] AC 1014 – the newly elected Conservative-controlled Tameside Metropolitan Borough Council (Greater Manchester) abandoned the former Labour Council's planned reorganisation of the borough's secondary schools shortly before its scheduled introduction. When the Labour Minister ordered that the reorganisation should proceed, the Borough's challenge was upheld in the House of Lords, which ruled that the Local Education Authority's action had not been unreasonable.
Derbyshire and Lancashire CCs v Secretary of State for the Environment [1994] 4 All ER 165 – the two County Councils succeeded in JR claiming the minister had acted illegally in trying to steer the Local Government (Reorganisation) Commission towards making recommendations for unitary, rather than two-tier, solutions for future local government in England.

@ **Visit the book's companion website to test your knowledge**

❖ Resources include a subject map, revision tip podcasts, downloadable diagrams, MCQ quizzes for each chapter, and a flashcard glossary
❖ www.routledge.com/cw/optimizelawrevision

9

Grounds for Judicial Review

Revision objectives

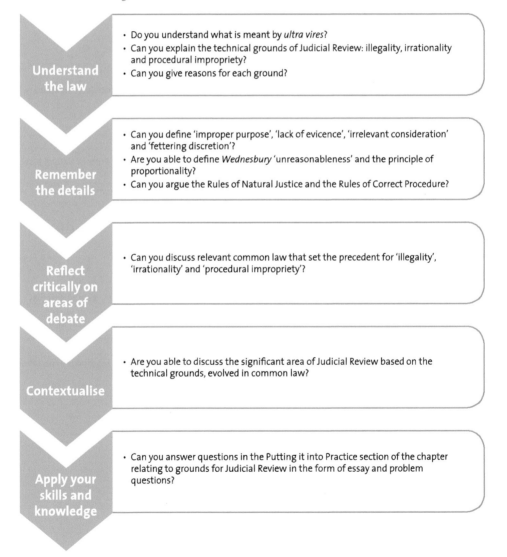

Understand the law
- Do you understand what is meant by *ultra vires*?
- Can you explain the technical grounds of Judicial Review: illegality, irrationality and procedural impropriety?
- Can you give reasons for each ground?

Remember the details
- Can you define 'improper purpose', 'lack of evicence', 'irrelevant consideration' and 'fettering discretion'?
- Are you able to define *Wednesbury* 'unreasonableness' and the principle of proportionality?
- Can you argue the Rules of Natural Justice and the Rules of Correct Procedure?

Reflect critically on areas of debate
- Can you discuss relevant common law that set the precedent for 'illegality', 'irrationality' and 'procedural impropriety'?

Contextualise
- Are you able to discuss the significant area of Judicial Review based on the technical grounds, evolved in common law?

Apply your skills and knowledge
- Can you answer questions in the Putting it into Practice section of the chapter relating to grounds for Judicial Review in the form of essay and problem questions?

Chapter Map

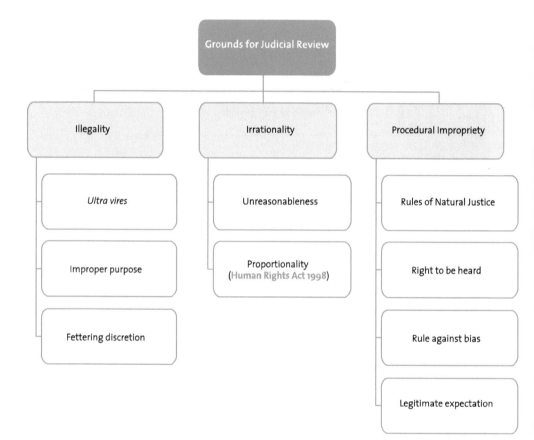

Grounds for Judicial Review

Illegality
- *Ultra vires*
- Improper purpose
- Fettering discretion

Irrationality
- Unreasonableness
- Proportionality (Human Rights Act 1998)

Procedural Impropriety
- Rules of Natural Justice
- Right to be heard
- Rule against bias
- Legitimate expectation

Traditional and modern grounds of Judicial Review

In Chapter 8, you were introduced to the topic of Judicial Review (JR) and the main legal means by which the decisions and actions of Government Departments, regulators and other public bodies can be challenged in the Administrative Court. We looked at the Government bodies and decisions that can be challenged and the remedies available to the courts. We also examined the JR process of **standing** (*locus standi*) and which individual or group action would successfully proceed to full JR if they can show at leave stage that the applicant has **sufficient interest** in the administrative decision complained of. You also saw that JR is not directly concerned with the **merits of the decision** (was it a good or a bad one?) but whether the decision was reached in a proper manner and is within the range of permissible outcomes in law. That is, was the procedure in reaching a decision properly followed? Did the public body act within the law? Or did the administrative authority act outside its statutory powers (*ultra vires*)?

This chapter deals with the technical grounds on which decisions can be challenged. We know now that in a JR claim it is the court's job to decide whether the decision in question was lawful. Although the grounds are fluid and developing with ever-increasing case law, the main technical grounds for JR are categorised as follows:

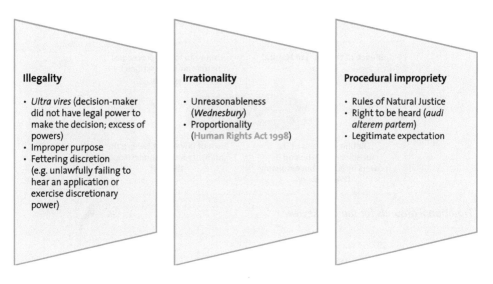

Illegality

- *Ultra vires* (decision-maker did not have legal power to make the decision; excess of powers)
- Improper purpose
- Fettering discretion (e.g. unlawfully failing to hear an application or exercise discretionary power)

Irrationality

- Unreasonableness (*Wednesbury*)
- Proportionality (Human Rights Act 1998)

Procedural impropriety

- Rules of Natural Justice
- Right to be heard (*audi alterem partem*)
- Legitimate expectation

Traditional grounds for Judicial Review

Illegality

Until the mid 1980s, Public Law textbooks traditionally defined the grounds for Judicial Review as being '*ultra vires*'. This meant that a decision could be *ultra vires* because the decision-maker simply did not have the power (statutory or otherwise) to make the decision in question. Or, because the public body or Government Department had not met the pre-conditions or criteria for exercising their powers (particularly in the case of statutory powers). This can be described as 'simple *ultra vires*' (see *Attorney-General v Fulham Corporation* [1921] 1 Ch 440 – the Corporation did not have the power to set up a municipal laundry; it only had power to provide public baths and self-service laundries under the Baths and Wash Houses Acts 1846).

In the past (pre *GCHQ* case), the constitutional theory of JR was dominated by the doctrine of *ultra vires*, under which a decision of a public authority could be set aside if it exceeded the powers granted to it by Parliament. For example, an Act of Parliament may have provided that a minister could only take action in specified circumstances; if he acted in a case where those circumstances did not exist, then he was acting outside his powers (i.e. *ultra vires*).

Increasingly, the role of the courts in JR has been seen as crucial, by enforcing the 'will of Parliament' in accordance with the doctrine of **Parliamentary Sovereignty** (see Chapter 3). Traditionally, then, *ultra vires* only meant errors in law. More recently, the courts have moved towards 'illegality' as grounds for JR, including the fact that even the **Royal Prerogative** is judicially reviewable (see Chapter 4). *Ultra vires* traditionally meant a number of things:

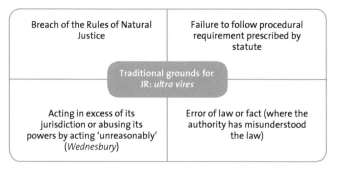

Traditional grounds for Judicial Review

Modern grounds of Judicial Review

The modern era of Judicial Review developed further grounds on a case-by-case basis over time, starting with the landmark judgment by Lord Diplock in the *GCHQ* case (see *Council of Civil Service Unions v Minister for the Civil Service* [1985] AC 374). In *GCHQ*, the Civil Service staff argued that the minister had failed to consult them over not allowing staff to belong to trade unions (see *O'Reilly v Mackman* [1983] 2 AC 237). Judicial Review has come a long way since the early days of challenges purely under *ultra vires* (see *Congreve v Home Office* [1976] QB 629; *R v Lord Saville of Newdigate ex parte A* [1999] 4 All ER 860; *R v Parliamentary Commissioner for Administration ex parte Balchin* [1997] COD 146). Today, a decision or action will be regarded as 'illegal' if it is contrary to **EU law** (see Chapter 2) or the **European Convention on Human Rights** (ECHR) (see Chapters 7 and 8). Therefore, it seems that today the constitutional position of JR is dictated by the need to prevent the abuse of power by the Executive as well as to protect individual (human) rights. Modern grounds of JR now include:

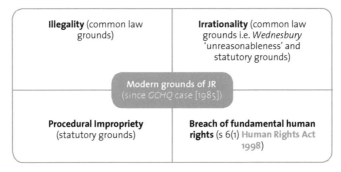

Modern grounds for Judicial Review

Case precedent – *Council of Civil Service Unions v Minister for the Civil Service* [1985] AC 374 (*GCHQ* case)

Facts: Since 1947, staff employed at the Government Communications Headquarters (GCHQ – the British intelligence agency) had been permitted to belong to a trade union. On 22 December 1983, the Minister for the Civil Service (Mrs Margaret Thatcher, Conservative) gave an instruction under Art 4 of the **Civil Service Order in Council 1982** to Civil Service staff that they would no longer be permitted to belong to national trade unions. The applicants, a trade union and six individuals, sought Judicial Review of the minister's instruction on the ground that she had been under a duty to act fairly by consulting those concerned before issuing it. Glidewell J granted the applicants a declaration that the instruction was invalid and of no effect. The Court of Appeal allowed an appeal by the minister and the trade union appealed to the House of Lords, who dismissed the applicants' appeal. The House of Lords ruled that the executive action by the minister was not immune from JR merely because it was carried out in pursuance of a power derived from Prerogative Power (common law) rather than a statutory source. A minister acting under a Prerogative Power is under the same duty to act fairly as in the case of action under a Statutory Power. However, it was for the Executive and not the courts to decide whether the requirements of national security outweighed those of fairness. The evidence established that the minister showed that her instructions were justified on grounds of national security. Belonging to a trade union and the risk of strike action would have disrupted the operation at GCHQ and revealed vulnerable areas of operation. The minister's decision therefore outweighed the applicants' legitimate expectation of prior consultation.

Principle: Lord Diplock classified the (modern) grounds for JR as: illegality, irrationality and procedural impropriety. He also said that further grounds may be added as the law develops on a case-by-case basis (Lord Diplock, *GCHQ* case at 401).

Application: Failure by an administrative body to observe the procedural rules that are expressly laid down in statute ('the legislative instrument') amounts to a denial of natural justice.

From *Wednesbury* 'unreasonableness' to 'irrationality'

Although Judicial Review is principally concerned with the lawfulness and not the merits of a decision being challenged, it has long been accepted that a decision may be so **unreasonable** as to be one that a decision-maker could not lawfully have reached.

> 'What, then, is the power of the courts? They can only interfere with an act of executive authority if it be shown that the authority has contravened the law.'
> (Lord Greene MR in *Wednesbury* [1948])

What is *Wednesbury* 'reasonableness'?

Traditionally, this ground has been very limited in its application, with the courts giving public authorities a wide margin of discretion as regards what is 'reasonable' in their decision-making. This was first established in the *Wednesbury* case (see *Associated Provincial Picture Houses Ltd v Wednesbury Corporation* [1948] 1 KB 223 (CA)) (see below).

Case precedent – *Associated Provincial Picture Houses Ltd v Wednesbury Corporation* [1948] 1 KB 223 (CA) (*Wednesbury*)

Facts: In November 1947, the owners and licensees (claimants) of the Gaumont Cinema in Wednesbury, Staffordshire, were granted a cinema licence by the defendant local authority, the Wednesbury Corporation, under the Cinematograph Act 1909 for performances on Sunday. But the licence was granted subject to a condition that 'no children under the age of fifteen years shall be admitted to any entertainment whether accompanied by an adult or not'. The cinema owners brought an action in JR for a declaration that the condition was *ultra vires* and unreasonable. The Court of Appeal dismissed the appeal and held that the local authority had **not** acted unreasonably or *ultra vires* in imposing the condition.

Principle: In considering whether an authority having so unlimited a power has acted unreasonably, the court is only entitled to investigate the action of the authority with a view to seeing if it has taken into account any matters that ought not to be or disregarded matters that ought to be taken into account. The court cannot interfere as an appellate authority to override a decision of a public authority.

Application: A court can only act as a judicial authority to see whether a public body has contravened the law by acting in excess of its power (illegally; *ultra vires*).

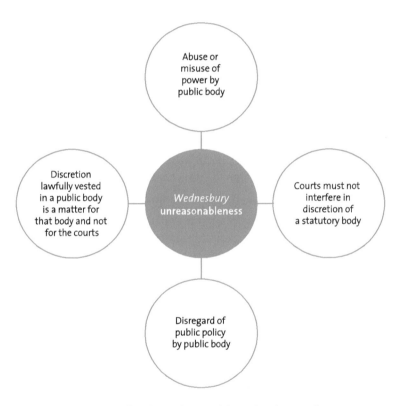

Wednesbury unreasonableness (traditional ground for Judicial Review)

Irrationality

The common law developed from the *Wednesbury* (1948) 'reasonableness' test towards the 'irrationality' test, first formulated by Lord Diplock in the *GCHQ* case (1985) (see *Council of Civil Service Unions v Minister for the Civil Service* [1985] AC 374 – see above). Since then there has been a trend towards a more critical consideration of the 'reasonableness' of a decision towards 'irrationality', which is now a new ground for JR.

'... this applies to a decision which is so outrageous in its defiance of logic or of accepted moral standards that no sensible person who had applied his mind to the question to be decided could have arrived at it.'

(Lord Diplock in *GCHQ* [1985])

Irrationality (modern ground of Judicial Review)

What does 'exercising discretion reasonably' mean and how does it relate to irrationality?

More recently, courts have indicated that *Wednesbury* **'unreasonableness'** (see above) is not a single test and offers different levels of scrutiny depending on the type of case and decision the court is dealing with. In practice, this means that the courts will require less justification from a public body where a decision has a high political content. In these cases, courts tend not to interfere with the administrative authority and tend to defer (i.e. defer the decision back for reconsideration to the public authority). Lord Cooke made this clear in *R v Secretary of State for the Home Department ex parte Daly* [2001] UKHL 26, when he called the *Wednesbury* test 'an unfortunately retrogressive decision in English administrative law'.

Today this means that the courts will be less intensive with political decisions and less so in ordinary decisions (e.g. planning applications). The problem is that the common law has not provided any definitive guidelines as to how intensive JR will be and how much discretion can be allowed to a public body when making a decision in any given case. There is no legal certainty. It is now well established that the court is entitled to review the **rationality** of a decision, that is, whether the decision-maker has taken into account the relevant (and only the relevant) considerations, exercising their discretion 'reasonably'. In summary, irrationality has become the modern ground for unreasonableness.

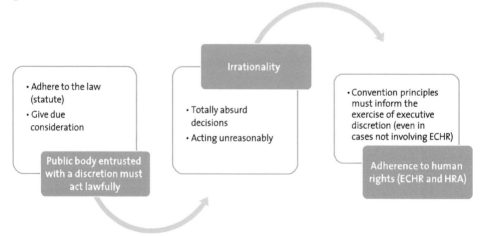

What does 'exercising discretion reasonably' mean?

Proportionality

In cases that engage issues of **EU law** or **Convention rights**, the court's scrutiny in this regard can be more intense, where it is required to consider the proportionality of the decision, which involves the balancing of the various considerations (see also Chapter 8). Nevertheless, for both constitutional and practical reasons, the court remains anxious not to substitute its own views for those of the body charged with making a judgment on the matter in question and so will afford the decision-maker a wide margin of appreciation on matters of discretion (see *ex parte Smith* – Chapter 8).

Procedural impropriety

A decision or action may be unlawful if the process followed was unfair when judged against the public law standards of **procedural fairness**. These standards, developed by the court in case law, apply irrespective of any statutory procedural requirements, but the standard imposed will depend on the circumstances and the nature of the matter. The standard of fairness (or 'procedural impropriety') is higher in a quasi-judicial context, such as a tribunal hearing or prisoner adjudication. Procedural impropriety may typically arise where there has not been proper consultation, where one party to a hearing or decision-making process is biased towards the individual affected by the decision, or where the defendant authority has breached a **legitimate expectation** as to the procedure to be followed (see also: *R (on the application of 'Save our Surgery Ltd')v Joint Committee of Primary Care Trusts* [2013] EWHC 1011 ('the *JCPCT* case').

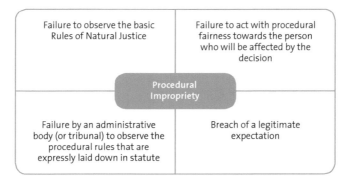

Rules of Natural Justice

The Rules of Natural Justice include the **rule against bias** (*nemo judex in causa sua*) and the **right to a fair hearing** (*audi alterem partem*). The term **natural justice** is now part of 'procedural fairness' and more generally (in the decision-making process or tribunal hearing) a 'duty to act fairly'. Fairness depends on context (*McInnes v Onslow-Fane* [1978] 1 WLR 1520). There is a duty of the decision-maker to act fairly in judicial procedure (including tribunals). In the employment case of *Ridge v Baldwin* [1964] AC, the House of Lords extended the doctrine of natural justice to become a technical ground for administrative decision-making and JR meaning procedural fairness.

In this case, Chief Constable Ridge had been wrongfully dismissed; the decision was quashed because he had not been given the opportunity to present his defence at the tribunal hearing.

'Natural Justice is but fairness writ large and juridically. It has been escribed as "fair play in action".'

(Lord Morris of Borth-y-Gest in *Furnell v Whangarei High Schools Board* [1973] (HL))

Right to a fair hearing (*audi alterem partem*)

The right to a fair hearing requires that individuals should not be penalised by decisions affecting their rights or legitimate expectations unless they have been given prior notice of the case, a fair opportunity to answer it, and the opportunity to present their own case. The mere fact that a decision affects rights or interests is sufficient to subject the decision to the procedures required by natural justice as grounds for JR. Administrative decisions have to guarantee a right to a fair hearing (trial or tribunal) under Art 6(1) **European Convention on Human Rights**, in addition to common law provisions.

Cases involving 'right to a fair hearing'	
Cooper v Wandsworth Board of Works [1863] 143 ER 414	Opportunity to be heard
Glynn v Keele University [1971] 1 WLR 487	Right to a hearing notice
R v Gaming Board for Great Britain ex parte Benaim and Khaida [1970] 2 QB 417	Right to know opposition's case
R v Thames Magistrates Court ex parte Polemis [1974] DC	Right amount of time necessary to prepare
R v Board of Visitors of Hull Prison ex parte St Germain (No. 2) [1979] QB 425	Right to cross-examine

Rule against bias

The basis for the rule against bias is the need to maintain public confidence in the legal system. Actual bias is very difficult to prove, but if it can be proved that there was imputed bias this will result in a decision being void. The leading case is the *Pinochet* case. The case set the precedent for Rules of Natural Justice, i.e. the rule against bias. This includes the judiciary, which has to be seen to be independent and unbiased. It was for this reason that the House of Lords held in *Pinochet No. 2* (2000) that a decision it had given had to be set aside and the appeal before it heard again by a panel of different Law Lords. It had come to light after the original decision that one of the Law Lords (Lord Hoffman) might have given an appearance that he was not independent and impartial because of a connection with a campaigning organisation (Amnesty International) which was involved in General Pinochet's case. In those circumstances, and even though there was no suggestion that the Law Lord was not in fact independent or impartial, the decision could not stand.

Case precedent – *R v Bow Street Stipendiary Magistrate ex parte Pinochet Ugarte (No. 2)* (2000) 1 AC 119 (HL) (*Pinochet* case)

Facts: General Augusto Pinochet was accused of international crimes of torture in Chile during his time in power (1973–1990). In 1998 he fled to the UK and Spain demanded his extradition so he could stand trial. Pinochet was arrested in October that year. Pinochet's lawyers argued diplomatic immunity. The question before the Divisional Court was whether the former Chilean President could claim state immunity, alleging that he would be tortured in Spain once extradited. The Divisional Court ruled that Pinochet had state immunity. The House of Lords (by a 3 to 2 majority) overruled the judgment, and held that Pinochet did not have state immunity and should stand trial for genocide, torture, hostage-taking and crimes against humanity committed during the armed conflict in Chile in 1973. As head of state he was responsible. However, the House of Lords' decision was set aside due to bias. One of the Law Lords, Lord Hoffman, was a member of Amnesty International. The General was allowed to return to Chile in March 2000, after Labour Home Secretary Jack Straw said he was not well enough to stand trial. In July 2002, all charges against General Pinochet were dropped, after the Supreme Court upheld the House of Lords ruling that he was mentally unfit to stand trial (*Pinochet No. 3*).

Principle: The House of Lords in *Pinochet No. 2* took the unprecedented decision to overturn its own judgment because of the possibility of bias in one of its judges.

Application: The *Pinochet* case is significant because of one of the Law Lords' bias (belonging to a human rights organisation involved in Pinochet's case); the Rules of Natural Justice demanded that the appeal be heard again before a new panel of Law Lords who had and gave the appearance to reasonable well-informed observers that they were independent and impartial.

Legitimate expectation

A legitimate expectation only arises in exceptional cases in Judicial Review – though it is fair to say that there is a general expectation that a public body will act fairly. We have already established that JR is a remedy of last resort. Only when a decision has been made which was substantively contrary to what the claimant legitimately expected (i.e. an express promise from the public body or local authority to an entitlement) will that applicant have standing on the grounds of 'legitimate expectation' (as part of the ground of procedural impropriety). The doctrine of **substantive legitimate expectation** was established in the *Coughlan* case (see *R v North and East Devon Health Authority ex parte Coughlan* [2001] QB 213). This case concerned a severely disabled woman who had been receiving long-term nursing care from the National Health Service, and who had sold her house after the promise was made by the local health authority that she would have a 'home for life' at Mardon House, a specialist facility run by the NHS Trust. The court ruled in favour of Mrs Coughlan, as she had a substantive legitimate expectation. Lord Woolf MR stated:

'Where the Court considers that a lawful promise or practice has induced a legitimate expectation of a benefit which is substantive, not simply procedural, authority now establishes that here too the Court will in a proper case decide whether to frustrate the expectation is so unfair that to take a new and different course will amount to an abuse of power.'

(Lord Woolf MR in *ex parte Coughlan* [2001])

But not every applicant citing 'legitimate expectation' as a ground for JR will be as successful as in Mrs Coughlan's case. In the *Heather Begbie* case, a statement made by a politician as to his intentions on a particular educational matter (grant-assisted places in public schools) if elected could not create a legitimate expectation as regards the delivery of the promise after the General Election, even where the promise would directly affect individuals, and the costs of a child's education. The Court of Appeal held that the consequences of a failure to keep a promise by a public body (or minister) must remain political and does not create a legitimate expectation (see *R v The Department of Education and Employment ex parte Begbie (Heather Charis)* [2000] WLR 1115); (see also *R (on the application of Hurley and Moore) v Secretary of State for Business, Innovation and Skills* [2012] EWHC 201 (Admin) – increase of student tuition fees to £9000 pa).

Human rights and grounds for Judicial Review

We have already established in Chapter 7 that the Human Rights Act 1998 (HRA) has impacted substantially on British legislation and administrative legal procedure. We have also established that Judicial Review is concerned not with the merits of the decision, but whether the public body has acted lawfully. One of the main purposes of the HRA in public (administrative) law has been to improve public access to the rights and freedoms guaranteed under the **European Convention for the Protection of Human Rights and Fundamental Freedoms** (ECHR), which has substantially influenced JR and its procedure.

The HRA imposes a duty on the Government to ensure that both primary and subordinate legislation (i.e. Acts of Parliament and Statutory Instruments made under such Acts) are compatible with the Convention and requires public authorities to act in a manner that is compatible with the Convention. Section 6 Human Rights Act 1998 makes it unlawful for a public authority to act in a way that is incompatible with a Convention right. The HRA makes Convention rights enforceable in the UK courts, in particular:

s 2 HRA 1998	s 3(1) HRA 1998	s 6(1) HRA 1998
❖ Requires a court or tribunal determining a question which has arisen in connection with a Convention right to take into account specified decisions, declarations and opinions	❖ Requires primary and secondary (subordinate) legislation to be compatible with Convention rights (ECHR)	❖ Provides that it is unlawful for a public authority to act incompatibly with a Convention right

Aim Higher

In a discursive essay you may be asked how the grounds for Judicial Review have developed and changed over time, from the traditional (and very narrow) *ultra vires* and *Wednesbury* 'reasonableness' (1947) to modern grounds of illegality, irrationality and procedural impropriety. You should argue that administrative law has come a long way since then, taking into account the coming into force of the **Human Rights Act 1998** (in October 2000) and EU law. You should link this back to the Separation of Powers and the role the judiciary plays in keeping checks and balances on the Executive. You should then discuss increased judicial awareness of human rights as part of JR and how public authorities and ministers have had to comply with the European Convention and adhere to fundamental rights imposed by the ECHR when making decisions that affect individuals (or groups). It is important for you to discuss that Convention rights and principles are now expressly part of the domestic statutory fabric and the courts take account of Strasbourg jurisprudence (case law) in determining any question concerning a Convention right. When concluding your essay, you might mention that *Wednesbury* 'unreasonableness' (now: irrationality) does no longer have an automatic place at the Public Law top table, though the core *Wednesbury* principle of proper statutory compliance is still sound, particularly where Convention rights are not directly an issue. Summarise that there is no doubt that the ECHR has substantially influenced the exercise of administrative discretion. However, the courts have made clear that where pure Convention rights are at issue, these should be decided by the Strasbourg Court (ECtHR) as was held in *ex parte Smith*.

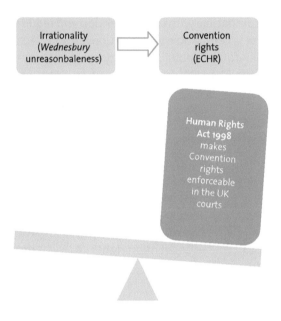

Putting it into practice

Essay questions are likely to relate to one of the following:

❖ The ability to argue the grounds for Judicial Review (JR)
❖ Arguing the difference between the elements of illegality, irrationality and procedural impropriety
❖ The ability to select relevant case law and apply these to complex arguments as grounds for JR have developed over time (e.g. from *Wednesbury* to *GCHQ* to human rights law)
❖ Why are grounds for JR needed?
❖ The continuous evolution of common law and grounds of JR in the light of EU and ECHR jurisdictions
❖ Discuss the problems related to JR grounds in the light of academic commentary (this can often be compared with, for example, the USA and Continental European jurisdictions such as Germany or France) (the discussion will usually feature on the 'free standing' ground of 'proportionality')

Problem questions: step-by-step guide

The following format usually works for answering problem questions in an exam that are concerned with the grounds for JR:

1. **Grounds for JR**: illegality, irrationality and procedural impropriety
2. **Illegality** includes: *ultra vires*; improper purpose; irrelevant considerations; lack of evidence; unlawfully failing to exercise a discretionary power

3. **Irrationality** → *Wednesbury* 'unreasonableness' → now linked to principle of proportionality (EU and HRA 1998)
4. **Procedural impropriety**: focus on Rules of Natural Justice and failure to observe procedural rules:

   a) **Right to a fair hearing** including: right to be heard; adequate notice; right to answer the allegations made
   b) **Duty to give reason**: there is no right to this; the authority does not have to give reason for its decision (now there are significant exceptions to this rule → HRA 1998)
   c) **Does the public authority have the power to make a decision**? What is the empowering statute?
   d) **What does the statute say?** (look at the [often fictitious] statute in the question!). Does the 'Act of Parliament' determine the nature and extent of the public authority's (or minister's) powers? (This can also be used for discussing *ultra vires*)
5. Detailed knowledge of case law is essential if you want to gain high marks in this area of law. In your answer you **must** cite relevant case law and link it to the problem question.

Aim Higher

When answering problem questions in the exam on 'grounds' for JR, you should create a structure to follow before discussing what particular procedural protections are needed for the individual (or group) in the problem question seeking redress in JR. You should ask the following:

i) What type of decision is it? (i.e. judicial or a tribunal or an 'informal hearing').
ii) What type of interest is at stake? (will the claimant lose his or her job? Loss of liberty –see *R v Board of Visitors of Hull Prison ex parte St Germain (No. 2)* [1979] QB 425).
iii Does the decision affect their livelihood? (see *R v Barnsley Metropolitan Borough Council ex parte* Hook [1976] 1 WLR 1052).
iv) Will the claimant lose his or her reputation? (see *R v Secretary of State for the Home Department ex parte Al Fayed* [1998] 1 WLR 763).
v) What is the severity of the sanction? (e.g. dismissal; bad references; loss of employment; loss of earnings; loss of home – see *R v North* and *East Devon Health Authority ex parte Coughlan* [2001] QB 213).

Essay

What is the difference between 'unreasonableness' and 'irrationality' as grounds for Judicial Review? Can you see any problems arising with 'irrationality'? Discuss.

Feedback on putting it into practice

a) Note that the question is divided into three parts. First, discuss the *Wednesbury* 'reasonableness' (or 'unreasonableness') and second the modern development since Lord Diplock's ruling in *GCHQ* towards 'irrationality' as a ground for JR. Finally, discuss any problems that you might foresee when the courts are faced with grounds of 'irrationality'. To attain high marks, you must answer all elements of the question and substantiate your argument by case law.

b) Introduce your essay with the availed technical grounds of JR. Discuss the meaning and application of *Wednesbury* 'unreasonableness' as a branch of administrative law, meaning abuse or misuse of power (*Associated Provincial Picture Houses Ltd v Wednesbury Corp* [1948] 1 KB 223 (CA)).

c) You should make the point that in JR it is the court's duty not to interfere with a discretion which Parliament has entrusted to a statutory body or an individual but to maintain a check on excesses in the exercise of discretion (checks and balances of the Executive by the Judiciary).

d) Do not discuss the facts of either the *Wednesbury* or the *GCHQ* case, just the principles established for grounds of JR.

e) Discuss Lord Green's principles in *Wednesbury*, i.e. that there must be a real exercise of discretion on behalf of the public authority and that the courts must focus on the proper statutory requirements and purpose of (a given) statute to determine whether any abuse of power (*ultra vires*) has taken place.

f) Conclude the first part of your essay by stating that judicial intervention only takes place if the Executive (i.e. the public body or Government Department) has acted unreasonably, 'so unreasonable that no reasonable authority could ever have come to it [the decision'] (Lord Greene in *Wednesbury*).

g) *Wednesbury* set the administrative court's interference threshold very high.

h) Start the second part of your essay by stating that public law has developed extensively since *Wednesbury*, and common law (since *GCHQ*) has developed modern concepts of 'proper statutory purpose' and 'abuse of power' derived from Lord Diplock's judgment in *GCHQ*.

i) Now: courts will not intervene to review the decision of a minister (or public body or tribunal) where the requirements of national security outweigh other matters.

j) A body entrusted with a discretion must direct itself properly in law.

k) To allow 'irrationality' as a ground for JR (and therefore quash the decision), the courts must give due consideration and pay attention to all relevant matters in the case. If a public body has not obeyed statute or acted unreasonably (i.e. irrationally), the decision would be judicially reviewable.

l) If you are writing a coursework essay, you could quote Warrington JJ in *Short v Poole Corporation*: '[in a decision] there may be something so absurd that no sensible person could ever dream that it lay within the powers of the authority'. An example of an irrational or totally absurd decision would be that the red-haired teacher was dismissed because she had red hair. You would explain that this is an unreasonable decision in that extraneous matters have been taken into consideration. As Warrington JJ continues to explain in this case: 'It is so unreasonable that it might almost be described as being done in bad faith; and, in fact, all these things run into one another'.

m) Complete your essay by addressing the final part of the question: what problems could you foresee with 'irrationality' as a ground of JR?

n) For this you should look at the case of *ex parte Smith* carefully (*R v Ministry of Defence ex parte Smith and Grady* and *R v Admiralty Board of the Defence Council ex parte Beckett and Lustig-Prean* [1996]).

o) Though the soldiers cited 'irrationality' as ground for their JR (for being dismissed due to their sexual orientation), the Court of Appeal decided that this was not a matter and ground for JR, but should have been taken to the European Court of Human Rights (ECtHR) 'with whom the responsibility for deciding this issue lay'.

p) Cite Sir Thomas Bingham MR in *ex parte Smith*: the greater the policy content of a decision (here the Ministry of Defence) and the more remote the subject matter of a decision from ordinary judicial experience, the more hesitant the courts will be to make a judgment and will defer the case.

q) Conclude that case law in this area is complex and unclear, though UK judges have applied 'proportionality' – especially when dealing with Community law issues (EU law) (see Lord Slynn in *R (Alconbury Developments Ltd) v Secretary of State for the Environment, Transport and the Regions* [2001] 2 WLR 1389).

r) *Wednesbury* unreasonableness (now 'irrationality') no longer has an automatic place in UK public law; Convention rights are now expressly part of JR (administrative law).

Problem question

Freshmen University has powers under the New University Consolidation Act 2013 to discipline and dismiss students in accordance with the University Regulations 2013. Sabine, a student in the Department of Food Preparation and Health Studies, has received a letter from Smallchops, the Registrar, summoning her to a disciplinary hearing the following day to answer 'serious allegations' of theft. The letter advises that Sabine must attend the hearing alone. She attends the hearing the following day before Professors Hake and Hamburger. Sabine knows she has had previously adverse encounters with Hake when he gave her a formal warning for being late for lectures and Sabine had called him 'incompetent'. Professor Hamburger presents the case against Sabine, saying that she stole a laptop computer from the Food Prep store room. At the hearing, two fellow students from Sabine's course, John and Edward, give evidence, saying that they saw her enter the store room, smuggling the laptop out in her rucksack. Sabine is not allowed to cross-examine them at the hearing. Professors Hake and Hamburger briefly retire to consider their decision, returning after five minutes to announce that Sabine is to be expelled with immediate effect from the University. They also tell her that there is a right of appeal under the 2013 Regulations;

that this must be done within three days to the Principal, the Comedy Actress. However, the Comedy Actress has already announced at her inauguration last year that, as a matter of principle, she will always support her educational staff in enforcing discipline and that any student appeals would be dismissed in any case. Sabine asks a legal friend for advice, but tells her that an appeal would probably be pointless. Advise Sabine.

Feedback on putting it into practice

a) Is it a judicial decision? Yes, the university is set up by (fictitious) statute and secondary legislation (the 2013 Regulations); this is an administrative decision and is least protected by grounds for JR.
b) Has the university acted *ultra vires*? No. Not if you look at the powers of the statutes.
c) What are the grounds for JR? You should consider procedural impropriety.
d) Do Rules of Natural Justice apply to such a decision?
e) How serious is the interest of the applicant? The allegations are 'serious' against Sabine, i.e. allegations of theft which could result ultimately in a criminal conviction (not just the loss of a university place and future job references).
f) Sabine is not given an adequate 'right to be heard' (*audi alterem partem*), i.e. the time limits are too short; she has had no time to prepare her case or seek advice; she is not allowed to take anyone along to the hearing; she is presented with a fait accompli without adequate evidence.
g) Alice, i.e. she must be given an opportunity to be heard (*Cooper v Wandsworth Board of Works* [1863]).
h) Are fundamental human rights at stake? Article 6 **European Convention of Human Rights** (ECHR) states 'right to a fair trial' (or hearing) re: theft of the laptop from the storeroom.
i) What is the severity of the sanction? Very serious, i.e. expulsion from the University and possibly criminal charges to follow.
j) What rights are at stake? Rules of Natural Justice (she has been told to attend alone).
k) Right to cross-examine: serious sanctions are at stake, there is a right (*ex parte St Germain (No. 2)* [1979] QB 425). Sabine is not permitted to cross-examine the two fellow students, John and Edward.
l) Legal points are not explained to her (i.e. she studies Food Preparation and is not a law student) – you should discuss whether she is allowed legal representation at the hearing. In *ex parte Tarrant* (*R v Secretary of State for Home Department ex parte Tarrant* [1985] 1 QB 251), Webster J set out six factors to be considered when deciding whether to allow representation by Counsel:

❖ the seriousness of the charge and the potential penalty;
❖ whether any points of law are likely to arise;
❖ whether the applicant is capable of presenting her own case;
❖ whether there are any procedural difficulties faced by applicants in conducting their own defence;

❖   whether there is reasonable speed in making the adjudication;
❖   whether there is a need for fairness between applicants and the authority.

m) You need to make the point that *Tarrant* involved a prisoner and therefore legal representation was definitely required; for Sabine at this stage it would not be appropriate to have legal representation at the hearing (unless she really did take the laptop!) – but she should be able to take a friend along to the hearing. Are there any points of law arising at the hearing?

n) Rule against bias: the evidence given by her two fellow students, John and Edward, needs to be contested and Sabine should have the right to cross-examine them (for which she may need legal representation or a member of the student union could assist).

o) Professor Hake may also be adversely biased against Sabine, because she has called him 'incompetent' – and he has already given her a formal warning. The hearing should possibly be conducted by someone else from the same department.

p) How serious is the decision? – expulsion and possible theft charges. The right to legal representation was also addressed in *Pett v Greyhound Racing Association* [1968]; *Enderby Town FC v FA* [1971].

q) Article 6 ECHR 'right to a fair trial (hearing)' should be mentioned.

r) Right to appeal: Sabine thinks an appeal would be pointless because the Principal of the University, the Comedy Actress, has made that public statement. Therefore, at this stage, Sabine may well need legal representation (see above).

s) However, you need to point out that there is no automatic right to an oral hearing; written evidence and justification will suffice (*Lloyd v McMahon* [1987]); though any blanket policy of 'no oral hearings' may be struck down by courts (*R v Army Board ex parte Anderson* [1991] 3 WLR 42).

t) Conclusion: the university has not acted illegally (*ultra vires*) but it has not acted with procedural fairness; there has been procedural impropriety in that Sabine has not had a fair hearing and should have been legally represented due to the serious allegations of theft. However, the university does not have to give reason for its decision and the decision may well be upheld after Sabine has been granted a 'fairer' hearing. Discuss Rules of National Justice

Chapter summary

❖   Traditional and modern grounds of Judicial Review
❖   Identification of: illegality, irrationality and procedural impropriety
❖   Knowledge of *Wednesbury* and *GCHQ* cases in relation to 'irrationality'
❖   Reasons for the different grounds and intensities of Judicial Review
❖   Human rights and Judicial Review
❖   Evolving ground of 'proportionality' in Judicial Review
❖   Judicial Review and the continuous evolution and development in common law

Table of key cases referred to in this chapter

Case name	Area of law	Principle
Cooper v Wandsworth Board of Works [1863]	Rules of Natural Justice; right to a fair hearing	The right to be heard (*audi alterem partem*)
Associated Provincial Picture Houses Ltd v Wednesbury Corporation [1948] (CA) (*'Wednesbury'*)	Unreasonableness; abuse of statutory powers (*ultra vires*)	It is the court's duty not to interfere with statute, but to maintain checks and balances on the Executive (here: excesses in the exercise of discretion) (Lord Greene MR)
Ridge v Baldwin [1964]	Rules of Natural Justice; right to a fair hearing	Doctrine of natural justice must be applied to all administrative decisions
McInnes v Onslow-Fane [1978]	Rules of Natural Justice; procedural fairness	Fairness depends on the context
O'Reilly v Mackman [1983] (HL)	Right to a fair hearing (*audi alterem partem*)	Failure to consult amounts to procedural impropriety
Council of Civil Service Unions v Minister for the Civil Service [1985] (*GCHQ* case)	Modern grounds for Judicial Review	Illegality, irrationality and procedural impropriety (Lord Diplock in *GCHQ*)
R v Bow Street Stipendiary Magistrate ex parte Pinochet Ugarte (No. 2) (2000) (*Pinochet* case)	Rules of Natural Justice	Rule against bias. If successful the decisions will be struck out (void). Judges must be seen to be independent and unbiased
R v North and East Devon Health Authority ex parte Coughlan [2001]	Legitimate expectation	Once the legitimacy of the expectation is established, the court will weigh the requirements of fairness against any overriding interest relied upon by the claimant

---

@ **Visit the book's companion website to test your knowledge**

❖ Resources include a subject map, revision tip podcasts, downloadable diagrams, MCQ quizzes for each chapter, and a flashcard glossary

❖ www.routledge.com/cw/optimizelawrevision

10

Commissioners for Administration

Revision objectives

Understand the law

- Do you understand the role and function of Ombudsmen in general?
- Can you explain the difference between the Ombudsman and ADR schemes and court action (Judicial Review)?
- Are you able to describe the main roles and functions of the Parliamentary and Health Ombudsman (PHSO)?

Remember the details

- Can you define the term 'maladministration' in relation to public authorities?
- Are you able to identify the limitations of the Ombudsman system?
- Can you define the investigatory powers of the Parliamentary and Health Ombudsman?

Reflect critically on areas of debate

- Are you able to discuss the advantages and disadvantages of the Parliamentary Ombudsman system?
- Can you characterise the main differences between court action (Judicial Review) and the Parliamentary Ombudsman system?

Contextualise

- Can you relate the sources of law to the function of the Parliamentary and Health Ombudsman within the British constitutional framework?
- Are you able to discuss the proposed reforms to the Parliamentary Ombudsman system in relation to academic sources?

Apply your skills and knowledge

- Can you answer questions in the Putting it into Practice section of the chapter relating to the Ombudsman system including limitations and remedies in the form of essay questions?

Chapter Map

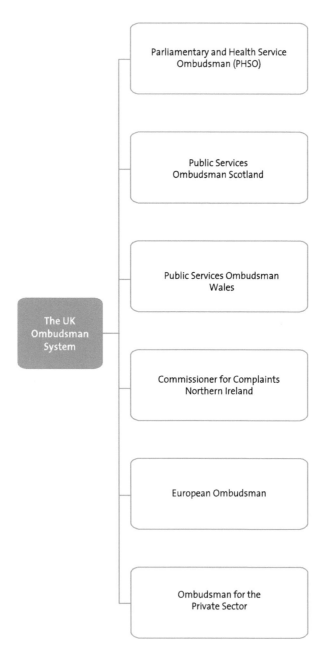

The UK Ombudsman System

- Parliamentary and Health Service Ombudsman (PHSO)
- Public Services Ombudsman Scotland
- Public Services Ombudsman Wales
- Commissioner for Complaints Northern Ireland
- European Ombudsman
- Ombudsman for the Private Sector

Introduction: Ombudsmen

Using an Ombudsman is a way of trying to resolve a complaint without going to court. This chapter is primarily concerned with the public office of **Parliamentary Commissioner for Administration** (or 'Parliamentary Ombudsman'), now referred to as **Parliamentary and Health Service Ombudsman** (PHSO) (see below). The Parliamentary Ombudsman is an independent office that can help citizens make a complaint against a public authority. The system was first created in the UK in 1967, set up under the Parliamentary Commissioner Act 1967 (as amended by the Parliamentary and Health Service Commissioner Act 1987 and the Parliamentary Commissioner Act 1994).

Why do we need an Ombudsman system?

Arguably, Judicial Review has increased to such an extent that the role of the Ombudsman is a powerful one because it involves no court action and is therefore less costly for an individual. Ombudsmen are independent, free of charge and impartial – that is, they do not take sides with either the person who is complaining or the organisation being complained about. In most cases, the individual must complain to the organisation first, before making a complaint to the Ombudsman. If an Ombudsman finds that the complaint is justified, they will recommend what the organisation should do to put things right. But an Ombudsman cannot force an organisation to go along with their recommendations. Although investigations by an Ombudsman can take a long time, the Ombudsman route often seems a more accessible remedy for those who have reason to complain against the administration of public or private bodies (like the energy or telecommunications industries). This is often referred to as **Alternative Dispute Resolution** (ADR). This means in theory citizens have a more immediate and direct recourse via either the Ombudsman system or to other non-judicial means of seeking redress, such as ADR. However, in both cases a remedy may be refused or is not necessarily available, compared with court action. Today, there exist a large number of different Ombudsmen systems in both private and public sectors in the UK, including:

UK Ombudsmen	
The Parliamentary and Health Service Ombudsman (PHSO)	Investigates complaints about Government Departments and other public bodies; also investigates complaints about NHS hospitals and community health services
The Local Government Ombudsman	Investigates complaints about local councils
The Financial Ombudsman Service	Deals with consumer complaints about personal financial matters

UK Ombudsmen	
The European Ombudsman	Investigates maladministration in European Community institutions (i.e. European Commission, Council of the European Union and the Court of Justice)
The Legal Ombudsman	Deals with complaints about services provided by legal advisers, including solicitors, barristers, legal executives, licensed conveyancers and notaries
The Property Ombudsman	Deals with disputes involving estate agents, letting agents, residential managing agents, valuers and auctioneers
The Housing Ombudsman	Deals with complaints about maladministration by social housing landlords (i.e. local authorities, housing associations and trusts)
The Prison and Probation Ombudsman	Considers complaints about most aspects of a prisoner's treatment in prison; also deals with complaints by people on probation
The Ombudsman Services: Energy	Deals with all energy suppliers as last resort (private companies)
Telecommunications Ombudsman	Deals with all telecommunications providers as last resort (private companies)

Note: this list is not exhaustive. For further information, see The Ombudsman Association at http://www.ombudsmanassociation.org.

The Parliamentary and Health Service Ombudsman

The office of Parliamentary Commissioner for Administration (commonly known as the 'Parliamentary Ombudsman') was set up under the Parliamentary Commissioner Act 1967. The Ombudsman is appointed by the Queen and is independent of both Government and Parliament.

The Parliamentary Ombudsman's office was extended to become the **Parliamentary and Health Service Ombudsman** (PHSO) under s 1 Parliamentary and Health Service Commissioners Act 1987 (as amended by the Parliamentary Commissioner Act 1994). The office of PHSO now comprises the offices of the **Parliamentary Commissioner for Administration** (PCA) and the **Health Service Commissioner for England** (HSC). The Ombudsman is responsible for considering complaints by members of the public against UK Government Departments, public authorities and the National Health Service (NHS) in England that have not acted properly or fairly, have provided a poor service or have acted unjustly (known as 'maladministration' – see below). Dame Julie Mellor DBE held the office of

Ombudsman (PHSO) in 2013. The offices of the PHSO are at Millbank Tower, London (see http://www.ombudsman.org.uk).

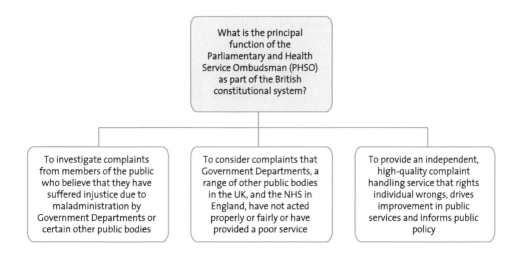

Investigatory powers of the Parliamentary and Health Service Ombudsman

The main role of the PHSO is investigatory, that is, his or her department investigates and if necessary resolves individual complaints about **maladministration** in the public sector (see below). Recently, a large number of complaints have been recorded against the National Health Service (NHS) as well as against the UK Border Agency, concerning asylum and immigration matters. The Ombudsman is accountable directly to Parliament and oversight of the work of the Ombudsman is undertaken by the **Public Administration Select Committee**. It is the PHSO's primary function to consider complaints against Government Departments and other public authorities, as well as the NHS in England. All reports and resolutions are published and available online. For example, following some 478 immigration and asylum-seeking complaints in 2010, the PHSO, Ann Abraham, investigated the UK Border Agency and upheld 97% of complaints (see 'Fast and Fair?' A report by the Parliamentary Ombudsman on the UK Border Agency Session 2009–2010. Presented to Parliament pursuant to s 10(4) Parliamentary Commissioner Act 1967, 8 February 2010). In January 2011, Ann Abraham criticised three Government agencies (HM Revenue and Customs, the Child Support Agency and the Department for Work and Pensions) for collectively failing to put things right when a data-sharing mistake led to Ms M's personal and financial information being wrongfully disclosed to her former partner and her child support payments being reduced without her knowledge.

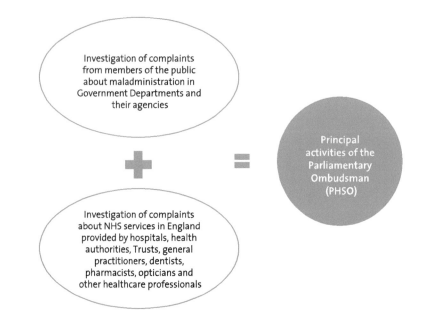

Decision by the Parliamentary Ombudsman – 'Debt of Honour': Complaint about the Ministry of Defence and the Service Personnel & Veterans Agency (2011)

Facts: In 2000, the British Government established an ex gratia compensation scheme to make payments to surviving members of British groups interned by the Japanese during the Second World War. It was clear from the outset that this compensation scheme was intended to provide tangible recognition of the 'debt of honour' that the UK owed to British prisoners of war and civilian internees. Mr A and his siblings thought they met the eligibility criteria and duly applied. However, they were all refused payment on the basis of what was described as the 'bloodlink criterion' – a test of the closeness of people's connection to the UK. This test had not been referred to in the Minister's Statement in November 2000 and was introduced much later, many months into the operation of the scheme. In 2007, the minister announced a further ex gratia compensation scheme, the 'injury to feelings scheme', with payments of £4000 to compensate people like Mr A and his siblings, whose applications to the original scheme had been rejected unlawfully on grounds of national origin.

Findings: The Ombudsman's investigation found injustice as a consequence of maladministration in the way the scheme was announced, devised and implemented. The Ombudsman made a number of recommendations for remedy, some of which the Ministry of Defence (MoD) did not initially accept, but all of which were eventually complied with, following a report by the Public Administration Select Committee and a series of legal challenges.

Recommendations: The Ombudsman's recommendations for remedy included:

(i) The MoD pay Mr A's widow, and each of Mr A's four siblings, the £4000 injury to feelings payment to which they were entitled, together with interest from the date they were incorrectly denied this payment.

(ii) The MoD pay Mrs A on Mr A's behalf, and each of Mr A's four siblings, £5000 in recognition of the outrage and distress they have suffered as a result of the Ministry and the Agency's maladministration.

(iii) The Secretary of State for Defence write a personal apology to Mr A's widow and to each of his siblings, apologising for the shameful way that the Ministry and the Agency have dealt with these matters, and for the impact of their maladministration on Mr A and his siblings; and outlining the Ministry's plans to ensure that other individuals in the same situation will be compensated appropriately.

(iv) The MoD review all other applicants under the injury to feelings scheme and, where it identifies individuals who are in the same position as Mr A and his siblings, that they should also receive the £4000 payment, with interest. The MoD also agree to review the internal mechanisms in place that allowed senior civil servants to get things so wrong, for so long, and which have had such a devastating impact on individuals who deserved so much better.

All of which were accepted by the Ministry of Defence.

(see 'Defending the Indefensible'. Report by the Parliamentary Ombudsman on an investigation of a complaint about the Ministry of Defence and the Service Personnel & Veterans Agency. Seventh Report of the Parliamentary Commissioner for Administration Session 2010–2012. Presented to Parliament pursuant to Section 10(4) of the Parliamentary Commissioner Act 1967, September 2011).

Maladministration

The Parliamentary Commissioner Act 1967 resulted from the **Crichel Down Affair** in 1954, where pre-existing remedies were found not to be an adequate redress for members of the public who had suffered maladministration in central Government (see Chapter 2). The Office of **Parliamentary Commissioner for Administration** (PCA) (as it was called then) was set up to have the ability to investigate a wide range of complaints by members of the public. The role was given wide-ranging independent investigatory powers to consider 'maladministration' under s 10(3) of the 1967 Act. Once maladministration is found, the Parliamentary Ombudsman has to show that this caused 'injustice' under s 10(3) of the Act. However, the Ombudsman may not investigate the merits of a decision taken (s 12 (3)) (see *R v Parliamentary Commissioner for Administration ex parte Balchin (No. 2)* [2000] 79 P & CR 157). Labour Cabinet Minister Richard Crossman, who championed the Parliamentary Commissioner for

Administration Bill through Parliament in 1966–67, explained the terms 'maladministration' and 'injustice' when he said:

'We have not tried to define injustice by using such terms as "loss or damage". These may have legal overtones which could be held to exclude one thing which I am particularly anxious shall remain – the sense of outrage aroused by unfair or incompetent administration, even where the complainant has suffered no actual loss … We have left both words – maladministration and injustice – undefined in the Bill. We believe that the meaning of the words will be filled out by the practical processes of case work.' (Richard Crossman, 1967)

What is maladministration?

The terms and concepts of 'maladministration' and 'injustice' were not defined in the Parliamentary Commissioner Act 1967, and Parliament has left it to the Parliamentary Ombudsman to develop this concept over the past nearly 50 years in common law and practice. In *R v Commissioner for Local Administration ex parte S* [1999] EWCA Civ 989, the court held that 'it must be established that there has been some prejudice to the complainant before a finding of injustice can properly be made. That prejudice may be no more than the loss of an opportunity … and certainly it is not required that any particular damage be established. Indeed, it is quite plain that the word "injustice" was used with a view to indicating something wider than is covered by the concept of damage, and also perhaps to avoid the need to delve into questions of causation which might otherwise arise in certain cases.'

Case precedent – *R v Parliamentary Commissioner for Administration ex parte Balchin (No. 2)* [2000] 79 P & CR 157

Facts: The petitioners (landowners whose land had been blighted by a County Council's Road Order) complained that the Secretary of State for Transport was guilty of maladministration in confirming 'Road Orders' without seeking an assurance from Norfolk County Council that the Balchins would be given adequate compensation for the effect of the road on their home. The Parliamentary Commissioner (the Ombudsman) had rejected their complaint and they sought Judicial Review of a second report, challenging the Ombudsman's report that found no maladministration. The court quashed the report and held that the role of the Parliamentary Commissioner 'as an investigator is not limited to the strict terms of the issue posed by the complaint'. Sedley J accepted that injustice had been widely interpreted: 'so as to cover not merely injury redressible in a court of law, but also "the sense of outrage aroused by unfair or incompetent administration, even where the complainant has suffered no actual loss"'. It followed 'that the defence familiar in legal proceedings, that because the outcome would have been the same in any event there has been no redressible wrong, does not run in an investigation by the commissioner'. Dyson J said that a 'reasons' challenge would succeed wherever there had been a failure to give reasons for findings on a 'principal controversial issue'. The state of knowledge of the Department was such an issue and the Ombudsman had only cited unspecific evidence for his disputed conclusion that the Department was aware of Council powers to purchase blighted land. Also, the Ombudsman's failure to mention the applicant's sense of outrage indicated that, as regards his finding of no injustice, the reasons given would not withstand scrutiny.

Principle: *Balchin No. 2* makes a requirement of 'reasons' that the Ombudsman must give (see also *ex parte Balchin (No. 1)* [1997] PLR 1 – that it is for judges to determine the relevance of any fact to an Ombudsman's report).

Application: The question of whether any given set of facts amounts to maladministration (or injustice) is for the Ombudsman alone to decide.

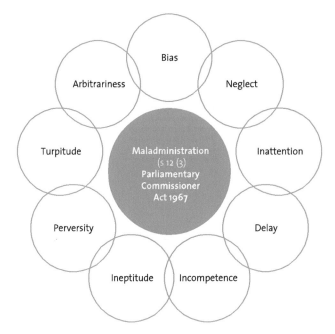

What is maladministration?

Remedies available to the Parliamentary and Health Service Ombudsman

The Parliamentary and Health Service Ombudsman (PHSO) has a set of principles outlining remedies available to him or her in the event he or she finds against a public body on grounds of maladministration and/or injustice. Common law has developed general principles necessary for good administration. These are:

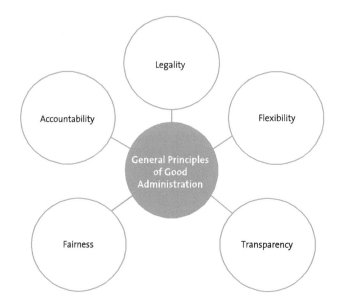

The Parliamentary Ombudsman has three general principles with regard to remedy:

1. Getting it right
- Quickly acknowledging and putting right cases of maladministration that have led to injustice or hardship.
- Considering all relevant factors when deciding the appropriate remedy and ensuring fairness for the complainant.

2. Being customer focused
- Explaining the maladministration and apologising.
- Understanding and managing people's expectations and needs.
- Providing remedies that take account of people's individual circumstances.

3. Being open and accountable
- Operating a proper system of accountability and providing fair remedies.
- Keeping record of what public bodies have decided on remedies and why.

Remedies: General Principles

Principles for remedy

What happens when the Ombudsman finds maladministration?

Where maladministration has led to injustice or hardship, the Ombudsman recommends that the public body responsible *should* take steps to provide an appropriate and proportionate remedy (note the word 'should' because the

Ombudsman has no direct enforcement or punishment powers in law). Ideally, the public body should:

❖ Return complainants and, where appropriate, others who have suffered injustice or hardship as a result of the same maladministration or poor service, to the position they were in before the maladministration or poor service took place.
❖ If that is not possible, compensate them appropriately.

The public body should also ensure they keep any commitments to provide remedies, including ensuring they do not repeat any failures in similar cases. In many cases, an apology and explanation may be a sufficient and appropriate response.

Case precedent – *R (on the application of Bradley and Others) v Secretary of State for Work and Pensions; the Parliamentary Commissioner for Administration and the Attorney-General* **[2008] EWCA Civ 36**

Facts: A report on final salary pension schemes by the Parliamentary Ombudsman was published in March 2006 ('Trusting in the Pensions Promise: Government bodies and the security of final salary occupational pensions' HC 984). The Ombudsman made three findings of maladministration, alleging that the Department of Work and Pensions (DWP) had provided misleading official information about final salary pension schemes. The Court of Appeal concluded that the findings of the Ombudsman that maladministration had occurred were not binding on the Secretary of State and that recommendations of the Ombudsman are not binding. However, the judgment concluded that it was not sufficient for the Secretary of State to simply reject a finding of maladministration: the decision to reject had to be rational. The court found that the Secretary of State had not provided sufficient reasons to show why he had decided to reject the maladministration finding and, therefore, the judgment in the High Court that the rejection was irrational should stand.

Principle: Findings by the Parliamentary Ombudsman are not binding on the Executive (here Secretary of State for the Department of Work and Pensions). If the minister decides to reject the Ombudsman's findings, he has to provide reasons for doing so. It was not a matter of the minister's discretion or choice because the minister had to act rationally in the *Wednesbury* sense.

Application: A Government Department found guilty of maladministration in an Ombudsman's report is under **no** obligation to judicially review it where it contests the findings. But if the minister proposes to reject a finding of maladministration he must do so on *reasonable* grounds, i.e. he has to give reasons for rejecting a finding that the Ombudsman has made.

Limitations of the Parliamentary Ombudsman system

A major weakness of the Parliamentary Ombudsman system is that the 1967 Act does not confer any power to impose an enforceable remedy. There are certain matters and departments which the Ombudsman cannot investigate. For example, the Ombudsman cannot investigate where a legal remedy exists (see *R v Local Commissioner for Local Administration ex parte Croydon London Borough Council* [1989] 1 All ER 1033). Furthermore, the Government Department or other public authority is free to ignore the Ombudsman's recommendations. Simply put: the Ombudsman has no sanctions or powers of enforcement, as was proven in the *Equitable Life* action when some 200,000 investors in the life insurance company lost £4.3 billion when *Equitable Life* collapsed in 2000. In 2008, following complaints by policyholders about the life insurer's maladministration, Ombudsman Ann Abraham recommended that *Equitable* investors be compensated by the Government. Ann Abraham's damning report (December 2001) on the debacle cast a spotlight on the shortcomings of regulatory bodies (such as the Financial Services Authority – FSA). The FSA ignored the Ombudsman's recommendations and so did the Government (under Labour and Gordon Brown's Premiership). In January 2009, the Labour Treasury Minister, Yvette Cooper, announced in Parliament that *Equitable Life* policyholders **could** be entitled to compensation. By April 2013, the Government (via National Savings & Investments) had made 35% of the payments worth £577 million but had already spent 72% of its budget. The Government said it could not trace all policyholders. Questions were raised, such as 'what is the point of the Parliamentary Ombudsman if the Government can ignore her recommendations?'

Excluded matters include:

❖ The work of the police (see Independent Police Complaints Commission – IPCC)
❖ Private bodies (privatised industries, e.g. Network Rail, British Nuclear Power, Scottish Power, Thames Water)
❖ Prime Minister's Office
❖ Cabinet Office
❖ Parole Board
❖ Tribunals (see Tribunal Service)
❖ Bank of England
❖ Criminal Injuries Compensation Board
❖ Government transactions.

The MP filter

Under the Parliamentary Commissioner Act 1967, individual citizens can only submit complaints to the **Parliamentary and Health Service Ombudsman** (PHSO) through a Member of Parliament (MP). This means there is no direct access to the Ombudsman. This is known as the 'MP filter', which checks the legitimacy of complaints. In many cases, MPs attempt to solve the problem themselves. Since 2009, putting a complaint to the Health Service Commissioner (HSC) is simpler in that no MP filter is required. The MP filter requirement for MPs to refer someone's complaint to the Ombudsman has often been criticised as being too restrictive for the PHSO's ability to provide a fully accessible service to complainants. On the other hand, the MP filter reduces the number of frivolous complaints. In practice, this means that complainants must direct their complaint about a public body through their local MP; additionally, the complainant must first have put their grievance to the Government Department or public authority before raising the issue of maladministration with their MP. This remains the most criticised aspect of the Parliamentary Ombudsman system. Despite this, there remains a degree of resistance to removing the MP filter by some MPs themselves, who are concerned about a variety of issues, particularly maintaining a relationship with their constituents. Some argue that removing the MP filter – with a direct access and complaint route to the Ombudsman – would damage the role MPs play in supporting their constituents and holding Government to account. A direct route to the Ombudsman in Scotland and Wales already exists in their devolved public administrations (see Chapter 6).

Judicial Review and the Parliamentary Ombudsman

There is no right of appeal against the Ombudsman's decisions, apart from the use of Judicial Review. In *ex parte Dyer*, the court rejected the argument that the Ombudsman was amenable only to control by Parliament and not subject to review by the courts (see *R v Parliamentary Commissioner for Administration ex parte Dyer* [1994] All ER 375). During the period of 1994–2002, for example, there were three reported cases in which the Ombudsman's decisions had been subjected to Judicial Review. One of the most high-profile cases was the one concerning *Equitable Life* in 1994, when the High Court gave representatives of the 'Equitable Members Action Group' (EMAG) leave to challenge the Ombudsman's decision (see above). However, in December 2004, EMAG dropped its JR proceedings following the decision of the Ombudsman to conduct a further investigation into the matter.

How many complaints?

In 2011–12, the Ombudsman handled just under 24,000 enquiries about Government Departments and agencies and the NHS in England. Of these the Ombudsman's office resolved 23,889 enquiries, providing help and advice on 19,157 and looking closely at 4732. The Ombudsman rejects many complaints at first instance because they are not part of the PHSO's remit. In 2012–13, the Ombudsman's office received 26,961 enquiries – an overall increase of 13% on the previous year, including:

❖ 16,341 about the NHS
❖ 7811 about central Government Departments and organisations
❖ 2809 about organisations outside the Ombudsman's jurisdiction.

The largest percentage increase concerned Government Departments (21%) and the UK Border Agency. There were 12% more complaints about the NHS (see Ombudsman's Annual Report 2012–13 at http://www.ombudsman.org.uk/annual-report-2012-13/home).

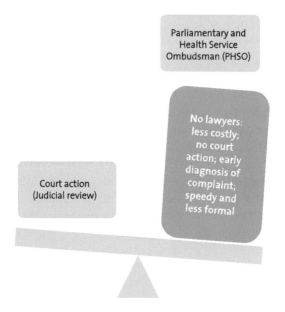

Advantages and disadvantages of the Parliamentary Ombudsman system

Advantages	Disadvantages
Early diagnosis of complaints	**Lack of enforcement power:** PHSO has no executive powers to alter a Government Department's decision, or award compensation (although the Ombudsman may suggest an appropriate remedy)
Speedy and appropriate levels of response	If there is a legal remedy, the PHSO must not take any action
Not a court or tribunal (no lawyers needed!)	The MP filter
Wide powers of discretion: PHSO has wide discretion based upon trust and shared understanding	**Duplication of work:** Some complainants pursue a matter through the courts (Judicial Review) **and** the Ombudsman
Powers to investigate: PHSO possesses significant power to investigate administrative procedures (independence from Government – the Executive)	**No right to appeal** to a decision made by the Ombudsman (except via JR).

PHSO has extensive discretionary powers (s 12(3) Parliamentary Commissioner Act 1967)	Ombudsman's decisions on cases cannot be overruled by a Government Minister or a Parliamentary Committee

Reform of the Parliamentary Ombudsman system

Parliamentary Ombudsman reform is very topical. The Law Commission's report on Public Services Ombudsmen recommends a number of changes to modernise the legislation governing the UK Parliamentary Ombudsman, including reform of the MP filter. The Law Commission also recommended that the Government establish 'a wide-ranging review of the public services ombudsmen and their relationship with other institutions for administrative redress, such as courts and tribunals' (see 'Administrative Redress: Public bodies and the citizen', *Law Commission Consultation Paper No. 187*, July 2008).

Criticisms of the system including lack of public awareness

One of the strongest criticisms of the system is that members of the public generally do not know about the Ombudsman system or the MP filter. A number of criticisms of the Parliamentary Ombudsman system have been identified over the years, summarised below:

Common Criticisms of the Ombudsman System	
Public confusion about the role and remit of the Ombudsman's office	PHSO rejects large number of complaints as inappropriate for investigation
MP filter	Reduces number of complaints to PHSO, i.e. overall volume of work does not compare well with Ombudsmen in other jurisdictions or private sector
Too many Ombudsmen	Public confusion about separate jurisdictions; public ignorance about access to Ombudsman's complaint system
Confusion about Government Departments and proliferation of different adjudication systems within departments	Many departments have their own independent complaints examiner or adjudicator and complaints handling arrangements
Statutory bar to investigate	Preventing the Ombudsman from investigating a case where the complainant has recourse to the courts (Judicial Review) (s 5(2) Parliamentary Commissioner Act 1967)

Aim Higher

If you are going to answer a question in the exam or as part of your coursework on the 'Parliamentary Ombudsman' system, you need to be factually correct in order to present a well-informed discursive composition. Weak students tend to waffle and choose this kind of essay as a 'last resort'. Make sure you have read the supporting documentation on the PHSO's website and the publications and academic discussions about the topic of reforming the Parliamentary Ombudsman system, particularly the MP filter. The Government's White Paper 'Open Public Services' (2012) proposes exploring the jurisdiction, resources, powers, profile and transparency of Ombudsmen in general (see http://files. openpublicservices.cabinetoffice.gov.uk/HMG_OpenPublicServices_web.pdf).

In an answer on reform of the Ombudsman system, you could suggest that the Government removes the MP filter, allowing direct access to the 'Parliamentary Ombudsman'. You could compare the 'Westminster' system with that of devolved Governments such as Scotland, Wales and Northern Ireland where direct access to their local government Ombudsmen already exists (check their websites). How could this be achieved in the UK? What do MPs think of the removal of the MP filer? You could suggest that the Government either amends the present legislation that governs the Parliamentary and Health Service Ombudsman (PHSO), or takes on board the recommendations of the Law Commission (see: The Law Commission Report: Public Services Ombudsmen [2011] HC 1136).

Privatisation of public services

When the Conservatives came to power under Prime Minister Margaret Thatcher in 1979, many services formerly in the public sector were privatised, including the energy companies, water, telephones and public transport (networked services). Under successive Governments a large proportion of council housing was sold off and parts of HM Prison Service were contracted-out (such as prisoner transport and at least four prisons) under Private Finance Initiatives (PFI). In England many schools are now outside of local government control. Most residential homes for older people are now privately provided. The first private sector Ombudsman was the Insurance Ombudsman Bureau established in 1981 and others quickly followed suit, such as the voluntary Ombudsmen schemes established in the banking, insurance and investment sectors. These were brought together by law to form the Financial Ombudsman Service in 2001. Statutory private sector Ombudsman schemes now exist as a form of ADR. But not all such schemes have penalties or legally binding force.

How can the individual seek redress against private companies who run public services?

Some are judicially reviewable, which often involves lengthy court action and expensive legal services (see hybrid public bodies – Chapter 8). The office of the

Parliamentary Ombudsman (Parliamentary and Health Service Ombudsman – PHSO) has therefore become increasingly important when an individual seeks redress against private or independent sector providers. Some of the services are within the remits of the public sector Ombudsman. The Parliamentary Ombudsman service in England has had its remit extended so that people who pay for their own care can still complain to the Ombudsman if they cannot resolve their concerns locally (the same is available for citizens in Wales, Scotland and Northern Ireland). Although the PHSO has extensive powers to investigate maladministration, their recommendations do not have legally binding powers, while private sector Ombudsmen do. In a hybrid model, binding powers are only valid when taken to a court of law, i.e. Judicial Review.

Aim Higher

A typical essay which you might have to write is on the Parliamentary Ombudsman's relationship with the Executive. For this you need to do some detailed background research via the Parliamentary and Ombudsman's websites, read Hansard Reports (Debates in Parliament), study your legal textbook and read academic commentary on the matter. This is well worth doing if you want to gain high marks in this kind of essay. Getting your facts right will add to your marks. You would then argue that since the late 1980s, there have been some major stand-offs between the Parliamentary Ombudsman and Government over the refusal of individual Departments to accept recommendations by the Ombudsman. You should study and mention the following:

(i) The case of the *Rochester Way*, part of the A2 in Kent: refusal to meet late claims for compensation (see *Rochester Way, Bexley, Parliamentary Affairs* January 2008).

(ii) Report into the *Barlow Clowes Affair* (a financial investment firm which became insolvent), in which the Government stated its disagreement with the Ombudsman's conclusions, but accepted them nonetheless (*Barlow Clowes Affair*, HC 76, 1989–90).

(iii) Report on the *Channel Tunnel Rail Link* (HC 193, 8 February 1995).

(iv) Administration of the *ex gratia* payment scheme to former prisoners-of-war of Japan ('*A debt of honour*' HC 324, 12 July 2005).

Putting it into practice

Essay questions are likely to relate to one of the following:

❖ The reasons for setting up the Parliamentary Ombudsman system

* The legislation covering the system
* The advantages and disadvantages of the Ombudsman system
* The nature and meaning of 'maladministration' (and 'injustice')
* Advantages and disadvantages of the MP filter (no direct access to the Parliamentary Ombudsman)
* Remedies and powers of enforcement
* Reform of the Ombudsman system

Essay 1

In *ex parte Bradley* (2008), the Court of Appeal held that a Government Department found guilty of maladministration in a Parliamentary Ombudsman's report is under NO obligation to judicially review it. Does this not make a mockery of the Ombudsman system and Alternative Dispute Resolution (ADR) in general? (see *R (on the application of Bradley and Others) v Secretary of State for Work and Pensions; the Parliamentary Commissioner for Administration and the Attorney-General* [2008] EWCA Civ 36).

Feedback on putting it into practice

a) This essay addresses the service provided by the Parliamentary and Health Service Ombudsman (PHSO) (or 'Parliamentary Ombudsman') service and its conflict with the Executive (in the *ex parte Bradley* case, the Department of Work and Pensions).

b) It is imperative you read the case; it will show in your discursive essay if you have not actually consulted the law report and read the decisive judgments.

c) In your introduction you should discuss the services the PHSO provides and their independence from Government; also give reasons why the office of the Ombudsman was set up in law in the first place in 1967.

d) The Ombudsman is meant to provide independent scrutiny of Government (and related authorities') maladministration and 'injustice'.

e) You should cite the advantages of the Ombudsman's system and office, particularly in relation to the out-of-court action and speed with which an individual can seek redress; you do need to mention the MP filter though!

f) You need to go online and look at some of the Ombudsman's recent reports of maladministration and their recommendations (see the links above). Did the Ombudsman's recommendations stand up in law? Did Parliament take notice?

g) Do not ignore the fact that the question also asks you to define ADR and the means by which a citizen can seek redress against a private sector company.

h) As an example, you could cite the recommendations by the Ombudsman in the *Equitable Life* investment scandal and how the Government and the FSA simply ignored the Ombudsman's report and recommendations. What happened next?

i) You may well agree with the question that the present system **does** make a mockery of the Parliamentary Ombudsman system. Give reasons and cite reports and academic commentary.

j) Your final paragraph should suggest ways of improving the system and ways forward to reform – this could be either by way of amending the present legislation (Parliamentary Commissioner Act 1967) or taking on board the Law Commission's recommendations (2008).

Essay 2

Discuss the main advantages and disadvantages of the Parliamentary Ombudsman system versus the effectiveness of legal redress in the administrative law arena.

Feedback on putting it into practice

a) For this question you must read and quote sections from the statute (Parliamentary Commissioner Act 1967), followed by a discussion of relevant case law.

b) This question requires you to make the distinction between the Ombudsman system and procedure (i.e. investigation into maladministration of Government Departments, etc.) compared with seeking redress via Judicial Review (see Chapter 8).

c) Discuss the role and duties of the Ombudsman and their statutory provision under the Parliamentary Commissioner Act 1967 (as amended by the Parliamentary and Health Service Commissioner Act 1987).

d) Discuss the Ombudsman's extensive discretionary powers (s 12(3) of 1967 Act) and the advantages of the system, such as their unlimited and independent powers to investigate maladministration (provide examples).

e) Discuss the Ombudsman's (limited) powers of redress and remedy and how they find a resolution to complaints.

f) You should then conclude by stating whether the Parliamentary Ombudsman system ought to be reformed, giving reasons; for this you need to read academic commentary on the subject and your prescribed textbook (e.g. Barnett, H., 2013, *Constitutional and Administrative Law*, 10th edn.).

g) Consult some Parliamentary Select Committee Reports such as 'The Parliamentary Ombudsman: Withstanding the test of time'. 4th Report Session 2006–2007, HC 421, 24 March 2007.

Chapter summary

❖ The Parliamentary Ombudsman system under the Parliamentary Commissioner Act 1967 (as amended by the Parliamentary and Health Service Commissioner Act 1987)

❖ The characteristics of the system as extended to the Parliamentary and Health Service Ombudsman ('Parliamentary Ombudsman')

- ❖ Investigatory powers of the Parliamentary Ombudsman
- ❖ The meaning of 'maladministration' in public services, public authorities and the NHS (England)
- ❖ The MP filter system
- ❖ Matters excluded from the Parliamentary Ombudsman system
- ❖ Remedies and redress
- ❖ Advantages and disadvantages of the system

Table of key cases referred to in this chapter

Case name	Area of law	Principle
R v Local Commissioner for Local Administration ex parte Croydon London Borough Council [1989]	Conflict: Ombudsman v judicial remedy	The Ombudsman must not investigate where a legal remedy exists
R v Parliamentary Commissioner for Administration ex parte Dyer [1994]	Judicial Review	Decisions by the Ombudsman are subject to Judicial Review
R v Commissioner for Local Administration ex parte S [1999]	Maladministration (injustice)	Some prejudice to the complainant must be established before a finding of injustice can properly be made
R v Parliamentary Commissioner for Administration ex parte Balchin (No. 2) [2000]	Maladministration	The question of whether any given set of facts amounts to maladministration (or injustice) is for the Parliamentary Ombudsman alone to decide
R (on the application of Bradley and Others) v Secretary of State for Work and Pensions; the Parliamentary Commissioner for Administration and the Attorney-General [2008] **(ex parte Bradley)**	Judicial Review	A Government Department found guilty of maladministration in an Ombudsman's report is under **no** obligation to judicially review it

@ Visit the book's companion website to test your knowledge

- ❖ Resources include a subject map, revision tip podcasts, downloadable diagrams, MCQ quizzes for each chapter, and a flashcard glossary
- ❖ www.routledge.com/cw/optimizelawrevision

11

Police Powers and State Security

Revision objectives

Understand the law
- Do you understand what is meant by freedom of assembly in relation to the European Convention on Human Rights?
- Can you explain the types of public order act and terrorism offences in relation to the Public Order Act 1986?
- Are you able to explain how the Human Rights Act 1998 relates to public protest and public assembly jurisprudence?

Remember the details
- Can you define freedom of assembly, public protest and terrorism jurisprudence?
- Are you able to describe the common law power to prevent breach of the peace?
- Would you be able to explain and discuss the public order provisions in law for a police officer to keep the peace?
- Can you define police powers of stop and search and detention under the Police and Criminal Evidence Act 1984 (PACE)?

Reflect critically on areas of debate
- Would you be able to discuss the relationship between police powers, public order and human rights?
- Can you discuss relevant sources of law in relation to public protest, breach of the peace and freedom of assembly?
- Can you discuss how human rights law has influenced UK statutory provisions relating to public order and terrorism offences?

Contextualise
- Can you relate the sources of law to the fundamental principles of freedom of assembly and the right to peaceful protest in relation to police powers to keep the peace and prevent terrorism?

Apply your skills and knowledge
- Can you answer questions in the Putting it into Practice section of the chapter relating to police powers and public order act offences in the form of problem questions?

Chapter Map

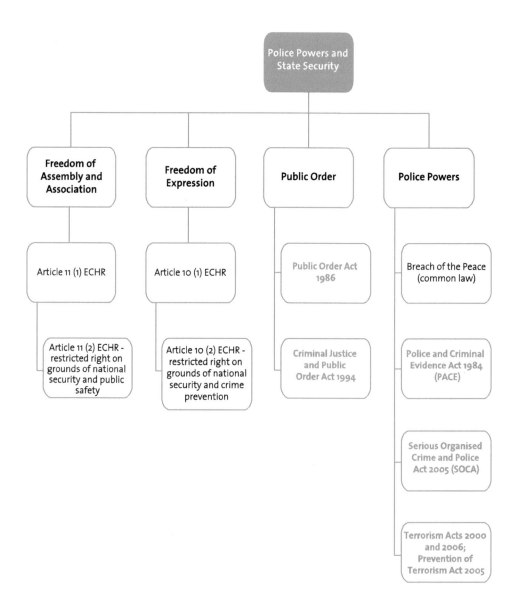

Introduction: freedom of speech, assembly and association

Chapter 7 introduced you to the **European Convention on Human Rights** (ECHR) and the Human Rights Act 1998 (HRA). This chapter sets out the legal background to the right to peaceful protest and the range of offences that can arise in the course of protesting. We will also look at human rights legislation, specifically **Art 11 ECHR**, the **right to freedom of peaceful assembly and association** and **Art 10**, the **right to freedom of expression**.

Every year London sees thousands of protesters marching either in front of the Palace of Westminster and Parliament Square or holding assemblies and rallies in Trafalgar Square to demonstrate or hold speeches about a large number of causes. The vast majority of protest marches and assemblies pass off peacefully. There have been infamous riots – such as the Anti-Poll Tax Riot on 31 March 1990 in central London when 45 police officers were among the 113 people injured as well as 20 police horses. A total of 340 people were arrested, as cars were overturned and set alight. There were the student riots between 6 and 10 August 2011 against tuition fees introduced by the Labour Party. The resulting chaos spread to all parts of London and generated looting and arson as mass police deployment tried to curb the rioting young people, many of whom were from middle-class backgrounds. These were called the 'BlackBerry riots', because people used mobile phones and social media to organise them. The riots escalated following the death of Mark Duggan, who was shot dead by police on 4 August 2011.

Positive and negative human rights

Article 10 ECHR ('freedom of expression') includes the right to hold and express opinions yourself as well as to receive and impart information and ideas to others (see *Handyside v UK* [1976] ECHR 5 – see below). Both Arts 10 and 11 ECHR are **qualified rights**, which means they are not absolute rights. This means that formalities, conditions, restrictions or penalties may be imposed on the exercise of this right if they are prescribed by law, pursue a legitimate aim and are necessary in a democratic society. Article 10(2) ECHR sets out the limitations by which the state can legitimately curtail or stop freedom of expression if it feels necessary in the interest of public safety or security to do so. Similarly with Art 11(2), which balances the rights of the individual against the broader interests of the community and society. Article 11(2) can lawfully restrict freedom of peaceful assembly and association to protect national security, public safety, the prevention of disorder or crime, or the protection of the rights and freedoms of others, if the state feels it 'necessary in a democratic society' to do so. These restrictions must be proportionate, meaning that the measures taken are the least restrictive necessary to achieve the legitimate aim.

Article 10(1) ECHR	Article 10(2) ECHR
❖ Right to freedom of expression ❖ Freedom to hold and express opinions ❖ Without interference from public authorities	❖ Right can be restricted by the state ❖ For legitimate aims ❖ In the interests of national security, territorial integrity or public safety ❖ Prevention of crime and disorder

Article 11(1) ECHR	Article 11(2) ECHR
❖ Right to peaceful assembly ❖ Right to freedom of association with others ❖ Without interference from public authorities	❖ Right can be restricted by the state ❖ For legitimate aims ❖ In the interests of national security, territorial integrity or public safety ❖ For the protection of health or morals ❖ Protection of the rights and freedoms of others

Case precedent – *Handyside v UK* [1976] ECHR 5; EHRR 737

Facts: Publisher Richard Handyside had published 'The Little Red Schoolbook' in 1971 (written originally in Danish in 1969 by Søren Hansen and Jesper Jensen). The 'Little Red Book' was intended for school children of age 12+. The book contained chapters on sex, including subsections on issues like masturbation, contraceptives, menstruation, pornography, homosexuality and abortion. In March 1971, the Metropolitan Police executed a warrant, searched Mr Handyside's premises and seized 1069 copies of the book under s 3 of the Obscene Publications Act 1959. The copies were destroyed and the book withdrawn from the market because of its 'obscene' nature. Mr Handyside claimed the book was meant as a reference text for teachers and parents and the confiscation and destruction of the copies amounted to a breach of Art 10 ECHR ('freedom of expression'). His appeals against his conviction failed. He appealed to the Strasbourg Court, the issue being whether the interference by the state (police) had been 'necessary in a democratic society' in accordance with the legitimate aim of 'protecting morals', under Art 10(2) ECHR. The ECtHR held that the police action was 'not necessary' under Art 10(2) ECHR. Therefore, the court could find no violation of the applicant's right to freedom of expression.

Principle: The ECtHR held that freedom of expression constituted one of the essential foundations of a democratic society and one of the basic conditions for its progress and development of every person. It also made clear that Art 10 ECHR applied not only to information or ideas that are favourable and inoffensive but also to those that offend, shock or disturb the state or a sector of the population.

Application: When Art 10 ECHR ('freedom of expression') is challenged, the court will look at the publication – for example – whether the state can derogate from the principles of Art 10, in respect of 'protecting public morals'. The ECtHR held in *Handyside* that it is impossible to find a uniform European conception amongst the contracting states of what amounts to 'obscene' material and equally what amounts to 'public morals' in a particular state. The court held that domestic courts must apply a margin of appreciation proportionate to the country's laws and religious perception.

The right to peacefully protest

The purpose of public order law is to ensure that individual rights to freedom of speech and freedom of assembly are balanced against the rights of others to go about their daily lives unhindered. To be able to peacefully protest is a vital part of a democratic society and has a very long and respected tradition in the United Kingdom. It can be a very powerful campaign tool and many of the rights and freedoms we enjoy today were gained because people were prepared to go out on the streets and protest. For centuries, the UK Parliament has resisted the notion of positive rights in the field of public protest and political expression. The Human Rights Act 1998 (HRA) presented a constitutional shift that fundamentally altered this position. However, the right to peacefully protest under Art 11 ECHR is not absolute. Article 11(2) ECHR makes this perfectly clear. Additionally, there is now a great deal of legislation in place which the state can use against protesters, increased by terrorism legislation since 9/11 (11 September 2001) and the London terrorism bombings on 7 July 2005. The Terrorism Acts 2000 and 2006 and the Prevention of Terrorism Act 2005 made it illegal for terrorism groups to operate in the UK. Since the 2005 Act, the police have been given very wide powers to control and restrict the actions of protesters.

Public order offences

Particular checks on public protest are offered by criminal law in respect of public order offences, intended to punish the use of violence and/or intimidation by individuals or groups. The principal public order offences are contained in Part I of the Public Order Act 1986 (POA). Additionally, there is the offence of 'drunk and disorderly behaviour' (s 91 Criminal Justice Act 1967) and so-called 'bind-overs'. Offences involving public disorder are often a precursor to, or part of, the commission of other offences such as an assault, unlawful possession of a weapon or the causing of criminal damage.

Public Order Offences	
s 1 Public Order Act 1986 (POA)	Riot (indictable)
s 2 POA	Violent disorder (either way)
s 3 POA	Affray (either way)
s 4 POA	Fear or provocation (summary)
s 4A POA	Intentional harassment, alarm or distress (summary)
s 5 POA	Harassment, alarm or distress (summary)
s 91 Criminal Justice Act 1967	Drunkenness in a public place ('Drunk and disorderly') (summary)
s 31 Crime and Disorder Act 1998	Racially or religiously aggravated disorderly behaviour with intent to cause harassment, alarm or distress (either way)
Bind overs (Justices of the Peace Act 1361)	Courts' power to bind over offenders to keep the peace against a surety

Riot (s 1 POA – indictable only)

Under s 1 of the Public Order Act 1986 (POA), it must be proved that the following criteria are met:

Riot is defined as:

Twelve or more persons, present together, used or threatened unlawful violence (all charged must use), for a common purpose that the conduct of them (taken together) was such as to cause a person of reasonable firmness, present at the scene, to fear for his personal safety.

An offence under s 1 POA is a serious indictable only offence (i.e. Crown Court, judge and jury). The maximum penalty on conviction is 10 years' imprisonment and/or a fine of unlimited amount.

Aim Higher

In a problem question, you may well have to deal with more than the one principal 'rioter'. Look at the above conditions for 'riot'. Providing all of these are met in the problem question, **each** of the persons using unlawful violence for a common purpose will be guilty of riot. If you are not sure, you could lay different charges; say, 'the police will charge X with the offence of aiding and abetting' (riotous behaviour), counselling or procuring the use of violence, e.g. encouraging, planning, directing or coordinating the activities of those involved in the violent action in the problem question. The police can then charge these as joint principals. This approach will gain you higher marks.

Violent disorder (s 2 POA – triable either way)

Under s 2 Public Order Act 1986 (POA), it must be proved that the following criteria are met:

Violent disorder is defined as:

Three or more persons, present together, used or threatened unlawful violence so that the conduct of them (taken together) would cause a person of reasonable firmness, present at the scene, to fear for his or her personal safety.

An offence under s 2 POA is an 'either-way' offence, meaning it can be tried either at the Magistrates' Court or the Crown Court (the mode of trial is decided by the magistrates depending on the seriousness of the alleged offence). The maximum penalty on summary conviction (Magistrates' Court) is 6 months' imprisonment; when tried on indictment, a maximum of 5 years' imprisonment.

Examples of Violent Disorder (s 2 POA)		
Fighting between 3 or more people involving the use of weapons, between rival groups in a place to which members of the public have access (town centre; crowded bar) causing severe disruption and/or fear to members of the public	Outbreak of violence; potential for significant impact on a moderate scale on non-participants	Serious disorder at public event; missiles are thrown at police and other civil authorities

Aim Higher

You should only consider the offence of 'violent disorder' in a problem question if there is evidence of serious disorder (three or more people). The difference between a riot and violent disorder is clearly the number of people taking part in a riot (12 or more). Look at how many people are involved in the question. How much planning is involved in the protest (particularly in relation to violent disorder)? Riots often flare up following minor incidents and lead to serious disorder sufficient to meet the requirements of s 2 POA. The offence may be committed in a **public or private place**. Violence can be against a person or persons or against property. You will gain a higher mark if you can mention some case law (e.g. *R v Mahroof* [1988] 88 Cr App R 317; *R v Fleming and Robinson* [1989] 153 JP 517; *R v NW* [2010] EWCA Crim 404).

Affray (s 3 POA – triable either way)

Under s 3 Public Order Act 1986 (POA), it must be proved that a person has used or threatened:

Affray is defined as:

Unlawful violence towards another and his conduct is such as would cause a person of reasonable firmness present at the scene to fear for his personal safety. The seriousness of the offence lies in the effect that the behaviour of the accused has on members of the public who may have been put in fear. The offence may be committed in a public or private place. There must be some conduct, beyond the use of words, which is threatening and directed towards a person or persons. Mere words are not enough.

An offence under s 3 POA is an 'either-way' offence. On indictment, a person guilty of affray is liable to a maximum of 3 years' imprisonment or an unlimited fine; on summary conviction, to a maximum of 6 months' imprisonment.

Note: It is often difficult to distinguish between a section 3 (affray) offence and a section 4 (insulting or abusive words) offence under the 1986 Act. Affray should be considered in circumstances of **serious and indiscriminate** violence (for further guidance, see www.cps.gov.uk).

Examples of Affray (s 3 POA)		
A fight between 2 or more people in a public place (e.g. pub, disco, restaurant, street); violence must put people in substantial fear (even though the fight is not directed towards them)	Throwing of objects directed towards a group of people in circumstances where serious injury is likely to be caused	Wielding of weapon, likely to cause people substantial fear for their safety; person brandishes a weapon and threatens to use it against police or others

Aim Higher

If you are not sure what 'affray' means or constitutes, you should apply the 'hypothetical bystander' test to a problem question and apply case law as was defined in *R v Sanchez* [1996] Crim LR 572. You will gain high marks if you assert that it is the notional bystander (and not the [potential] victim) who has to be put in fear for his or her personal safety. BUT: apart from the hypothetical bystander, there must be present a 'victim' against whom the violence is to be directed (see *I & Others v DPP* [2002] 1 AC 285 (HL)). Read the question carefully: there has to be violence of such a kind that a bystander would fear for his safety. Where the violence is focused solely and exclusively on the victim, such that it would be incapable of causing a person of reasonable firmness present at the scene to fear for his safety, then the offence is not made out (see *Leeson v DPP*, unreported (2010)).

Public order offences: offences of violence – summary

Riot (s 1 POA)	Violent Disorder (s 2 POA)	Affray (s 3 POA)
12 or more people and common purpose	3 or more people	1 person (or more)
threaten unlawful violence for a common purpose	who are present together use or threaten unlawful violence	uses or threatens unlawful violence towards another
10 years maximum prison sentence	5 years maximum prison sentence	3 years maximum prison sentence

What is the difference between harassment, racial and religious hatred offences and drunk and disorderly?

Offences contrary to ss 5, 4A and 4(1)(a) Public Order Act 1986 ('public order act offences causing harassment, alarm and distress') and s 91 Criminal Justice Act 1967 ('drunk and disorderly') overlap considerably in the conduct required to commit any one of these offences and can be difficult to make out when faced with a problem question (imagine how difficult it is for the police and the CPS to charge!). Whether behaviour can be properly categorised as disorderly is a question of fact. 'Disorderly behaviour' does not require any element of violence, actual or threatened; and it includes conduct that is not necessarily threatening, abusive or insulting. It is not necessary to prove any feeling of insecurity, in an apprehensive sense, on the part of a member of the public (see *Chambers and Edwards v DPP* [1995] Crim LR 896).

Examples of Disorderly Behaviour		
Causing a disturbance in a residential area or common part of a block of flats	Persistently shouting abuse or obscenities at passers-by; pestering people waiting to catch public transport or otherwise waiting in a queue	Rowdy behaviour in a street late at night which might alarm residents or passers-by; alarming or distressing vulnerable citizens (e.g. the elderly); members of an ethnic minority

Elements required for 'disorderly behaviour' (s 91 Criminal Justice Act 1967 **and ss 5, 4A and 4(1)(a)** Public Order Act 1986**):**

	Drunk and disorderly (s 91 CJA)	s 5 POA	s 4A POA	s 4(1)(a)
Disorderly or abusive behaviour?	disorderly behaviour	threatening, abusive or insulting words or behaviour or disorderly behaviour	threatening, abusive or insulting words or behaviour or disorderly behaviour	threatening, abusive or insulting words or behaviour towards another person
Public or private space?	in any public place	in a public or private place (but not when confined to a dwelling house – see note below)	in a public or private place (but not when confined to a dwelling house – see note below)	in a public or private place (but not when confined to a dwelling house – see note below)

Intention?	while drunk	With intention or awareness that behaviour may be disorderly; or with intention or awareness that such behaviour may be threatening, abusive or insulting	With intent to cause and thereby causing	Either: with intent to cause that person to believe that immediate unlawful violence will be used against him or another by any person **or**: with intent to provoke the immediate use of unlawful violence by that person or another **or**: whereby that person is likely to believe that such violence will be used **or**: it is likely that such violence will be provoked
Victim?		within the hearing or sight of a person likely to be caused		
Effect on victim?		harassment, alarm or distress	harassment, alarm or distress	

Incitement to religious hatred

This offence falls under the Racial and Religious Hatred Act 2006 and is aimed at those who stir up hatred against persons on religious grounds. The 2006 amended s 64 Public Order Act 1986. This potential offence is often referred from the police to the Special Crime and Counter Terrorism Division.

Incitement to religious hatred:
Requires that the words behaviour, written material, recordings or programmes must be threatening and intended to stir up religious hatred.

Defines religious hatred as hatred against a group of persons on the basis of their religious belief or lack of religious belief.

Amends the Police and Criminal Evidence Act 1984 (PACE) so that the powers of citizen's arrest do not apply to the offences of stirring up religious and racial hatred.

The Human Rights Act 1998 and Public Order Offences

The introduction of the Human Rights Act 1998 (HRA) incorporated Arts 10 and 11 **European Convention on Human Rights** (ECHR) into UK domestic law. This represented a constitutional shift in the domestic protection of the right to freedom of expression and peaceful assembly.

Section 3 HRA ('interpretation of legislation') requires courts to interpret both primary and subordinate legislation to be compatible with the Articles of the European Convention (ECHR). This interpretation goes far beyond normal statutory interpretation and includes past and future legislation. This means that there is no implied repeal of the HRA by subsequent contradictory legislation. This means that Parliamentary Sovereignty has been curtailed and limited (see Chapters 3 and 7). Section 3 is rather vague and has therefore invited a number of legal challenges.

Section 6 HRA ('acts of public authorities'): s 6(1) HRA provides: 'It is unlawful for a public authority to act in a way which is incompatible with a Convention right.' This section makes it unlawful for a public authority to act incompatibly with Convention rights (ECHR) and allows for a case to be brought in a UK court or tribunal against the authority where it does so. However, a public authority will not have acted unlawfully under the Act if, as the result of a provision of primary legislation, it could not have acted differently. Where it is not possible to do so, a court may:

❖ quash or disapply subordinate legislation
❖ give a declaration of incompatibility for primary legislation, thereby
❖ allowing a minister to make a remedial order to amend the legislation to bring it into line with the Convention rights.

The HRA also requires UK courts and tribunals to take account of the Strasbourg case-law (jurisprudence).

Police powers
Breach of the peace in common law
A breach of the peace is not in itself a criminal offence, but the police and any other person have a power of arrest where there are **reasonable grounds** for believing a

breach of the peace is taking place or is imminent. Breach of the peace goes back to the Justices of the Peace Act 1361, which defines the powers of Justices of the Peace (Magistrates) and states that there 'shall be assigned for the keeping of the Peace, one Lord, and with him three or four of the most worthy in the County, with some learned in the Law, and they shall have Power to restrain the Offenders, Rioters, and all other Barators who have offended said peace.' The term was clarified in common law in *R v Howell* [1982] QB 416 (see below); the Court of Appeal defined a breach of the peace as being 'an act done or threatened to be done which either actually harms a person, or in his presence, his property, or is likely to cause such harm being done'. This power of arrest potentially conflicts with Art 5 ECHR ('the right to liberty and security'), Art 10 ('the right to freedom of expression') and Art 11 ('the right to freedom of assembly and association').

> '[A breach of the peace is] an act done or threatened to be done which either actually harms a person, or in his presence, his property, or is likely to cause such harm being done.'   (Watkins LJ in *R v Howell* [1982])

Case precedent – *R v Howell (Errol)* [1982] QB 416 (CA)

Facts: The appellant, Errol Howell, was tried on indictment on two counts of assault occasioning actual bodily harm on two police constables. The prosecution's case was that a disturbance had occurred in the early hours of the morning as people congregated in a street from a house where a party was being held and the police were called. Howell repeatedly swore at the two police officers, who subsequently charged him with breach of the peace. The appellant continued to swear and one police constable took hold of the appellant, but before he could explain why he was arresting him, the appellant struck him in the face and together with the others set on the two policemen. Howell was convicted of the assault on a police officer. He appealed against conviction on the grounds, *inter alia*, that his arrest was unlawful because no breach of the peace had been proved against him, and accordingly, on the supposition that he had, contrary to his own evidence, struck the police constable, he had been acting lawfully in escaping from a wrongful arrest in that he had used no more force than had been necessary. The Court of Appeal dismissed the appeal stating that the original Recorder in the trial had correctly stated the ingredients of the offence of a breach of the peace in his ruling on the submission of 'no case to answer' and in his directions to the jury, it could not be said that the verdict of the jury was unsafe or unsatisfactory and the conviction for assaulting a police officer stood.

Principles: (1) A police constable or ordinary citizen has power of arrest without warrant where there is reasonable apprehension of an *imminent* breach of the peace even though the person arrested has not at that stage committed any breach. The person making the arrest must reasonably and honestly believe that such a breach would be committed in the immediate future.

(2) The behaviour that causes a constable to believe that a breach of the peace has occurred or will occur has to be related to violence and such a breach occurs whenever harm has actually been done or is likely to be done to a person, or in his presence, to his property, or a person is put in fear of being harmed through an assault, affray, riot, unlawful assembly or other disturbance.

(3) That where an arrest is made for an anticipated breach of the peace it is sufficient that the constable states that it is for 'a breach of the peace' and, since the defendant either knows why he is being arrested or has prevented the constable from telling him the reason for the arrest, the arrest is valid.

Application: When such a power (arrest for breach of the peace) is exercised by a police officer, it has to be established that the apprehension is imminent, it has to be based on an honest (albeit possibly mistaken) belief that violence has occurred or is imminent, but that it was a belief which was founded on reasonable grounds.

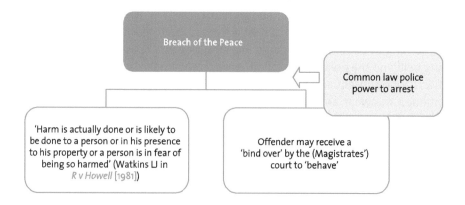

Bind over

A breach of the peace in the context of Magistrates' powers to bind a person over to keep the peace under s 115 Magistrates Courts Act 1980 has to involve violence or the threat of violence. The violence does not have to be committed by the defendant himself; it is sufficient if his conduct is such that violence will be feared by a third party as a natural consequence of the defendant's action, with some real possibility of actual danger to the peace.

Up for Debate

Since the atrocious terrorism acts on 9/11 in the USA and on 7 and 22 July 2005 in London, Parliament has granted the police additional stop-and-search powers and powers of detention and arrest in addition to powers already granted under the **Police and Criminal Evidence Act 1984** (PACE). Have a look at the police shooting dead the 27-year-old Brazilian, Jean Charles de Menezes, on 22 July 2005 at Stockwell Underground Station. Would you say that police powers have gone too far? In order to enhance an essay in this area, you need to study the law and the facts. Take a look at the following legislation, and discuss whether the scope of police powers (in addition to PACE) severely restricts the free movement of protestors and the free expression of political protest (see s 140(1)(c) **Criminal Justice Act 1988**, s 60 **Criminal Justice and Public Order Act 1994**, s 44 **Terrorism Act 2000** and s 1 **Criminal Justice Act 2003**).

Processions and assemblies

The Public Order Act 1986 (POA) refers to marches as 'processions' (s 11) and to all other static demonstrations as 'assemblies' (s 12). A 'procession' is simply defined as people moving together along a route; the law does not provide a minimum number to constitute a procession. Even a handful of people going to a County Hall to hand in a petition will constitute a procession. The POA gives the police extensive controls over processions. Organisers of most processions must give advance notice to the police. The police may impose conditions on processions and, in limited circumstances, have them banned. Failure to comply with these provisions is a criminal offence.

PUBLIC PROCESSION (MARCHES)	PUBLIC ASSEMBLY (DEMONSTRATIONS)
Advanced written notice to police (s 11 POA 1986)	No advance notice required
Senior officer can 'give [any] directions' if trigger conditions satisfied (s 12(1) POA)	Senior officer can 'give directions' as to Location Duration Numbers If trigger conditions are satisfied (s 14) (Conditions)
Knowingly failing to comply with a direction is an offence (ss 12(4)(5), 14(4)(5) POA) **BUT** Defence to prove that the failure arose from circumstances beyond organiser's control. Blanket bans possible (s 13 POA)	

Notification requirements

The law on notification requirements for marches ('processions') is set out in s 11 Public Order Act 1986. The organisers of a march are required to give advance written notice of the march to the local police force. Notice can be in the form of a letter to the local police station (recorded delivery or by hand) and must be at least **one week before the march**. The notice must state:

> ❖ Date and start time of the proposed march and its route
> ❖ Name and address of at least one of the organisers

Anyone who organises a march and does not give the required notice commits an offence for which they can be fined up to £1000. The law recognises some exceptions to the notice period, because a march has to be organised speedily in response to an unexpected event (e.g. student protest against increase in tuition fees). Section 11 POA provides that it is possible to give shorter (i.e. a full week's) notice as long as it is 'reasonably practicable'.

Demonstrations ('public assembly')

A **'public assembly'** is an assembly of **two or more people** in a public place that is wholly or partly open to the air. This can extend to privately owned land that the public generally has access to.

There is no requirement to give the police advance notice of demonstrations (see *R (on the application of Morris, E. and T.) v Chief Constable of Kent Police* [2009] EWHC 2264 (Admin) – see below). However, many people choose to give the police advance warning so that they are not surprised by the demonstration and can make arrangements to police it.

> ### Case precedent – *R (on the application of Morris, E. and T.) v Chief Constable of Kent Police* [2009] EWHC 2264 (Admin)) (*Kingsnorth Power Station* case)
>
> **Facts:** In August 2008, three activists ('Camp for Climate Action'), including two 11-year-old twins, were stopped and searched under s 1 PACE by police officers who had 'reasonable suspicion' that the individuals were carrying prohibited weapons or articles that could be used to cause criminal damage at Kingsnorth Power Station, Kent. At the height of the week-long climate camp, the number of protesters was estimated at 1800 to 2000. Police required people who wanted to join the protest to pass through a cordon of multiple stops and searches, with officers conducting a total of 8218 searches. Hundreds of people's possessions were seized, from walking sticks to crayons to health and safety supplies. Dave

Morris, an activist, and the 11-year-old twins brought Judicial Review proceedings against Kent Police. It was held that the 'blanket group' stop and search was 'unlawful' and 'should not have happened' and that Kent Police's widespread use of stop and search at the protest was 'disproportionate'. The court also held that the applicants' Art 11 'right to peaceful protest' was violated. In January 2010, the protesters received compensation after Kent Police admitted they had been unlawfully stopped and searched and violated the protesters' rights under Arts 8, 10 and 11 ECHR.

Principle: The submission of each of the three claimants was that there was no reasonable suspicion to carry out the stop and search and that the approach of the police to them and the general approach of the police to the stop and search of other people on the ground demonstrated that there was a blanket policy of searching individuals without there being reasonable suspicion as required by s 1 of PACE.

Application: (i) each stop and search by the police must not exceed police powers under s 1 of PACE and must be 'on reasonable grounds' for searching the individual; and (ii) each stop and search of an individual must be lawful and not violate the individual's rights under Arts 8 ('respect for private life'), 10 ('freedom of expression') and 11 ('freedom of assembly') ECHR. There is no requirement to give police notice of demonstrations.

Conditions on marches and demonstrations

Sections 12 and 14 Public Order Act 1986 give the police the power to impose conditions on marches and any demonstration that comes within the definition of a 'public assembly' (i.e. three or more people in the open air on public or private land). Conditions imposed in advance have to be put in writing. The power to impose conditions in advance can only be exercised by the **Chief Constable** (or the Metropolitan Police Commissioner or the Commissioner of the City of London Police). This power can be delegated to an Assistant Chief Constable (or Assistant Commissioner). Once a march or demonstration has started to assemble or a demonstration is under way, conditions can be imposed by the most senior police officer present. These can be given orally. The Chief Constable/senior officer present can only impose conditions if they consider that the march or demonstration may result in serious public disorder, serious damage to property or serious disruption to others, or that the purpose of the organisers is to intimidate others into doing or not doing something. An organiser of a march or demonstration who fails to comply with conditions commits an offence for which they can be fined up to £2500 or sentenced to up to 3 months' imprisonment. Someone taking part in the march/ demonstration who knowingly breaches a condition commits an offence for which they could be fined up to £1000.

A Chief Constable can ban a march under **s 13** POA 1986 if he or she has grounds to believe that imposing conditions will not be enough to prevent the march leading to serious public disorder. The decision to ban the march must be approved by the local council (unless the march is in London) and, in all cases, the Home Secretary. If a ban comes into force, it applies to all marches in the area for the duration of the ban. This power is used very sparingly but has been used recently to prevent English Defence League (EDL) marches in Woolwich in June 2013, after Drummer Lee Rigby was murdered on 22 May 2013 by a Muslim extremist.

Conditions imposed by the police can include:

Marches ('public procession') (s 12 POA)	Demonstrations ('public assembly') (s 14 POA)
Taking a certain route only	location
Entering only certain areas	duration
Banning a march (s 13 POA)	maximum number of people

Obstructing the highway

The law provides a specific right to use a public highway: the right to pass and re-pass along the highway (including the pavement), and the right to make ordinary and 'reasonable use' of the highway. This means a peaceful assembly will be seen as a 'reasonable use' of the highway (in addition to Art 11 ECHR – 'the right to peaceful assembly').

Section 137 of the Highways Act 1980 makes the unreasonable obstruction of the highway a criminal offence. The section is vague and provides the police with extensive powers over public gatherings, simply describing persons 'without lawful authority or excuse' who 'in any way wilfully obstruct the free passage along a highway' will be guilty of an offence and liable to a fine. In this respect, police powers have been increased to 'on the spot fines' of up to £100. The police use s 137 to remove sit-down demonstrators ('sit-ins'), to keep marchers from leaving the agreed police route or to control picketing. Often the police will give a warning to move before making an arrest, although there is no legal requirement to do so. The offence can be tried in the Magistrates' Court only (summary). The maximum penalty is a fine up to level 3 (currently £1000). There is no power to send a person convicted of highway obstruction to prison.

Human kettling

In the controversial 'human kettling' case of *Austin and Others v United Kingdom* (Appl. Nos. 39692/09, 40713/09, 41008/09) (2012), the Strasbourg Human Rights Court (ECtHR) ruled by majority in favour of the London Metropolitan Police in the case brought by demonstrator and bystanders over a 2001 incident in Oxford Circus during an anti-capitalist protest. The case took more than a decade to come to court. The police had placed a cordon around thousands of protesters at 2 pm during the May Day protest (known as 'kettling') due to significant violence and threats from some members of the crowd. The ECtHR agreed with the High Court ruling in the original Judicial Review that the situation was correctly assessed by the police as 'substantially dangerous', which necessitated the imposition of the cordon. The *Austin* ruling was seen as a major setback for activists, who argued that kettling is a disproportionate tactic that infringes protest rights and discourages people from taking part in demonstrations.

However, in *Mengesha (Susannah) v Commissioner of Police of the Metropolis* [2013] EWHC 1695 (Admin), a legal observer and volunteer barrister with the Bar Pro Bono Unit, who was kettled during a public sector trade unions demonstration march against government cuts in London's West End in November 2011 won a High Court declaration (Judicial Review) that the police acted unlawfully when kettling her with some 100 other people, filmed her and made her hand over personal information before she was released. Mengesha described the police action as oppressive, aggressive and intimidating. The London Metropolitan Police justified their actions on the grounds that it would help any subsequent post-incident investigation to identify people involved in criminal activity. Lord Justice Moses and Mr Justice Wyn Williams ruled that the demonstrators and legal observers had been lawfully contained but that officers had exceeded their powers in the conditions they set in order for people to be allowed to leave. This ruling means that human kettling remains lawful.

Up for Debate

Michael Mansfield QC argues that we need greater clarity on when the use of 'kettling' is permitted before people's freedom to protest is severely curtailed. Would you agree following the two cases of *Austin* (2012, ECtHR) and *Mengesha* (2013, Judicial Review at the High Court)? In a coursework essay of this kind you need to define the legitimate police powers first (which are extensive in the area of public protests, marches and demonstrations) before you define human rights and the remit of Arts 10 and 11 ECHR. You could look at the actual and perceived violence which triggers human kettling by the police. You could question the 'trigger' threshold which converts into the restriction of personal liberty and how police officers assess situations within their legal remit. Mansfield would argue that police powers in crowd control are 'totally arbitrary and confused' (*Guardian*, 1 May 2012). You might argue that a perfectly peaceful crowd may be contained for hours in a 'kettle' to prevent future violent disorder.

Protests on private land

The right to assembly under Art 11 ECHR generally only applies in public places. Private bodies, whether companies or individuals, are not required under the Human Rights Act 1998 (HRA) to act compatibly with the **European Convention on Human Rights** (ECHR) when refusing to allow a protest or demonstration on their land. This means that individuals cannot challenge under Judicial Review or invoke the HRA (e.g. Canary Wharf, London or a privately owned shopping centre) (see *Appleby v United Kingdom* (App no. 44306/98) (2003)). If you protest on private land without the permission of the occupier, you will be trespassing. Trespassing is not normally a criminal offence, but it is a tort (a civil wrong). This means that the occupier can sue the trespasser, or apply for a court order for possession, but the police cannot normally arrest someone merely because they are trespassing. In the *Appleby* case, the owners of the privately owned shopping mall 'The Galleries' in Washington, Tyne and Wear, Postel Properties Ltd, refused to give a Mrs Appleby and her community group permission to canvas for signatures in the mall. The applicants argued before the Strasbourg Court (ECtHR) that the law should recognise some privately owned land as 'quasi public'. The community group lost their case, and the ECtHR held that the applicants' rights under Arts 10 and 11 were not infringed.

Up for Debate

In the case of *Appleby v UK* (2003) (see above), Mary Eileen Appleby, acting chair of 'Washington First Forum', had written to the manager of the *Galleries* shopping centre, asking for permission to canvas views from the public. Though the local Council had granted planning permission for the new town centre shopping mall, that centre was privately owned and managed. That means that the public authorities also bore some responsibility for decisions about the nature of the area and access to and use of it. If you were to use this case in a coursework essay or exam question, would you not agree that the decision in *Appleby* was rather harsh? Surely the shopping area in question is in essence a public forum and arguably a 'quasi-public' space (as indeed Mrs Appleby argued before the Strasbourg Human Rights Court). Should the law be changed in this respect? And who could change it? Why, in your opinion, were the applicant's Art 10 and 11 rights not breached?

Putting it into practice

Problem questions are likely to include:

❖ Controls on public protest by the police (e.g. breach of the peace; statutory provision)

❖ The different public order offences under the Public Order Act 1986 (POA)
❖ The difference between 'public assembly' and 'public procession' and the requirements under the POA (e.g. ss 11, 12 and 14)
❖ The need to consider ss 3 and 6 Human Rights Act 1998 in relation to the claimant's possible problems in relation to marches, protests and assemblies
❖ The demands of Arts 10(1) ECHR ('right to freedom of expression') and 11(1) ECHR ('right to freedom of assembly and association)
❖ Any other Convention violations (e.g. Art 8 ECHR 'right to privacy and family life')
❖ Trespass on public and private land (public highway offences)
❖ The likely derogations by the state (either by the police or the Secretary of State) to invoke Arts 10(2) and/or 11(2) ECHR for reasons of state security and the preservation of law and order
❖ Legal challenges under human rights legislation

Step-by-step guide to assess violent conduct

1. Have the normal forces of law and order broken down? (s 1 POA 1986 – riot)
2. Consider which category the behaviour complained of falls into
3. Understand the difference between public procession and public assembly and controls attached to them
4. Understand the key elements of public order offences
5. Understand breach of the peace
6. How intense are the attacks on police and other civilians and their property?
7. Have emergency services been impeded by mob activity (s 1 – riot)
8. How severe and ferocious is the disorder?
9. Are there severe disruptions and fear caused to members of the public? (s 1 – riot)
10. Is this an organised or spontaneous act? Is it a peaceful protest? Or large-scale act resulting in unlawful violence?
11. Offences contrary to ss 5, 4A and 4 of the Public Order Act 1986 ('public order act offences causing harassment, alarm and distress') and s 91 Criminal Justice Act 1967 ('drunk and disorderly') overlap considerably in the conduct required to commit, therefore,
12. refer to the relevant paragraph(s) in the question to identify which offence may be appropriate to charge (remember it is the CPS that charges an offender, not the police)
13. Impact ECHR has had on these controls and the degree to which they comply with ECHR

Problem question 1

The *Movement Against Nuclear Power* is an organisation opposed to any further expansion of nuclear power stations in the UK. Its supporters have for several months held a vigil on the pavement outside the headquarters of *Energy For All* (EFA) in Central London, an energy company who have been given a 25-year contract by the Government to build and manage 14 new nuclear power stations across the UK. The thirty campaigners, who regularly man the protest, often hold banners and pictures which show nuclear damage to people following the accident at the Fukushima Nuclear Power Station in Japan on 22 March 2011. The protesters carry slogans such as 'Our Toxic Millionaires' and 'Death to the Nuclear Killers'. The pictures are upsetting many EFA workers. The EFA management contact the police wondering if they can stop the protestors and remove them from the pavement outside their offices. Discuss the public order issues which arise from this scenario.

Feedback on putting it into practice

a) You should first assess the situation and note that it must be a public 'assembly' (two or more people) and notice of the 'sit-in' to the London Metropolitan Police is not required under s 11 Public Order Act 1986 (POA).

b) Make the point that the protestors have held their vigil on a public pavement for months; this raises the issue of whether the protestors are obstructing the public highway under s 137 Highways Act 1980?

c) Can the police move them on? Is there an *unreasonable* use of the public highway contrary to s 137? An unreasonable obstruction of the highway is a criminal offence. Make the point that the police use s 137 to remove sit-down demonstrators.

a) It was held in *Hickman v Maisey* [1900] (CA) that a man resting at the side of the road or highway was not a trespasser. In this case, a racing tout used the public highway which crossed the plaintiff's property to watch racehorses being trained on the plaintiff's land. Held: the defendant's activities fell outside the ordinary and reasonable use of the highway and so amounted to a trespass. Make the point that the public highway could only be used to pass and repass.

b) The problem question is similar to the *Margaret Jones* case (see *DPP v Jones (Margaret)* [1999] 2 AC 240). On 1 June 1995, Dr Jones and 21 other protesters gathered on the roadside verge of the A344, adjacent to the perimeter fence of Stonehenge. Some were bearing banners stating 'Never Again', 'Stonehenge Campaign 10 years of Criminal Injustice' and 'Free Stonehenge'. Salisbury District Council had made an order under s 14A POA prohibiting all trespassory assemblies for 4 days covering a four mile radius around Stonehenge. Police Inspector Mackie concluded that they constituted a 'trespassory assembly'. They were arrested and charged for 'trespassory assembly' under s 14B(2) POA. Their appeals to the Salisbury Crown Court succeeded. The court held that neither of the appellants, nor any member of their group, was being destructive, violent, disorderly, threatening a breach of the peace or doing anything other than reasonably using the highway. The DPP appealed the decision. The House of Lords held in favour of the DPP and existing laws as per the ruling in *Hickman v Maisey*.

c) You should make the point that the House of Lords ruling in the *Margaret Jones* case raises an issue of fundamental constitutional importance: what are the limits of the public's rights of access to the public highway? Are these rights so restricted that they preclude in all circumstances any right of peaceful assembly on the public highway? The ruling in *Jones* was very narrow (i.e. you can only pass and reasonably repass on a public highway, otherwise the assembly will be held unlawful).

d) You now apply the two cases to the present problem outside the EFA headquarters and the 30 protesters who are staging the sit-in on the pavement. Does their ongoing protest plus their banners amount to offences under ss 4, 4A or 5 of the POA? The nuclear damage pictures are in themselves not 'threatening, abusive and insulting', but the 'Death to the Nuclear Killers' posters amount to threatening words. The House of Lords held in *Brutus v Cozens* [1972] All ER 1297 (QBD) that insulting words or threatening behaviour amount to a breach of the peace and do not amount to any further interpretation. The defendant had interrupted a tennis match at Wimbledon by blowing a whistle and throwing leaflets in his protest about apartheid in South Africa.

e) In assessing the possible criminal offences under the Public Order Act 1986 of the anti-nuclear protestors, their action is unlikely to fall within the remit of a s 4 POA offence; the protestors have been there for several months and there is no evidence of any violence, which makes it unlikely to establish there was 'intent to cause that person to believe unlawful violence would be used towards them' (make sure you quote exactly from the statute at this point)

f) It is more likely that they could be charged under s 4A POA with possible intent to provoke immediate violence; taking into account the threatening signs and placards they are carrying (s 4A(1)(b)), *intending* to cause harassment, alarm and distress; you may also consider s 5 POA in relation to the banners and signs in the sight of persons likely to be caused harassment. The police can arrest the protestors for carrying the signs and banners in a public place (not the seemingly peaceful protest sit-in).

g) You will gain higher marks for discussing relevant case law, plus mention Art 10 ECHR ('right to freedom of expression') – as the demonstrators' defence (see also *Percy v DPP* [1995] 3 All ER 124) – where banners and violent words amounted to a breach of the peace).

h) Can the protest outside EFA headquarters be stopped under s 14A POA ('prohibiting trespassory assemblies')? This (police) power only applies if more than 20 persons are gathered (s 14A(9) POA); this is satisfied here – there are 30 protestors.

i) You need to make the point that s 14A only applies to gatherings *in open air* in public spaces (not private land) (s 14A(1) POA).

j) Clearly, the pavement is a public highway and the public only have a right of reasonable protest (see *DPP v Jones* – above); you may well conclude that the protestors have been there for months and the placards are threatening violence.

k) But what if the pavement is owned by EFA? Then this is private property and the protestors have no right to be there and cannot invoke the HRA (or indeed the ECHR). It is unlikely though that the pavement is 'private' since it is located in Central London; you should nevertheless make the point about private land, which will gain you higher marks.

l) EFA must reasonably believe that the protestors are there without permission; if they have been granted permission to protest by the police (mention the notice period here), then you would argue on EFA's behalf that the protest is now in excess of permission **and** amounts to a 'trigger condition' for the police to be lawfully allowed to move the protestors on and remove the banners. You should argue that this condition has been met here: the assembly is 'likely to cause serious disruption to the life of the community' (evidenced by the reaction of the workers to the signs). For additional marks you should discuss Arts 10 and 11 ECHR in the protestors' defence.

m) It is likely that the police will move the protestors on from the pavement protest. If the protestors do not move, the police can make the necessary arrests and charge.

Problem question 2

The *Campaign for Free Access to Pornography on the Internet ('FreePorn')* decides to march from their campaign headquarters in North London to the Home Office to lobby the Secretary of State for the Home Department ('the Home Secretary') in London's Victoria in opposition to her proposed legislation to regulate adult pornography on the Internet. There are some 35 *FreePorn* supporters on the march. Anti-pornographic protestors ('*Anti Porn*') and Government supporters ('*The Grey Foxes*') gather near the Home Office to intercept the '*FreePorn*' march. When the first FreePorn supporters reach the vicinity of the Home Office they are attacked by a group of five *Grey Foxes* with cricket bats and golf clubs, shouting 'you pervs'. To avoid further confrontations the police surround the remaining *FreePorn* protestors with a cordon and keep them in a small area for six hours, until the *Grey Foxes* and *Anti Porn* supporters have dispersed. Each of the *FreePorn* protestors is asked for their name, address and contact details, and as a matter of security the police take photos of each of the protestors. Discuss the scenario.

Feedback on putting it into practice

a) You should first establish whether the organisers of the *FreePorn* march have given written notice under s 11(1) POA. Advance notice must be given by one organiser of the march under s 11(1)(a) POA to the Metropolitan Police Chief. This is clearly a 'public procession': *FreePorn* is demonstrating 'opposition . . . to the actions' of the Government (s 11(1)(a)), and/or publicising their campaign (s 11(1)(b)).

b) And if the *FreePorn* organiser did not give notice to the police chief, why not? Was it impracticable to do so? Too short notice? Good students will spend some time discussing the necessary notice period and question whether it was 'not practicable to do so' (s 11(3)–(6)). It is a criminal offence to organise a public procession without satisfying the necessary notice requirements (s 11(7)).

c) The *Grey Foxes* are guilty of an offence of violent disorder under s 2 POA (you may also lay additional charges of assault under s 47 Offences Against the Person Act 1861).

d) You should also note that the *Grey Foxes'* gathering is an 'assembly' under s 14 POA. Point out that they do not need to give notice.

e) You should take some time to discuss the issue of 'kettling' by the police and their asking for the personal ID and taking photos of the *FreePorn* protestors. Is the action taken by the police lawful?

f) Discuss 'stop and search' powers under Police and Criminal Evidence Act 1984 (PACE) first of all, and additionally the extensive common law powers under 'breach of the peace' and under subsequent more recent legislation.

g) Note that the question states that the police took the kettling action to 'stop further confrontations'. This may mean that the police can take actions to prevent a breach of the peace and to prevent violent behaviour. Such common law powers exist when the police have a **reasonable belief** that there is an imminent threat of violence (*R v Howell*). You should discuss whether there is 'imminence' (violence has occurred and is likely to reoccur given the *Grey Foxes'* and *AntiPorn*'s reputations) (see *Austin and Others v United Kingdom* (2012) ECtHR; *Mengesha (Susannah) v Commissioner of Police of the Metropolis* [2013])

h) The actions by the police must be reasonable in all the circumstances and police can take actions other than arrest including containment (kettling) (see above two cases in g).

i) Police action must comply with human rights legislation and the requirements of proportionality since the protester's rights under Arts 10 and 11 ECHR are at stake. Containment of *FreePorn* members must only be continued for as long as necessary.

j) Consider the high profile Judicial Review case of *R (on the application of Hannah McClure and Joshua Moos) v Commissioner of Police of the Metropolis* [2012] EWCA Civ 12, where Climate Camp protestors during the G20 summit in April 2009 were kettled for over four hours. The Court of Appeal held this unlawful, there being no reasonably apprehended breach of the peace sufficient to justify such action. The court further held that the concerted use of force by officers wearing riot gear, who pushed the crowd 20–30 metres back when putting the containment in place, was also unlawful.

k) The police must consider whether their actions are really necessary or whether their action interferes with the protestors' Convention rights? Could the police have taken alternative action?

l) You should also discuss the common law offence of breach of the peace and (extensive) police powers that can be used against protestors to whom violence is threatened rather than who threaten it; case law in this area is somewhat contradictory (see *Beatty v Gillbanks* [1882]; *Redmond-Bate v Director of Public Prosecutions* [1999] EWHC Admin 732; *Bibby v Chief Constable of Essex Police (2000) The Times, April 24 2000* (2000) (CA) – appears to suggest that it is unlawful to impose breach of the peace constraints on peaceful protestors).

m) You could argue that *FreePorn* organised a peaceful assembly and that the police action of kettling them breached their Art 11 right of 'peaceful assembly' and their Art 10 right of 'freedom of expression' (though in *Austin* this was held to be lawful).

n) For additional high marks you ought to conclude that there are two clear breaches of Convention rights, that the police are a 'core' public authority under s 6(1) HRA and the lawful protestors would have standing to bring an action in Judicial Review (s 3 HRA).

Chapter summary

❖ The provisions of the Public Order Act 1986 (POA).
❖ Human rights legislation in relation to freedom of assembly and public protests in general (Arts 10 and 11 ECHR).
❖ Bringing legal challenges under ss 3 and 6 Human Rights Act 1998 (HRA).
❖ Police powers in relation to marches and demonstrations.

Table of key cases referred to in this chapter

Case name	Area of law	Principle
Hickman v Maisey [1900] (CA)	Protests and demonstrations; sit-ins	A man resting on the side of the road or highway is not a trespasser
Brutus v Cozens [1972]	Threatening and abusive words (including banners and placards)	No need for further interpretation
Handyside v UK [1976] (*Little Red Schoolbook* case)	Art 10 ECHR ('freedom of expression')	Art 10 not only applies to information or ideas that are favourable and inoffensive but also to those that offend, shock or disturb
R v Howell [1982]	Breach of the peace	An arrest for breach of the peace must be made by a constable in the honest and reasonable belief that violence has occurred or is imminent

R v Mahroof [1988] 88 Cr App R 317; *R v Fleming and Robinson* [1989]	Violent disorder (s 1 POA)	Defendant was **one of the three** or more involved in the commission of the offence
R v Sanchez [1996]	Affray (s 3 POA)	Hypothetical bystander test
DPP v Jones (Margaret) [1999]	Protest and demonstrations on the highways	You can only pass and reasonably repass on a public highway, otherwise the assembly will be held unlawful (upholding *Hickman v Maisey* [1900] – above)
I & Others v DPP [2002]	Affray (s 3 POA)	There must be a victim present to find guilty of affray
Chambers and Edwards v DPP [1995]	Disorderly behaviour (ss 4, 4A and 5 POA)	'Disorderly behaviour' does not require any element of violence, actual or threatened; it includes conduct
Appleby v United Kingdom (App no. 44306/98) (2003) ECtHR	Private bodies and human rights (demonstrations and marches)	Private bodies do not have to adhere to HRA
R (on the application of Morris, E. and T.) v Chief Constable of Kent Police [2009] *(Kingsnorth Power Station case)*	s. 1 PACE ('stop and search'); demonstrations; notice period	(i) Each stop and search by the police must not exceed police powers under s 1 of PACE and must be **on reasonable grounds** for searching the individual; and (ii) each stop and search of an individual must be lawful and not violate the individual's rights under Arts 8 ('respect for private life'), 10 ('freedom of expression') and 11 ('freedom of assembly') ECHR. There is no notice requirement for demonstrations
Austin and Others v United Kingdom (2012) ECtHR	Human kettling by the police; Art 11 ECHR	The situation was 'substantially dangerous', which necessitated the imposition of the police cordon; no breach of Art 11

Case name	Area of law	Principle
R (on the application of Hannah McClure and Joshua Moos) v Commissioner of Police of the Metropolis [2012]	Human kettling by the police; Art 11 ECHR	Containment of protesters must only be as long as is reasonably necessary
Mengesha (Susannah) v Commissioner of Police of the Metropolis [2013]	Human kettling by the police; Arts 10 and 11 ECHR	The protestor had been lawfully 'kettled', but the police had exceeded their powers in the conditions they set in order for people to be allowed to leave; human kettling remains lawful

---

@ **Visit the book's companion website to test your knowledge**

❖ Resources include a subject map, revision tip podcasts, downloadable diagrams, MCQ quizzes for each chapter, and a flashcard glossary

❖ www.routledge.com/cw/optimizelawrevision

Index